LOBBY
LIFE

LOBBY LIFE

INSIDE WESTMINSTER'S SECRET SOCIETY

CAROLE WALKER

Elliott&Thompson

First published 2021 by
Elliott and Thompson Limited
2 John Street
London WC1N 2ES
www.eandtbooks.com

ISBN: 978-1-78396-565-6

9 8 7 6 5 4 3 2 1

A catalogue record for this book is available from
the British Library.

Typesetting: Marie Doherty
Printed by CPI Group (UK) Ltd, Croydon, CR0 4YY

For Tony, Sophie and Gus

CONTENTS

PREFACE: GO TO THE LOBBY

It was on a cold, grey morning early in 1996 that I walked into Downing Street for my first Lobby briefing. I showed my freshly minted brown plastic pass to the policeman at the security gates and followed a small group of journalists in through the front door of No. 10. 'You had better go to the Lobby with John', had been the instruction from my new boss at the BBC's political unit. I did not know what she meant: the lobby of the House of Commons, or that of our offices close by? And which John was she talking about? In those days there were more BBC political correspondents called John than there were women lobby journalists.

'Yes, great,' was the obvious response. I was not going to reveal my ignorance. What she meant was that I should attend the Monday morning Lobby briefing from the prime minister's press secretary and the John, on this occasion, was John Sergeant, the BBC's chief political correspondent. It would be many years before his appearance on *Strictly Come Dancing* made him a national celebrity, but he was a big figure in Westminster journalism, known to his colleagues as Sergy, though I did not dare use such a familiar term at the time. I tagged along as he marched to Downing Street and launched into his assessment of the current state of British politics. The prime minister, John Major, was beleaguered after years of Tory divisions, scandals and rebellions, and his majority had dwindled to less than a handful of MPs. Sergy had plenty to say about the Conservatives' woes, but no explanation or advice as to what I should expect at the gathering we were about to attend.

Entering the front door of No. 10 we turned right, into a sitting room with a couple of sofas and a few chairs. There were not nearly enough seats for all of us and, as the political editors and senior correspondents bagged the comfortable spots, I sat on the floor wishing I had worn trousers. I was the only woman in the room. John Major's press secretary, Christopher Meyer, arrived with a posse of press officers. I had an excellent view of his elegant red socks as he gave us a list of the prime minister's plans for the week ahead and key announcements from other government ministers. There were questions about Home Office proposals for tougher prison sentences for burglars and drug dealers to be revealed later that week.

Christopher (now Sir Christopher) Meyer went on to become British ambassador to the USA, but he had already spent many years as a diplomat and was clearly at ease as he fended off difficult questions with well-polished charm. He delivered some key messages on the need to address public concerns about serious crime, without giving any details of the measures to be announced. I scribbled frantically, aware that my shorthand was rusty. There was no question of anyone recording his words. The briefing was strictly off the record; any comments were to be attributed to 'sources close to the prime minister' or 'Westminster sources'. I subsequently realised that certain journalists, keen to hint at their contacts in the inner circles of power, would use phrases such as 'I understand from senior sources' before trotting out quotes from a Downing Street Lobby briefing.

No one had explained any of this to me. Indeed, it was only when researching this book that I discovered that there was, in fact, a book of rules, entitled *Notes on the Practice of Lobby Journalism*, published in 1982. It included the instruction: 'DON'T TALK ABOUT LOBBY MEETINGS BEFORE OR AFTER THEY ARE HELD', in capital letters.

On the way back from Downing Street, I felt it wise to probe gently about the terms of the briefing Sergy and I had attended, without giving away how little I knew. He gave a lengthy and magnanimous explanation, enjoying his role as one of the elder statesmen of the Lobby. Back at the office, everyone gathered around as he gave a read-out of what we had been told, followed by his own fulsome assessment of what he believed were the real messages behind the words and how they were likely to be received.

I still had to be formally introduced as a member of the Lobby at the afternoon briefing at 3.45 p.m., which until recently took place in a small room at the top of a spiral staircase in one of Parliament's Gothic spires. Finding it through the maze of corridors, columns and steps was one of the first challenges for a new recruit. The format of the afternoon session was different from that at No. 10, with a senior journalist chairing the meeting and inviting Christopher Meyer to address the room. It was only after twenty-five minutes of questions and banter that I was formally welcomed as a new member. There was a low-key murmur of 'Hear, hear', before everyone scurried out to meet their afternoon deadlines.

Over the next twenty years, I attended hundreds of Lobby briefings. While these official gatherings could be a chore, sometimes lengthy and boring, they also yielded key lines signalling the fate of embattled ministers or gave the first hint of policy changes to come. Looking back, it seems extraordinary that the BBC's Westminster team would often have to wait for one of its senior correspondents to return from the Monday morning

Lobby briefing to discover that the foreign secretary was making a statement in the Commons that afternoon or that the environment secretary would be addressing farmers on Thursday.

Yet the announcement of government business at the start of each meeting was simply the prelude to the main performance – the chance to ask the prime minister's representative whatever you wanted, to follow up with specific queries and to glean unexpected gems from the questions of your colleagues from rival organisations. The spokesman, and it was a man for most of my time at Westminster, would often give cautious answers, repeat agreed lines or duck the subject completely. The gatherings could be tense and combative, with the assembled media trying to force admissions of mistakes or failings when a government was on the back foot. When I first arrived, with little experience of the inner workings of the political world, it was not always easy to spot the real significance of an apparently bland answer, but I learned to look out for the phrases that hinted at an imminent U-turn or lack of support for a minister in trouble.

By the evening of my first day as a political correspondent I thought I had at least learned what was meant by 'the Lobby'. In fact, it refers not only to these briefings from No. 10 and the group of political journalists who attend them, it can also mean the Members' Lobby: the grand hallway adjoining the Commons Chamber, surrounded by statues and busts of former prime ministers, and once the best location for catching a quick word with passing MPs and ministers. This unfettered access to politicians across all parties and shades of opinion is as important as the No. 10 briefings, perhaps even more so for any reporter wanting to tell the full story of the latest political drama. Such conversations would traditionally be on 'Lobby terms', meaning that the source of your off-the-record chats cannot be named.

While the importance of preserving the concept of 'Lobby terms' is restated in the latest version of the Lobby journalists' rules, others have evolved over the years, and some of the more idiosyncratic conventions have been dropped. The late Chris Moncrieff, former political editor of the Press Association news agency and a legendary Lobby figure, took a bold step back in the 1970s when he produced a notebook and pencil while talking to an MP in the Members' Lobby to jot down some key quotes, defying a long-held unwritten agreement that this simply was not done. He got away with it and other journalists quickly followed suit. This was a significant breakthrough.

Other obscure rules survive to this day. Another late, great journalist, Anthony Howard, who became editor of the *New Statesman* and deputy editor of the *Observer*, recalled the trouble that ensued when he sat down on one of the benches at the side of the Members' Lobby. 'All sort of hell was let loose,' he told the BBC. 'Policemen rushed forward and said, "You can't sit there, get up",' an episode he described as 'absolutely absurd'.[1] When the Lobby rules were updated in 2018, the ban on journalists sitting down in the hallowed hallway was amended to allow them to sit on one small bench by the doorway to what is known as 'the Ways and Means corridor'. Progress indeed.

For Howard, these seemingly trivial edicts reinforced his highly critical view of the Lobby, a club he refused to join. He believed the arrangement was cosy and corrupt, creating an incestuous relationship between politicians and the press. He is certainly not alone in that view.

Throughout its history, the Lobby has been the focus of numerous rows and controversies. Critics have argued that it allows the government too much power to manipulate the agenda, putting its own slant on announcements. They believe the system has encouraged lazy journalism and a herd mentality among its reporters. Its defenders insist that it has always been an important channel of communication between Downing Street and the media, an opportunity for correspondents to challenge the prime minister's spokesperson and to gain a better understanding, which they can pass on to their readers. After two decades working in the highly competitive environment of Westminster, among some of the most ambitious and well-connected journalists anywhere, I do not believe it would be feasible for any self-respecting reporter to rely on the daily briefings for anything more than one very specific aspect of a story: the view that those in power wish to convey.

I left the Lobby in 2017 when I decided to move on from my job as a BBC political correspondent to work as a freelance political commentator, journalist and presenter. It was only after I handed in that unobtrusive brown pass that I realised it was in fact a golden ticket that granted access not only to the most powerful people in the land, but to their rivals and opponents too. It gave me advance sight of sensitive information and allowed me to challenge one of the prime minister's closest advisers, day after day, whatever political storm was swirling. The system is undergoing radical change, but still provides an essential framework for those who seek to explain what is going on at the heart of our politics away from public view.

The Lobby may be a very different place today from its nineteenth-century beginnings, and a far more open institution than the one I left a few years ago. Nevertheless, there remain many tales to tell about this once highly secretive institution, which has been central to so many battles between journalists and government across the decades.

Drawing on interviews with former colleagues, politicians, spin doctors and critics of the system, as well my first-hand experiences, *Lobby Life* will give you an insight into the manoeuvrings behind the closed doors of Westminster, the efforts to hold our politicians to account and their struggles to shape the news agenda. I am enormously grateful to all those who have generously shared their experiences and perceptions of our political system, and I hope you will find it as intriguing as I have.

The Lobby remains a privileged club, one which I may yet seek to rejoin – if I am still welcome.

1 THE FIRST DRAFT OF HISTORY

'So, let us today drudge on about our inescapably impossible task of providing every week a first rough draft of history that will never be completed about a world we can never really understand.'

Philip L. Graham, publisher of the *Washington Post*, April 1963

'Now, for the very latest on this story, we can go live to Westminster and speak to our political correspondent Carole Walker, who has just come from a briefing by the prime minister's press spokesperson for Lobby journalists. Carole, what is the word from Downing Street?' That is the sort of introduction I heard on numerous occasions in my time as a BBC political correspondent. I would race to a live camera position outside Parliament to explain the government's response to the latest row, trying to focus on the key lines to emerge from an often lengthy and confrontational session. For decades it would have been a blatant breach of Lobby rules even to report that I had attended such an event, let alone broadcast the details of what

I had been told. Journalists who belonged to the Lobby were instructed not to mention that such briefings took place, even to their colleagues.

Chris Moncrieff told me that when he first worked at Westminster in the 1970s, he was warned that he should not tell even his wife about the regular gatherings he attended in Downing Street or the Commons. John Pienaar, the radio presenter and former deputy political editor of the BBC, said that when he first worked at Westminster in 1982 the Lobby was like MI6: 'Everyone knew it was there but it didn't formally exist, nor did the briefings, and the number-one rule was that you did not attribute anything to the spokesman, describing any information as from a Whitehall source, which was in itself misleading.'

Nevertheless, the regular briefings from the prime minister's spokesman, or more recently spokeswoman, are at the heart of the system of Lobby journalism. For many years, members of this club were instructed to attend, unless they had very good reason to be absent. Still, the journalists usually needed no such edict to seize the opportunity to question one of the leader's closest aides. Over many decades, before the advent of digital media, the lines delivered by No. 10 at these encounters would often become important ingredients of newspaper reports, to be preserved in cuttings libraries for decades and generations to come, serving as a public record of events. Which is why the briefings, and the reports that followed, have so often become the focus of battles between government and press, and also why this arrangement has survived for so long. As the historian and former Westminster journalist Lord Hennessy told me: 'There's this dreadful, compulsive mutuality of interest. It drives both sides mad, but they cannot do without it and indeed both sides are striving, are they not, to dominate the content of the first rough draft of history.'

Today, when we have so many sources of news and information on our phones and laptops, the power of the newspapers to control our knowledge and understanding of politics is diminished. Correspondents from the press, broadcasters and websites race to be the first to tweet the latest lines from the regular Lobby briefings. The rules, which had stipulated that nothing could be published or broadcast until the meeting was over, were recently relaxed so the words of the prime minister's spokesperson can be read online within moments. The message from No. 10 now reaches millions of people moments after it has been delivered. It still has the power to establish a first draft of history, however much that may change in the subsequent hours and days.

Yet this almost instantaneous dissemination of the government's case does not necessarily work to its advantage. If it subsequently decides on a different approach, performing the U-turn beloved of headline writers, the words and phrases from its official briefings stand as evidence of its lack of consistency.

While much has been written about the levels of vitriol and abuse that characterise many of our current debates, politics has always been about argument and dissent. Thus the briefings from No. 10 can only ever provide one element of any story. The Lobby reporters' right to wander freely into parts of the Palace of Westminster that are off-limits to anyone else, apart from MPs and parliamentary staff, is arguably even more valuable in the quest to explain the political mood of the moment, the opposition to the government's aims as well as its objectives.

Traditionally, a key stamping ground for political reporters was the Members' Lobby, the anteroom to the Commons Chamber. It is a venue that still provides good opportunities for journalists to catch a word with MPs as they stride across the Pugin tiles on their way into a debate or pause to chat to colleagues. Words uttered immediately after a key vote, all off the record of course, can still give vital colour, conveying the emotion of a historic moment.

I remember all too well the awkward social dance as I tried to catch the eye of a minister already in conversation with a colleague, or intercept a potential rebel on the way to a parliamentary division. These days, such all-important chats are more likely to take place in the glass-roofed courtyard of Portcullis House, which opened in 2001 to provide additional offices and meeting places for MPs and their staff. The coffee bar and canteen is usually teeming with politicians and journalists, though it has never been the best location if you want to keep your source secret. The setting is more informal, the social dance updated to involve complex manoeuvres over cappuccinos, but the chance encounters and casual chats still yield the quotes and tip-offs that have always been essential for anyone writing the political narrative of our times. Recently this task was made much harder, with many MPs working online and all human interaction on the parliamentary estate becoming masked and distanced due to Covid-19.

Still, although the majority of MPs tweet their views and announcements and update constituents on their own websites, today's political correspondents need those quiet conversations to root out stories and discover what is really going on behind the scenes. And every MP has a campaign, an issue or personal mission that they wish to bring to a wider audience, even if they do not want their names revealed. It's little wonder that the early efforts of Boris Johnson's aides to clamp down on such discussions never really succeeded. Reporters and politicians will always find ways to exchange news, views and gossip, even when it has to be done remotely.

During numerous crises over the decades, Lobby journalists were often the first to get wind of looming emergencies, either from embargoed official briefings or from contacts who were well placed to pass on sensitive information, provided they were not revealed as the source. Indeed, it was during the turmoil of the General Strike of 1926, when the government realised the importance of conveying a coherent message to the country, that the first collective Lobby briefings began. A dispute that started over the pay and working conditions of coal miners escalated as the unions brought more than 1.5 million workers out on strike. Public transport was crippled, the armed forces were deployed to protect food deliveries and fights broke out between police and pickets in cities across the UK. As the cabinet met to discuss the increasing chaos, Westminster journalists struggled through crowds of angry strikers outside Downing Street to try to catch a word with ministers. In an effort to get a grip on the situation, the government decided to invite them in separately from the rest of the press for 'guidance'.

It was a significant moment, establishing the exclusive right of members of the Lobby to get the inside track on the government's approach. Indeed, the Committee, which governs the Lobby, was keen to underline the fundamental principle that only its members should attend these conferences, as 'ministers often speak confidentially, and the Committee can only assure ministers that our own members will respect confidences'.[2] The suggestion that such briefings should be held regularly would come three years later.

The country's first Labour prime minister, Ramsay MacDonald, had been given a hard time by the largely right-wing press during his first brief spell in office in 1924. Despite, or perhaps because of, this, when he returned to power for a second term in 1929 he sought to formalise relations with journalists. The Lobby Journalists' Committee papers for that year show that it was approached by No. 10 'with a view to the provision of regular machinery for facilitating press enquiries'.[3] Arrangements were made for an MP called W. W. Henderson to act as liaison officer between the government and the Lobby. MacDonald's advisers clearly hoped to get a more positive account of his leadership into the papers, then the main source of news, but Mr Henderson provided little information at the gatherings and the arrangement soon lapsed.

Relations between government and journalists were further strained when one of the Lobby correspondents was interrogated and threatened with arrest under the Official Secrets Act. In the spring of 1930, Jack Kirk of the *News Chronicle* was questioned for five hours after reporting that the government had approved the arrest of Mahatma Gandhi for his civil disobedience campaign in India. Gandhi had a huge following among Indian citizens, and the British administration feared he was undermining its grip on the country. It was Frederick Truelove of the *Daily Sketch* who first got a tip-off that the cabinet had approved Gandhi's detention. He needed corroboration of such sensitive news, and managed to speak to the home secretary himself, J. R. Clynes, who was an old friend. Clynes gave him a clear signal that Gandhi would not be allowed the freedom to continue his protests for much longer. Truelove decided to share his story with Kirk and William Forse of the *Daily Telegraph*. It seems extraordinary that he would pass on his exclusive scoop, but such collaboration was not unusual then and it seems that Truelove was nervous about going it alone with such a big story. All three papers carried similar reports of 'decisive action' to be taken against Gandhi, with his arrest 'to be expected at any time', after the administration in India had sought and received the backing of ministers at Westminster. Within hours of publication, Scotland Yard officers turned up at the offices of the three newspapers, requesting information about the journalists involved in what they said were potential breaches of the Official Secrets

Act. While the editors of the *Telegraph* and the *Sketch* refused to co-operate, the deputy editor on duty at the *News Chronicle* provided Kirk's name and address. The officers swiftly moved on to Kirk's home, demanding to know the source of his story and continuing their questioning for many hours.

Shaken by the experience, Kirk phoned Truelove to tell him what had happened. Truelove then pulled strings with his contacts at the highest level, speaking to both Scotland Yard's chief inspector and to the home secretary, who had confirmed the story in the first place. Clynes informed the prime minister of his own role and the police investigation was called off. Seven days later, Gandhi was indeed arrested.

That was not the end of the matter, though. The Opposition raised the episode in the Commons, MacDonald lectured his cabinet about leaks from their meetings and Lobby journalists took up the battle for press freedom. The Lobby Committee set up a special sub-committee to consider the whole question of the interrogation of Lobby journalists under the Official Secrets Act. In its report, the following year, it declared that the Act 'should never be used except in cases of real importance and then only with caution. Certainly the Acts ought not to be used to interfere with the political and other news which is communicated to their newspapers by Lobby Journalists'.[4] Significantly, they also succeeded in getting an undertaking from the Attorney General 'that in future, where he found it necessary to make inquiries involving journalists under the Official Secrets Acts, he would personally see the journalist before police action was authorised'.

In addition, there was a commitment from government that senior members of the Lobby Committee would have the right to be present, and to make representations to prevent the abuse of the Act, if it was used against any of their members in future. Although the arguments over the Act continue to this day, it was a recognition of the importance of a free press and a moment when No. 10 was forced to realise the limits of its power.

It was in 1931, after this episode, that the Lobby Committee persuaded Downing Street that the government's relations with political reporters would improve if regular briefings from a designated liaison officer were reinstated. The prime minister's private secretary, Herbert Usher, agreed to be available to speak to them at No. 10 between 12 noon and 12.30 p.m. every day when Parliament was sitting, and in the House on other occasions. The arrangement fell apart as the political and economic crisis gathered pace, just as it became more important than ever for journalists to get a proper understanding of the immense problems gripping the nation.

The Wall Street Crash and subsequent Great Depression had a devastating impact on British industry, as exports slumped, sterling plummeted and unemployment soared. The Labour government collapsed, leaving journalists struggling to keep pace with events. The official briefings lapsed amid disarray over who was running the country and the media resorted to a dramatic surge into Downing Street to try to find out what was happening. The Lobby Committee's annual report bewailed the 'absence of machinery at the time of crisis', which it said was 'a handicap alike to politicians and journalists'. Its usually dry ledger conveyed the drama of the time: 'In practice it resolved itself into mass bombardment of the door of No. 10, Downing Street and Lobby journalists were compelled to take part in much undesirable questioning of cabinet ministers in Downing Street.'[5]

This surging crush sounds very similar to the media scrums of recent years, in which I have so often been a participant, with reporters and camera crews jostling to catch a word with ministers on their way to key meetings in Whitehall. These chaotic 'doorsteps', as they are known, add to the sense of drama, but they rarely provide ministers dodging the cameras with a proper chance to tell their side of the story. When Ramsay MacDonald controversially returned to power in 1931 at the head of a new National Government, including Conservatives and Liberals, he sought to avoid such scenes in future. A civil servant called George F. Steward was appointed as an additional private secretary who arranged what were described as 'conferences' with Lobby journalists at No. 10.

This was to be the start of regular Lobby briefings, where reporters were given embargoed information on matters such as the New Year's Honours List and the Revenue Returns. They were also granted informal meetings with the prime minister himself, 'relaxed social and personal chats, far removed from the formal, politically geared sessions which became the set style in later years'.[6] This is something that rarely happens today – aside from occasions such as the Christmas drinks reception at No. 10.

Although MacDonald was the first prime minister to introduce these regular briefings for Westminster journalists, the Lobby itself had already existed for almost fifty years. It is hard to imagine the scene back in the nineteenth century when anyone could wander into Parliament. It was, in those days, a noisy, crowded place with large numbers passing through to gaze at the architecture, accost their MP and soak up the atmosphere at the heart of our democracy. In 1870 the Speaker, John Evelyn Denison, wrote in his diary that the Members' Lobby was so crowded that 'members could not get to the Vote Office, or to the refreshment room, or to and from the House, without being pressed upon and thronged, not only by constituents, but by members of deputations and other strangers, to their excessive inconvenience'.[7]

It sounds remarkably similar to some of the scenes at Westminster during the crucial Brexit debates of 2019, when MPs were harangued by campaigners on opposing sides of the argument. However, most of these more recent confrontations happened outside Parliament, which is now surrounded by a formidable array of security measures, including solid-steel barriers, concrete bollards and towering wrought-iron fences, all patrolled by heavily armed police. You can get inside by arranging to attend a Commons debate or to visit your MP, but unless you are the holder of the magic brown Lobby pass you will need to provide identification and go through airport-style security scanning.

The precedent for this was set 150 years ago when Speaker Denison decided that only MPs should be allowed into the Members' Lobby, while the public would be able to meet their representatives in the Central Lobby. Special access for journalists was added soon after, when a list was drawn up of reporters who were permitted to keep their freedom to enter the Members' Lobby and speak to MPs outside the debating Chamber. It is unclear exactly when the arrangements were formalised, as many of the Lobby records were destroyed during the Second World War, but the process started early in the 1880s.

In 1885, the existing list of Lobby correspondents was scrapped, and new arrangements were drawn up by the Speaker, Arthur Peel. These severely curtailed the rights of journalists, who lost their access to the Members' Lobby and even had to seek special permission to get to the Press Gallery to report on the proceedings of the Commons.

There was an outcry from reporters, who declared that the restrictions would prevent them from doing their jobs. One of them said: 'The loss to the public would be immense if the press lost touch of each political situation as it arose.'[8] They resolved to take up the matter with the Speaker and it is worth noting that, even at this stage, they formed separate delegations. One consisted of parliamentary reporters, whose role was to provide accounts of debates and statements on the floor of the Commons and Lords. The other represented Lobby correspondents, who wrote stories on the wider political picture, often informed by their conversations in the Members' Lobby. Both groups succeeded in persuading Speaker Peel to change the rules once more. Restrictions on their rights of parliamentary access were lifted and newspapers were issued with tickets for the Lobby – just one per newspaper, with the exception of the London morning papers, which got two passes. The authorities had realised that proper coverage of the political life of the country was an essential element in the first draft of its history.

This formal allocation of tickets marked the creation of the Lobby List kept by the Serjeant at Arms, responsible for keeping order in the Commons, with the names of all the holders of the coveted Lobby passes. The new arrangements resulted in fewer passes overall, a development welcomed by those who did qualify and jealously guarded their privileges. As the *London Standard* put it at the time: 'None will be more pleased than those who have real work to do in the lobby to find it closed in future against the soi-disant leaders of opinion, the miscellaneous button-holers and the propagandist idlers who haunt the House on important occasions and pester Members with their trivialities.'[9]

For some, this moment in 1885 marks the official creation of the Lobby. However, there is some dispute over the precise date. The Lobby celebrated its own centenary in 1984 with a glittering lunch at the Savoy Hotel, where members were addressed by Prime Minister Margaret Thatcher. The respected journalist James Margach suggested an even earlier beginning, in 1881. He recalled how two of the Lobby's founding fathers, R. G. Emery of the *Morning Post* and Alexander Mackintosh of the *Aberdeen Free Press*, were entertained in style in 1931 on completing fifty years as accredited Lobby correspondents. Frederick J. Higginbottom, a Lobby journalist in the 1890s who went on to become editor of the *Pall Mall Gazette*, concurred with that earlier date: 'Lobbying by journalists began to be practised seriously in 1881, and ten years later had come to be tolerated, but by many members very grudgingly.'[10]

It is important to note, despite Higginbottom's use of the word, that Lobby journalists do not in fact do any 'lobbying' as we understand the term today. Lobbyists are employed by companies or commercial groups to try to persuade or influence legislators for the benefit of their businesses. Lobby journalists use their access to the corridors of power to get stories and intelligence on political developments, which they then publish or broadcast to inform a much wider audience.

It is clear that from these days in the Gladstone era, Lobby journalists prided themselves on pursuing a very different role from that of their colleagues in the Press Gallery, who reported on proceedings in Parliament. Higginbottom had this explanation:

> While the practitioners in the gallery are limited to writing about the daily debates, the lobby men must be forever looking for the events that are to come, anticipating and foreshadowing developments in policy and parliamentary tactics. The faculty of anticipation is cultivated by constant contact with members of all shades of opinion and every degree of influence: by conversation, observation and questioning, deduction and speculation.[11]

For all the huge changes in media and technology since then, this remains a pretty apt summary of the role of political correspondents today. Their contacts with 'members of all shades of opinion' are essential in establishing an accurate picture of our ever-changing political landscape. They would also identify with the difficulties faced by their nineteenth-century counterparts when trying to waylay reluctant ministers, though an account written a few decades later suggests parliamentarians did gradually accept the role of the Lobby journalist: 'The way of the lobbyist was hard in contrast with what it is today. Then one had to walk warily and calculate the chances of rebuff in approaching a minister or member for the first time; now, information is asked for and expected almost as a right and even ministers are canvassed for news with a freedom that forty years ago would have been resented.'[12]

This was written in the early 1930s, when George Steward had just been brought in by Ramsay MacDonald to liaise with reporters and became the first and only press officer in the whole of Whitehall. Journalists saw his appointment to this new role as a positive step in formalising relations with Downing Street and praised his 'personal helpfulness'. They were, however, wary of the 'danger that [this position] may become too much a personal service of the prime minister' and could have the effect of 'putting members of the Government further away from members of the Lobby'.[13]

The political journalists were quick to spot a move by Downing Street to control the narrative, discourage other ministers from speaking out of turn and provide their own lines for that first draft of a story. They were even more concerned with preserving the secrecy of the Lobby system and its private off-the-record briefings, issuing members with frequent reminders of the rules:

It is desirable that members should not talk in public of the source of their information, or discuss with others – especially those who did not attend a meeting and are, therefore, not bound by any pledge of secrecy – any information given at a confidential talk.

13

Nor should any phrase or word be used in the stories written which might indicate the source of information. Such expressions as 'I learn on the highest authority'; 'a member of the cabinet'; 'in ministerial quarters' should be avoided where concealment of source is especially desirable.[14]

The result was that as the government grappled with the economic crisis of the 1930s, stories would emerge without being attributed to anyone, although no one really objected at the time. Lobby journalists were happy to abide by the rules, as long as they were getting the guidance and information from No. 10 that was so important for their reports. The government was equally content to stick to an arrangement that allowed it to make its case without being accountable. It was a mutually convenient agreement that remained largely unchanged for almost sixty years, when the pressure for greater transparency finally resulted in Prime Minister John Major's press secretary being referred to as a 'Downing Street source'.

In the pre-war era Westminster reporters also had to contend with the suspicion of MPs, some of whom resented the power and access of journalists. As the Lobby briefings became more frequent, a Conservative MP named Sir Herbert Williams organised a rota of backbenchers to keep watch on the entrance to the meeting room and identify which ministers were entering and speaking. Questions were raised in the Commons as to whether members of the government should be disclosing information to the press before telling the Commons. Yet ministers batted away the criticism and the Lobby system survived, with successive governments seeing it as a crucial channel for getting their message to the wider public. George Steward served three different prime ministers: Ramsay MacDonald, Stanley Baldwin and Neville Chamberlain.

Chamberlain had been health secretary and chancellor before he became prime minister in May 1937, with a record of significant reform when it came to pensions and healthcare. His premiership, though, was dominated by his campaign for appeasement, his belief that the only way for Britain to avoid being involved in another war was to reach a deal with Hitler and Mussolini. History tells a damning indictment of that pursuit and of his extraordinary efforts to convince journalists that his strategy was working in the face of mounting evidence of the build-up to war.

Chamberlain had begun meetings with Lobby correspondents when he was chancellor and continued the practice when he became prime minister, determined to secure positive coverage of his policies. He began taking a select group of journalists from newspapers sympathetic to his cause to lunch at St Stephen's Club, considered a safe location as it was the exclusive preserve of Conservative MPs and other senior party figures. It is clear he set out to manipulate the media into supporting his plans by every possible means. As well as Steward's continuing briefings for Lobby journalists, Major Joseph Ball, a former head of MI5's investigation branch, became a party press officer, a political fixer who operated behind the scenes. What is perhaps most remarkable was the amount of time and effort Chamberlain devoted to dealing personally with Lobby journalists and their editors.

Initially, there was significant support for Chamberlain's views among the public and some newspapers. As war clouds gathered over Europe, and the prime minister faced rising opposition, not least from Winston Churchill and other high-profile Conservatives, he resorted to threats and, at times, lies about the international situation. James Margach, a Lobby correspondent at the time, knew Chamberlain long before he took office in 1937 and gave an eviscerating account of how the prime minister employed what he called 'news management on a grand scale', particularly when dealing with the Lobby behind closed doors:

> . . . he bitterly resented any critical – or even probing – questions whatever; he always felt they were inspired by opponents. Sometimes he would reply with a haughty sneer. Then he developed a more intimidating style. When he sensed critical undertones, he would pause deliberately and ask the correspondent if he would identify the name of the newspaper he represented – the implied blackmail being that the editor and proprietor would not take kindly to their Westminster man proving unfriendly and unpatriotic. He made no attempt to conceal his anger on such occasions.
>
> Alternatively, when asked a question that he resented he would attempt to snub a correspondent with frozen silence; after an eloquent pause, staring contemptuously at the questioner without saying a word in reply, he would turn aside, look in a different direction and snap 'Next question, please'.[15]

It has all the hallmarks of Donald Trump's approach to the US media eighty years later, though in Chamberlain's day there were no cameras present and none of his remarks would have been quoted directly.

The prime minister also took to wooing newspaper proprietors, editors and leader writers, many of whom did indeed write articles and stories supportive of his approach. His closest confidant was Geoffrey Dawson of *The Times*, who was clearly won over by Chamberlain's entreaties. He even wrote a letter to one of his foreign correspondents, saying he could not understand why the paper's coverage had annoyed the Germans, when he had been altering despatches 'night after night to keep out of the paper anything that might have hurt their susceptibility'.[16]

As late as March 1939, six months before the outbreak of the Second World War, Chamberlain himself met a group of Lobby journalists to give them his assessment of the situation. Under the headline 'Brighter Outlook', *The Times* reported: 'The more optimistic feeling in political circles is attributable not only to the consciousness of a swift growth in our armed strength, but also to an improvement in the international outlook. Difficulties and dangers enough remain, but in general the international situation seems now to give less cause for anxiety than for some time past.'[17]

Chamberlain's success in shaping the first draft of history in the crucial months leading up to the war seems astonishing today, particularly when rivals, including Churchill himself, were stepping up their warnings of the Nazi threat. There was, of course, no mass media; the BBC was in its infancy and the papers were still the main source of news.

The Lobby briefings were a crucial channel for Chamberlain's propaganda exercise as his message, delivered unattributably, was faithfully conveyed in column inches. Decades before anyone used the phrase 'fake news', journalists attending them succumbed all too often to the prime minister's powers of persuasion and intimidation as he insisted his efforts to broker a deal with the Führer were working:

In all situations and in all crises, however menacing, he always claimed that the outlook was most encouraging, with not a cloud in the sky; he claimed his contacts with Hitler and Mussolini were very good and that the dictators were responding with understanding and promise, and if only Left-wing newspapers would stop writing critical and insulting things about them, he was confident that Herr Hitler and Signor Mussolini . . . would co-operate with him in his peace initiative.[18]

Chamberlain would assure the political correspondents that they could go off on their holidays at Easter and Whitsun in 1939 without worrying about the world situation. Margach admits that all too often he and others were caught out, and that their reputations suffered: 'We would report Chamberlain's assessment in good faith, and write news reports and articles reflecting a strong mood of Government optimism on the eve of this or that recess. All too often we would be compelled to come rushing back within twenty-four or forty-eight hours as some new outrage by one or other of the dictators created a war threat which made nonsense of the Premier's dearest hopes.'[19]

In September 1938, Chamberlain flew three times to Germany to negotiate with Hitler, culminating in the infamous Munich Agreement, which he signed alongside the Führer and the leaders of France and Italy, declaring their mutual desire to resolve their differences though consultation to assure peace. The price of the agreement was the Sudetenland, a border region of Czechoslovakia that was annexed by the Nazis. Chamberlain was greeted by cheering crowds as he appeared at the window of Downing Street, waving the piece of paper that he said would bring 'peace with honour'. It was, he declared, 'peace for our time'.

The newspapers were broadly supportive of the deal he had struck. The *Guardian* reported that 'The pacificators of Munich returned home yesterday to receive greater gratitude than has ever been given to any returning conqueror. They have done something that has hardly ever happened before in history – the snatching of the world at the eleventh hour from a universal calamity, from a return to barbarism, from untold cruelty and misery.'[20] Yet the paper's editorial did set out its misgivings, warning: 'Politically Czecho-Slovakia is rendered helpless, with all that means to the balance of forces in Eastern Europe, and Hitler will be able to advance again, when he chooses, with greatly increased power.'

It was by no means the only warning that the Munich Agreement would not halt the Nazis' march across Europe. Yet Chamberlain continued to tell Lobby journalists how well his campaign of appeasement was progressing. Margach recalls the prime minister's words at a briefing as late as 9 March 1939, during which he declared that 'the situation had never been better; he was actually working towards halting the armaments race, he claimed, perhaps leading to an agreement later in the year; his relations with Herr Hitler were most cordial . . . he was on the point of bringing about improved relations between France and Italy. And so on and so on; everything going well in the best of all possible worlds.'[21]

Just six months after Chamberlain's infamous speech declaring 'peace for our time', his words looked hollow indeed as Germany seized the rest of Czechoslovakia in March 1939. His policy of appeasement fell apart and his optimistic briefings, so frequently reported by Lobby journalists, were exposed as utterly misleading. Chamberlain clung to power, but the newspapers finally turned against him, nursing wounds to their reputations from their often ludicrously upbeat assessments of the international situation, lines fed to them by the prime minister and, all too often, seemingly printed without question.

The Lobby does not emerge from the Chamberlain era with credit. The legendary William Deedes, a correspondent at the time who went on to become editor of the *Daily Telegraph* and a Conservative MP and minister, lamented the 'signal failure of national newspapers to discover and print the truth about Hitler's Germany' when 'proprietors and editors were induced by ministers – manipulated is not too strong a word – to suppress material, in the news or editorial columns, that might give offence to Hitler. Bluntly, the national press fell down on the job.'[22]

I find it hard to understand why so many highly esteemed journalists were taken in by the prime minister's spin, particularly when other powerful figures were arguing against Chamberlain's policies and his assessment of the international picture. I have found no accounts of any rows in these pre-war Lobby briefings, occasions when the reporters challenged the blatant untruths they were being told. Of course, the meetings were all off the record, and we do not know what went on behind closed doors, but there is no indication of any aggressive exchanges like those at many of the Lobby sessions I attended. Indeed, ministers as well as press secretaries often speak of their trepidation at facing an array of political journalists, but I have found no record of Chamberlain being given a hard time.

In May 1940, amid the shock of a devastating German offensive in the Low Countries, Chamberlain stood down, ushering in a very different political leader, Winston Churchill. He too would go to extraordinary lengths to try to control the media, justifying his approach as necessary to protect national security in wartime Britain while seeking to define, in his own words, the first rough draft of history.

2 CENSORSHIP, SECRECY AND SURVEILLANCE

'Careless talk costs lives.'
Wartime propaganda slogan

Less than a month after Winston Churchill became prime minister at the head of a coalition government, he stood in Parliament to deliver perhaps the greatest of his famous wartime speeches. It was 4 June 1940. He warned that large tracts of Europe had fallen into the grip of the Nazis and that Hitler had plans to invade the British Isles:

> We shall go on to the end, we shall fight in France, we shall fight on the seas and oceans, we shall fight with growing confidence and growing strength in the air, we shall defend our Island, whatever the cost may be, we shall fight on the beaches, we shall fight on the landing grounds, we shall fight in the fields and in the streets, we shall fight in the hills; we shall never surrender, and even if, which I do not for a moment believe, this Island or a large part of it were subjugated and starving, then our Empire beyond the seas,

armed and guarded by the British Fleet, would carry on the struggle, until, in God's good time, the New World, with all its power and might, steps forth to the rescue and the liberation of the old.

His audience was the Commons Chamber, with a handful of journalists in the Press Gallery to report his words. There was no advance briefing to the media, no spin doctors to point out the key phrases to the Lobby. Churchill believed in the power of his own oratory to strengthen the resolve of the nation and did not employ speech writers, spending long hours preparing his scripts himself and practising their delivery.

Churchill's attitude towards the media was as far removed from Chamberlain's as his stance on the Nazi threat. His focus was on winning the war that had begun eight months before he became prime minister: the only role he could see for the press was to report his grand speeches and policy announcements. These would be delivered in Parliament or in statements broadcast to the nation. There was no question of him chatting with Lobby correspondents or giving interviews to the newspapers. Yet alongside these stirring public pronouncements were some far-reaching measures intended to suppress anything that might potentially undermine the war effort, and these included frequent efforts to prevent the papers printing stories or comments which could be considered unhelpful to his overriding objective of defeating the Nazis.

Churchill's mindset is somewhat surprising, given that he was himself a journalist who'd been a war correspondent for the *Daily Telegraph*, and returned to writing articles for newspapers during his periods out of office. He had close personal ties with some of the press barons, notably Viscount Camrose, who owned a string of titles including the *Telegraph*, and

Lord Beaverbrook of the *Daily Express*, who was brought into the war cabinet as minister of aircraft production. Churchill did meet with a select number of newspaper editors, but he appears to have had almost no direct contact with political correspondents and never once briefed the Lobby in person. The records of the Lobby Committee for 1941–2 do note that there was a Lobby luncheon for the prime minister at the Savoy Hotel on Friday, 6 March 1941, the first to be held since the outbreak of war. Nearly 250 guests attended, including other members of the war cabinet. Sadly, there is no record of any of the speeches, let alone the conversations among those present.

Churchill liked to deliver his messages to the nation unfiltered and uninterrupted. He was highly reluctant to give news conferences, although he was persuaded to take part in a handful of on-the-record sessions with the press alongside President Roosevelt in the USA. Churchill handled these occasions with aplomb, winning applause and cheers from his mainly American audience, but his answers were wary to say the least. At the first of these gatherings, shortly after the attack on Pearl Harbor in December 1941, Churchill was asked how long he thought it would take to win the war. His response was: 'If we manage it well, it will only take half as long as if we manage it badly.'[1]

The British press – perhaps understandably – protested that they were never granted their own opportunities to question the prime minister. They were summoned to Southampton, where Churchill agreed to speak to them on his way back from another of his trips to the States. It did nothing to quell their frustration, as Churchill told them he could not speak about his American visit or his discussions with the president. Every question prompted brief though courteous replies along the same lines: 'I'm very sorry, I can't say anything on that until I have reported to Parliament.'

Back at Westminster, one political correspondent, James Robertson of the *Glasgow Herald*, plucked up the courage to try to catch a word with Churchill when he spotted him striding through the Lobby after questions in the House. Robertson humbly tried to introduce himself, mentioning that Scotland was very interested in his leadership. Churchill, though, was clearly affronted at being accosted by a mere reporter and demanded to know what right he had to do so. Other journalists and MPs paused to watch the tense confrontation. 'Out of my way,' growled Churchill as he stomped off, bringing the encounter to an abrupt end.

Despite his reluctance to engage with journalists, Churchill was certainly preoccupied with what they were writing. Like John Major, some fifty years later, he had the newspapers delivered to Downing Street as soon as they came off the presses, sending despatch riders to collect the first editions from Fleet Street so he could read them late at night. He was annoyed at the slightest criticism of his handling of events, but his greatest concern was wartime security and the need to prevent the spread of any information that might help the enemy. Even before he came to power, in the opening days of the war a Ministry of Information was established to distribute and censor all information concerning the conflict. Newspapers had to submit their stories to the censor, and any information of potential military significance, from weather reports to the location of troops, was removed. 'Defence Notices' could be issued to stop publication of stories that were deemed to breach official guidance. The new ministry also held briefings at its headquarters in Senate House at the University of London, with facilities for journalists to write their stories and have them checked by the censor at the same time. The system was intended to replace the off-the-record meetings with Lobby journalists.

It may have seemed a sensible arrangement, but within a week it fell into disarray. News leaked out from Paris that a British Expeditionary Force was on French soil. The story was picked up by international agencies and the Ministry of Information decided that, under the circumstances, it would allow publication to go ahead. When the British newspapers included far more information than anticipated, the War Office reacted with alarm and the Ministry of Information was forced into a late-night U-turn, banning publication retrospectively. The government's current website describes the situation then as one of 'chaos and complete confusion'; 'Scotland Yard were instructed to arrange the seizure of all newspapers, police officers were deployed to newspaper offices and wholesale newsagents throughout Britain, roadblocks were erected in Fleet Street and newspaper trains were stopped en-route from London.'[2] It is hard to imagine such an exercise today, and indeed it would almost certainly prove futile once stories had spread across the internet. There was further disarray when the Ministry of Information announced that the Queen had returned from a visit to Scotland with her daughters. It was then decided that it was a security risk for this to become public knowledge and once again there was a scramble to try to confiscate newspapers, only for the order to be reversed and the news reannounced hours later.

These incidents prompted Lobby journalists, who were already unhappy at the loss of their exclusive briefings, to write to the prime minister, urging a return to the confidential, off-the-record meetings at Westminster. Both sides realised the potential benefits of the unattributable Lobby meetings, and these not only resumed but were held without the presence of an official censor. The Ministry of Information continued to distribute information and oversee propaganda, but it had lost some of its power to control the news agenda.

Churchill had a low opinion of government communications officers and for a while did not even have a press office at No. 10. He did eventually appoint a press secretary, Fife Clark, to brief Lobby journalists and he ensured that they received embargoed copies of some of the prime minister's speeches. Clark, though, had little direct contact with his boss and he was unable to offer much detail or insight into the wartime leader's intentions. Far more powerful was the minister of information, Duff Cooper, who had been brought back into government after resigning from Chamberlain's cabinet over the Munich Agreement.

Cooper was a close ally of Churchill, but he was unhappy with the role he was given. In his autobiography he complained that when he appealed for support from the prime minister on his handling of the media, he seldom got it: 'He was not interested in the subject. He knew that propaganda was not going to win the war.'[3] Cooper's aggressive attempts to control the press using the tight censorship rules caused huge resentment among those trying to report the war, and his programme of 'Mass Observation' to gauge the public mood prompted comparisons with the networks of spies in Nazi Germany. The droves of staff he deployed to gather information on people's lives and attitudes came to be known as 'Cooper's Snoopers'. Their job, interviewing people around the country, was supposedly to assess morale, establish which government slogans were effective and gather information to help plans for food rationing and wartime supplies. Inevitably, some saw the questions as an unnecessary intrusion into their personal lives and habits, yet the programme went far beyond these face-to-face interviews. The authorities were concerned that people might conceal their real opinions, so investigators also eavesdropped on people's conversations, recording their unguarded remarks as 'overheards'. It is hardly surprising that many viewed this as a sinister exercise in surveillance, with some suggesting that the Ministry of Information was the model for the Ministry of Truth in George Orwell's novel *1984*.

The scale of the operation makes all the internal polling and focus groups conducted by Boris Johnson's government look pretty modest. In December 1939, a Home Intelligence Department was created under the leadership of a formidable former BBC producer called Mary Adams. It began by building a picture of life and attitudes in the Lancashire town of Bolton, known as 'Worktown' in its reports, but expanded to try to gather data more widely. By the summer of 1940 it was instructed 'to report daily on people's reactions throughout the country with special reference to morale, rumours and the reception of ministerial broadcasts and pronouncements'.[4]

While focus groups today usually involve a small number of people, selected to reflect a cross-section of society, the effort to find out what people thought of the war effort and the performance of their political leaders was on a vast scale, even if the methods may have lacked statistical rigour. Regional information officers across the country were instructed to report each day by telephone between 12 noon and 2.30 p.m. on morale in their area. An internal history of the department noted that their data was obtained 'partly by discussions with their own staff, partly by casual conversations initiated or overheard on the way to work, and partly by a hurried series of visits to public houses and other places where the public foregathered'.[5] BBC listener research was used, as was information from political parties. Postal censors also analysed the contents of some letters. A network was established to assess the mood in the capital. The department's internal history said it made contact with 'a number of people in all strata of society, who would be prepared, in response to a telephone call or personal visits, to report the feeling of those with whom they came into contact'. The recipients of these calls were 'doctors, dentists, parsons, publicans, small shopkeepers, newsagents, trade union officials, factory welfare officers, shop stewards, Citizens Advice Bureau secretaries, hospital almoners, businessmen and local authority officials'.[6]

Most people were unaware of the extent of the efforts to track their behaviour and attitudes and Lobby journalists had no access to any of the data. When the *Daily Herald* reported on the face-to-face surveys, just one part of the Mass Observation programme, there was a backlash from many of the newspapers. The *Daily Sketch* warned: 'This house-to-house questioning will throw the shadow of the Gestapo over honest and loyal creatures. The Ministry must abandon these ill-judged, amateurish inspirations,' while the *Observer* noted that: 'Nothing could be more unpopular or more futile.'[7] The hostility of the press was fuelled further by the fact that the Ministry of Information was also running what was known as a 'Silent Column' campaign, urging the public to join an imaginary regiment formed to combat rumours that could undermine morale or help the enemy. Several people were prosecuted for spreading alarm and despondency or for making defeatist remarks. The papers feared that the efforts to monitor morale could be used in a wider witch-hunt against innocent civilians. In July 1940, the Ministry of Information noted that the campaign against its activities continued in the press, but an inquiry designed to test public feeling found that while less than 10 per cent of employees in a large aircraft factory, and less than 5 per cent in an unspecified village, had heard of it, 'prosecutions for defeatist talk are a general topic of conversation and a large proportion of the public have been affected by rumours, fears and criticisms'.[8]

Duff Cooper, though, mounted a strong defence of his department's activities and the row appears to have subsided. There was clearly relief in government circles that the covert eaves-dropping on people's conversations was not revealed at the time. 'Though no deliberate efforts at concealment were made, Home Intelligence worked, as it were, in the shadow of the Survey, its doings unquestioned and its results confidential.'[9] The data has since become a valuable source for social historians, a trove of information on wartime habits and opinions, gathered by human endeavour decades before algorithms began to track our views and behaviour across the internet.

In 1941, after just a year as minister of information, Duff Cooper was replaced by another of Churchill's closest friends, Brendan Bracken. He was under no illusions about his role, describing it as 'one of the toughest jobs which has ever fallen to the lot of man!'. Within days of his appointment he said: 'I think that in a very short time I shall be joining the happy band of ex-ministers of information.'[10] Yet he did much to rebuild relations with the media, organising regular news conferences for ministers to provide updates to Lobby journalists on the progress of the war, though even these were often censored.

Churchill was not only prepared to take a tough line with any publication deemed to have threatened national security, but he also reacted badly to any criticism or negative comments in the papers. Cabinet papers record his fury at the tone of the *Daily Mirror*, which was hugely popular at the time, partly because of its irreverent attitude and willingness to poke fun at the author-ities. At one cabinet meeting in October 1940, the prime minister accused the *Mirror* and its sister paper the *Sunday Pictorial* of trying to 'rock the boat and to shake the confidence of the country in ministers'.[11] He did not see the funny side of some of their more subversive cartoons and the papers were warned that the government was prepared to take firm action against them, but it had little effect. Herbert Morrison, then home secretary, was despatched to give a final warning of suppression to the *Mirror*. He delivered a strongly worded statement in Parliament to reinforce the government's readiness to act. Other newspapers rallied round, declaring their determination to stand their ground in the face of such threats, and the *Mirror* survived. Nevertheless, several smaller journals, including the *Daily Worker*, which was owned by the British Communist Party, were banned.

The prime minister's celebrated wartime speeches to Parliament were generally reported in glowing terms, but he was not happy when critical interventions by other MPs were also included. In the early years of the war, the Ministry of Information began blacking out contributions to parliamentary debates that it deemed were likely to harm morale, including straightforward criticism of the government. This heavy-handed move, at a time when the country was fighting for freedom, prompted objections from press and parliamentarians. A group of senior Lobby journalists protested to Lord Beaverbrook. He arranged to meet them at the Dorchester to try to resolve the issue and agreed that Parliament should not be censored. When other ministers also took the journalists' side, the practice ceased. Churchill, though, resorted to alternative tactics. When he sensed that his critics in the House of Commons were going on the attack, one of his close allies would call out 'I spy strangers', which triggered the parliamentary procedure to ensure that the House sat in private. Journalists and members of the public were excluded, and it was a crime to report what had been said in the Chamber. While many reporters saw it as censorship by the back door, they found themselves outmanoeuvred.

Other restrictions on parliamentary reporting meant that no stories could be filed until after the House had adjourned, to prevent accounts that would reveal when the Commons was sitting, though this rule was gradually eroded and abandoned by

1941. More than thirty years before the first radio broadcasts of parliamentary proceedings, the public turned to the newspapers to learn about those wartime debates and statements, though the BBC played an increasingly important role as the conflict progressed.

The government swiftly realised the significance of the public broadcaster and took new powers to control its output, ensuring that press statements from ministers were carried in full, having first insisted they were cleared by the censors. When Brendan Bracken took charge at the Ministry of Information, he decided to limit the profile of ministers and ensure that Churchill himself took the lead in bolstering public mood, resulting in those memorable broadcasts direct to the nation.

Behind the scenes, the Lobby was still important when the government wanted to get information out unattributably. At a critical phase later in the war, British intelligence learned that the Nazis were about to step up their aerial attacks with pilotless planes and V-2 guided missiles, but it seems there was a lack of agreement across government over how to prepare the public for the new threat. James Margach, one of the great political correspondents at the time, recalls that Brendan Bracken came to brief Lobby journalists on the latest weapons, knowing that he would not be named as the source of their subsequent reports. Yet the plan fell foul of the censors from his own ministry, who blocked all the stories on the grounds they would depress public spirit. Furthermore, they then demanded to sit in on all future ministerial meetings with the Lobby. Once again, Lord Beaverbrook was called in to resolve the dispute. Once again, with his help, the journalists were able to see off the censors and their private off-the-record briefings resumed.

It is worth remembering that Parliament itself was an enemy target. Before the war, contingency plans were drawn up to evacuate it to Stratford-upon-Avon, though these were never put into practice. The Chamber of the Commons was virtually destroyed when it was struck in a German air raid on 10 May 1941. Proceedings had already been moved to nearby Church House, and though facilities were cramped, Lobby journalists were able to wander the corridors to speak to MPs about their views and concerns, though anything they reported would still have to be approved by the censors. Parliament then moved into the Lords, where proceedings continued throughout the rest of the war.

The election of the post-war Labour government under Clement Attlee ushered in significant reforms: the nationalisation of many industries, expansion of the welfare state and the creation of the National Health Service. Attlee's priorities and his attitude to the press reflected the rapid changes in society after the war and his character could hardly have been more different to that of his predecessor. He was described in the *Daily Sketch* as 'a man who tucked his personality behind a pipe and left colleagues and public to make what they could of all the smoke signals'. Whereas Churchill waited up to see the first editions and fretted over the coverage of his leadership, Attlee relied on his staff to provide official news digests and only took *The Times* for its crossword and announcements of births, deaths and marriages.

After a brief honeymoon of positive headlines, Attlee faced some of the most hostile coverage of any leader. The overwhelmingly right-wing newspapers had been wary of his socialist government from the outset and seized on the mood of anti-climax as rationing, unemployment and poor housing continued to blight the lives of many voters.

Attlee appeared to be undeterred by what the papers were saying, largely because he was unaware of much of it. He simply ignored the media and was reluctant to speak directly to journalists or their masters. Before the war, he had held weekly meetings with the Lobby to discuss Labour's approach to issues of the day. His style was to deliver brief, one-sentence answers to most questions and to dismiss any which he saw as irrelevant. In power he remained reluctant to engage.

Attlee appointed the former editor of the *Daily Herald*, Francis Williams, who had joined the Ministry of Information, as his press secretary and was happy to let him communicate the government's message – not only to Lobby journalists, but to the nation. In a groundbreaking move, Williams appeared on radio and television, prompting complaints that 'he seemed to have the status almost of a minister',[12] though his Lobby briefings remained strictly off the record.

Williams' famous story of the Downing Street newswire machine tells us much about the attitude of the prime minister. Williams wanted a telex machine at No. 10 to ensure he had instant access to the news agencies. It seems a pretty basic requirement these days, but he met some resistance from Attlee and only convinced him to give the go-ahead by telling him it would provide the latest cricket scores. A week after it was installed, a worried prime minister went to his press secretary. 'Francis, you know my cricket machine at the cabinet door?' he asked. 'When I checked it just now for the lunchtime score at Lords, it was ticking out the decisions and subjects discussed at the cabinet meeting this morning. How can it do that?' Williams explained that part of his job was to brief the Lobby on the main issues from these ministerial gatherings, which were then reported on the newswires. Attlee had been unaware that this was common practice but accepted the explanation without question or quarrel, telling his press secretary, 'I'll leave the show to you. Good work.'[13]

Censorship had been lifted and it was a time of huge political and social change. However, rather than moving to a more open, transparent arrangement, the first edition of the Lobby rule book, drawn up by the Lobby Committee, contained a long list of instructions to reinforce the formal and secretive nature of the club. These were intended to preserve its privileges and included the principle that briefings should be strictly off the record:

> Don't quote informants. Meetings of the lobby are on the same basis as individual lobbying and unless the informant gives special leave for his name to be mentioned, it should not appear. The policy of the lobby has always been against quotations from an informant, even if he has no objection to this course. It is felt that the individual member of the lobby should take personal responsibility for his own stories and that quotation reduces lobbying to mere reporting.[14]

The Code of Conduct was, of course, headed 'Strictly private and confidential'. It was only circulated to Lobby members and the rules remained in place for decades, despite numerous arguments over quotes and attribution.

In 1947, Williams suggested that the Downing Street briefings should be open to other journalists, an idea that was immediately rejected by the Lobby Committee on the grounds that it would be impossible to have the same 'confidence between informant and informed'. It would take more than fifty years before another Labour government, under Tony Blair, would introduce this modest reform. In the post-war era, the Lobby still operated under a cloak of secrecy with codes known only to its members. Obscure notes would appear on a noticeboard in a corridor leading to the press rooms within Parliament, with the words 'Red Mantle 4 p.m.' or 'Blue Mantle 2.30 p.m.'. The cryptic messages, preserving the exclusivity and mystique of the arrangements, informed Lobby journalists of briefings: Red Mantle if it was from Labour, Blue Mantle from the Tories. Decades later, these coded notices were still in use and, although their meaning was known more widely, they still bemused newcomers to the Westminster beat.

Beyond the authorised briefings, the Attlee government's relations with the media were further strained by two high-profile cases. The first concerned the revelation of the source for a series of stories in the *London Evening Standard* about the increasingly bitter rows at the weekly meeting of the Parliamentary Labour Party. Lobby journalists have always done their best to find out what goes on at these party gatherings. When I was a political correspondent, we would frequently hang around outside the committee room in which they were held to find out what we could about the latest internal arguments as MPs scurried away down the corridor.

In Attlee's day there was surprise at the extraordinary detail and verbatim accounts of the angry exchanges reported in the *Standard*. A Labour MP named Garry Allighan suggested that some MPs were being paid for information and others were being plied with booze in Westminster bars. In an article for the *World's Press News* he wrote: 'Under the influence MPs talk their heads off. They spill the beans. Easy my dear Watson!' The suggestion of bribery and corruption among MPs sparked an inquiry by the Committee of Privileges. The *Standard*'s editor, Herbert Gunn, admitted that he paid a small press agency £120 a month for stories from Westminster, and it was not long before it emerged that the agency was owned and controlled by none other than Garry Allighan himself. Under questioning, the MP confessed his role in telling the *Standard* what had happened in supposedly private meetings and he was subsequently expelled from the Commons. During the inquiry it emerged that the *Standard*'s rival, the *London Evening News*, had been paying another MP for help with its stories. A move to impose more severe sanctions in future, by excluding from Westminster any newspaper that paid for information, was defeated. The episode undoubtedly damaged the reputations of both journalists and parliamentarians, exposing the willingness of certain MPs to use their positions to earn extra cash and the methods used by some papers to get their stories.

A fortnight later there was a second episode that increased MPs' wariness when talking to Lobby reporters. The chancellor, Hugh Dalton, was on his way to deliver his Budget in November 1947 when he bumped into John Carvel, political correspondent for the *London Evening Star* and a long-standing friend. Carvel asked him what he had in store. Somewhat to his surprise, Dalton told him several of the main measures he was about to announce. I can imagine the journalist's excitement at his indiscretion, but Carvel calmly wished the chancellor luck with his speech before racing to the phone to file his story immediately: no more on tobacco, a penny on beer, something on dogs and pools but not on horses, an increase in purchase tax. It was a major scoop and made it into early editions of the paper, which were distributed to news-stands near Fleet Street minutes before the chancellor got to his feet.

It was a significant breach of procedure and, in a subsequent Commons debate on the leak, Dalton apologised and offered his resignation, saying: 'I take the blame for having committed an indiscretion in my relationship with this Lobby correspondent whom I have known, as we have known so many of the Lobby correspondents, over a period of years, and I do not think that it would be suitable for me to pass any judgement on him.'[15]

Attlee accepted Dalton's resignation and appeared character-istically unshaken by the row. In the midst of it all, he invited Mr and Mrs Carvel for a weekend at Chequers, the prime minister's country retreat, a surprising move from a politician not known for his warmth towards journalists. A subsequent inquiry found the leak had not had any serious economic consequences. In his evidence, Carvel said he was astonished at how comprehensive his story had proved to be and expressed his regret at what he called the 'tragic outcome for Mr Dalton'.

More than sixty years later, Carvel's grandson, also named John, wrote how the story had come about, describing the way that 'Dalton manoeuvred Carvel into a corner and told him the main points in the speech he was about to make, playfully making mock punches with each point.' He said Dalton never intended this as a leak, and Carvel never intended it as a story that would unseat a chancellor, yet it had made Budget secrecy 'a cardinal principle of British political life'.[16] He wrote the article on the day in March 2013 that all the key details of Chancellor George Osborne's Budget were published on Twitter by the *Evening Standard* before he stood up to deliver his statement. The paper apologised for what it said was a very serious mistake.

In the post-war years, senior Labour figures believed they needed to find a way of confronting what they saw as an institutional bias against the left from the mainly right-wing newspapers, owned by a handful of wealthy proprietors. Central to this was Herbert Morrison, then deputy prime minister, whose grandson Peter Mandelson was to play such a central role in tackling a similar task fifty years later. Morrison encouraged Labour MPs to push for a commission to investigate what he called the 'monopolistic tendencies' of the newspapers. After a debate and vote in Parliament, a Royal Commission was estab-lished in 1947 to inquire into the 'control, management and ownership' of the press. It rejected some of the most extreme accusations, but it did recommend the establishment of a body to oversee standards and ethics and establish a procedure for complaints. There followed years of argument over membership, powers and guidelines, but in 1953 the Press Council, the industry's first official watchdog, began work.

None of this curtailed the relentless criticism of Attlee's government. In the 1950 general election, Labour scraped to victory with a majority of just five seats. The party was riven with divisions and the following year, after another low-key campaign in which Attlee was driven around the country with his wife at the wheel, he was defeated. Winston Churchill returned to power, but by this time he was seventy-six years old and his health was failing. He still believed that it was nonsense to suggest anyone should speak for him. Yet within six months, the pressure from both the Lobby and from ministers and officials in government led to the reappointment of Fife Clark as his adviser on public relations. Clark, who'd been a government press officer, then became Churchill's spokesman. While the prime minister remained largely aloof from speaking directly to reporters, other ministers did give them off-the-record speeches and briefings. What is most extraordinary about this period, however, is the extent to which the prime minister's deteriorating health was kept secret.

In June 1953, Churchill had just finished an after-dinner speech at No. 10 when he suddenly slumped into a chair and was unable to speak or move. He somehow managed to hold a cabinet meeting the next day, though the chancellor, Rab Butler, later remarked that he had noticed the prime minister talked rather less than usual. Churchill was then taken to Chartwell, the family home in Kent, where doctors said he had suffered a severe stroke and might not survive. Downing Street issued a press release that hid the gravity of what had happened. It said 'The prime minister has had no respite for a long time from his arduous duties and is in need of a complete rest. We have therefore advised him to lighten his duties for at least a month.' In fact, he was out of public view for more than two months but had told his principal private secretary, Jock Colville, to prevent any news of his serious incapacitation from getting out. Colville summoned three of Churchill's close friends, who between them controlled a significant number of newspapers. Lord Beaverbrook, the proprietor of the *Daily Express* and *Standard*, Lord Camrose of *The Sunday Times* and *Daily Telegraph* and Brendan Bracken, who chaired the *Financial Times*, were all persuaded to prevent publication of the true state of the prime minister's health. There is no record of whether the issue was ever raised at the regular Lobby briefings, but his stroke was not revealed until Churchill himself referred to it in a speech in the Commons a year later. When Boris Johnson was taken seriously ill with Covid-19 in 2020, information on his medical condition was strictly limited, but the public was informed when he was taken into intensive care. During his recovery, the repeated briefings that he was 'in good spirits' gave us few details on the state of his health, but it is hard to imagine a prime minister nowadays being able to disappear for weeks on end with almost no explanation, as happened in 1953. Churchill eventually stood down two years later, though he remained in Parliament for almost another decade before his death after another stroke in 1965.

When Anthony Eden succeeded Churchill as prime minister in 1955, one of his first acts was to organise a reception for Lobby journalists. Although he'd been a significant figure inside and outside the cabinet for many years and had played a leading role in opposing Chamberlain's policy of appeasement, Eden had little direct contact with correspondents before he took the reins of power. Keen to get the media onside, he decided to brief the 4 p.m. afternoon gathering of the Lobby in person. Fife Clark sent him a memo warning him what to expect:

> the lobby meetings are very informal, and held in conditions of physical discomfort in a small room reached by an iron staircase at the very top of the House of Commons building. The traditional style for these weekly meetings is chatty, personal and not too heavy. On the other hand, every word said, particularly by a prime minister, is most carefully examined for all possible implications and may be 'written up' well above the level of ministerial intention.[17]

The memo suggested the prime minister should talk about a forthcoming summit and his industrial policies but warned against saying anything that might fuel speculation on a cabinet reshuffle.

Though this was a welcome opportunity for Lobby journalists to question the new prime minister directly, the strict rules still in place meant they were not allowed to reveal the source of their stories. Reports would begin: 'I understand . . .' or sometimes 'friends of the prime minister . . .'. Indeed, the correspondents were only allowed to tell their editors that they had even attended a Lobby briefing if they warned their bosses of the need for secrecy. In July 1956 the so-called 'Black Book' code was updated, but many of the key rules remained in place, including the importance of journalists preserving the anonymity of their informants. This was justified on the grounds that 'experience has shown that ministers and MPs talk more freely under the rule of anonymity'. The rule book added: 'Sometimes it may be right to protect your informant to the extent of not using a story at all. This has often been done in the past, and it forms one of the foundations of the good and confidential relationship between the Lobby and members of all parties.'

Despite his readiness to engage with influential journalists, Eden's honeymoon with the press was short-lived. He'd been a dashing, rising star on the political scene, the youngest foreign secretary for over a century, and was a fluent performer on the increasingly important broadcast media. Yet the long wait for the top job had taken its toll. Eden has been described as the Gordon Brown of his era, a politician who'd been waiting in the wings for more than a decade but whose term in power was swiftly terminated.

Eden had won a Conservative majority in the 1955 general election but faced a worsening economy, health problems and accusations of dither and delay. He did appear to have made a good decision when he appointed William Clark, a respected senior *Observer* journalist, as his press and broadcasting adviser, but Clark profoundly disagreed with his boss over his handling of the Suez crisis.

When Egypt's President Colonel Gamal Abdel Nasser took control of the strategically important Suez Canal in the summer of 1956, Eden treated the move as a power-grab by a dictatorial leader. He devised a secret plan for the Israelis to mount an operation to seize control of the canal, whereupon the British and French would intervene on the pretext of separating the combatants. The crisis divided opinion in both the press and the public and Eden became increasingly preoccupied with efforts to win over the media. He summoned groups of newspaper editors to No. 10 to brief them off the record and try to convince them it was their patriotic duty to support the military action. His nervous state and somewhat threatening approach did not work, and those who disagreed with his Suez policy resented the pressure to change their stance. When the papers were delivered to Downing Street at 6 a.m., Eden would phone some of the same editors and their proprietors. Once again it had little effect, yet he ignored advice to deal directly with political and defence correspondents.

Eden's position was made more difficult by Randolph Churchill, son of the former prime minister, who wrote a series of articles for the *London Evening Standard* deploring the government's approach and used his connections with the press barons to encourage wider criticism. Furthermore, he did not hesitate to attack Eden personally. Randolph's cousin Clarissa was married to Eden and he had no qualms about ringing her up to spell out, in forthright terms, his thoughts on her husband's disastrous leadership of the country, sometimes leaving her in tears.

The Labour Party opposed the government's plans for military intervention, and when the BBC reported Labour's stance in parliamentary debates and gave airtime to its leader, Hugh Gaitskell, to challenge the government, Eden was furious. He had hoped to use the BBC to bypass the hostile press and speak directly to the nation and had mistakenly believed this would not be a problem because, as he remarked, 'the Director General was my fag at Eton'.[18] He had misjudged the BBC, which stood its ground and defended its right to reflect both sides of the argument. As the row continued, Eden even considered emergency powers to take control of the broadcaster, though he was talked out of such drastic action.

Caught in the midst of all this was the prime minister's press secretary, William Clark. He believed the whole plan was a mistake but decided to stay in his post out of loyalty and, at his regular Lobby briefings, he continued to outline the government's case without revealing his own huge misgivings. Eden was aware of his press secretary's opposition to the venture, so he ensured that key journalists received additional briefings from his parliamentary private secretary, Bobby Allan. And as the situation at Suez began to ignite, the prime minister appears to have taken the extraordinary step of misleading his own spokesman as well as the wider world.

When British and French forces landed at the Egyptian city of Port Said to seize control of the area around the Suez Canal two days after the Israelis had invaded, Clark's line was hot with calls from journalists, including many from the Lobby. Clark contacted Eden, who told him he was 'very surprised' at the news, though the truth was that this was his strategy being implemented on his orders. Clark had little alternative but to relay the prime minister's response to reporters. Eden then broadcast a message to the nation, saying the deployment of British forces was necessary to 'put out the forest fire' of conflict between Israel and Egypt. He gave no hint that it had all been part of his plan. Meanwhile, Eden continued to try to convince the papers that his cabinet was united when even his defence secretary had come to the view that the policy was a mistake.

In the midst of the crisis, Clark described in his diary what he deemed the worst week of his life: 'The knowledge of collusion, the deception, the hypocrisy . . . I am getting a bit hysterical myself. It seems to me that the PM is mad, literally mad.' He wrote of his 'violent bitter contempt and hatred for a man who has destroyed my world and so much of my faith', adding: 'I long to be free as a journalist to drive this government from power and keep the cowards and crooks out of power for all time. God, how power corrupts.'[19] I can think of no other occasion when a spokesperson for the prime minister has disagreed with his boss so profoundly on such a serious issue and continued in the role. Yet Clark hid his deep misgivings and kept delaying his resignation until a ceasefire was agreed in November 1956. He later revealed the trauma over his personal role in the deception of Parliament and the public:

> Public opinion at home and particularly abroad was suffi-
> ciently potent that it could not be ignored, it had to be fooled.
> News management became news invention. This is not just
> moral judgement about deception; it is based on the know-
> ledge that the power of Government to deceive is so immense
> that fooling all of the people some of the time can success-
> fully and easily lead to fooling them all of the time. That is
> why a Press Officer who is being used for fooling the Press
> should break the rules of the Civil Service and resign.[20]

At the time, most of the newspapers accepted the government's case, despite the misgivings of some editors, and toed the patriotic line. The *Guardian* and *Observer*, however, not only declared their opposition to the entire strategy but conducted their own investigation, which discovered the truth about Eden's secret plan. The *Observer* accused the government of 'folly and crookedness'.

Eventually, after weeks of international brinkmanship, Britain was forced into an ignominious retreat when the USA refused to support the military action and several members of Eden's cabinet turned against him. The United Nations deployed peace-keeping troops to stabilise the situation on the ground. In the midst of the political fallout, the prime minister, who'd been in poor health for some time, flew to Jamaica to stay at Goldeneye, home of the James Bond author Ian Fleming. Downing Street told journalists his doctor had ordered complete rest, but the untimely holiday prompted further questions over his ability to lead the country. Eden had lost the support of his cabinet and in early January 1957 he was forced into a humiliating resignation.

William Clark described his time as Eden's press secretary as 'a story of disillusion'.[21] He rejoined the *Observer*, which had opposed the Suez campaign. Its deputy editor, John Douglas Pringle, said Clark was seen as something of a hero for resigning over the ill-fated episode. 'It was all the more impressive since it was well-known that he had thoroughly enjoyed his job as press adviser to Eden, which brought him so close to the centre of power in Britain. He was seen to be a man who could act with the greatest courage when he believed his principles were at stake.'[22] Clark went on to become a successful pundit who gave regular radio talks on the BBC.

Suez was not only a watershed for British foreign policy; it was also an episode in which the government's efforts to conceal its disastrous plans in a shroud of secrecy did not survive the events that unfolded on the ground. The censorship and surveillance of the war years had been swept away. The television age had dawned and pictures and words on camera were increasingly powerful in shaping our views. Yet, away from the cameras at Westminster, the Lobby would continue to play a powerful role in communicating the unfolding dramas throughout a new era of political turmoil.

3 SWINGING RELATIONSHIPS

'Who governs Britain?'

Prime Minister Edward Heath launching the election campaign, 7 February 1974

On election night, 15 October 1964, Harold Wilson, wearing his trademark Gannex raincoat, made his way through cheering crowds to take the train to London from his constituency of Huyton in Merseyside. 'If the past belongs to the Tories,' he declared, 'the future belongs to us, all of us.' Wilson's narrow victory that night brought to an end thirteen years of Conservative rule. The charismatic Labour leader, at ease with the cameras, had campaigned as a man of the people, a sharp contrast to his Tory rival, Sir Alec Douglas-Home, who was seen as an aristocratic and remote figure, out of touch with the fast-changing world around him.

In the Britain of the 1960s and 1970s, the political upheavals were as numerous and far-reaching as the social and cultural changes transforming the country. Against a backdrop of economic crises and industrial strife, political leaders sought to tap into the mood of the moment, promoting developments in technology and the importance of British music and fashion. They recognised the power of television as a means of connecting directly to the public, though a new generation of on-screen correspondents was determined to ensure the politicians would not go unchallenged. These early political broadcasters swiftly realised that they needed the off-camera briefings just as much as their counterparts working for the newspapers in order to understand fully the unfolding dramas in an era of swinging political fortunes.

Harold Wilson had worked hard to win over newspapers and broadcasters before he came to power. He understood how to handle journalists and was always ready with a sound bite for the television crews, happy to allow the cameras to film him mending his son's bicycle at home or walking near his bungalow on the Isles of Scilly. A BBC profile described him as 'the archetypal new man'.[1] Wilson made a point of finding time for local journalists covering his patch on Merseyside and for less experienced members of the press corps.

The journalist and author Peter Jenkins covered his successful campaign in 1964 and recalls: 'His style with the press was flattering to young reporters. He would single us out by Christian name at press conferences and refer to articles we had written in order to show that he had read them. He seemed to have read everything. He would seldom, on those long railway journeys or over a nightcap in his hotel room, ask for our opinions, but he was eager always for the gossip that newspaper men can retail to politicians.'[2]

Wilson seized every opportunity to reinforce his image as a man of the people, puffing on his pipe and sometimes enjoying a pint of beer, though in private he preferred brandy and a cigar. Yet he also wanted to be seen as a modern leader in an era of rapid change. In his party conference speech the year before the election he famously declared that if the country were to prosper, industry had to embrace the 'white heat' of scientific revolution.

He was frequently described as the first television prime minister, acutely aware of the power of the medium at a time when the handful of channels attracted vast audiences. Recently released BBC archives tell of an extraordinary episode that suggests that a scheduling decision by the boss of the corporation may have helped Wilson at a pivotal moment on polling day. When the Labour leader learned that an episode of popular comedy sitcom *Steptoe and Son* was due to be broadcast on the night of the 1964 general election, he feared that many working-class voters would stay at home to watch it rather than head out to the polling stations. He visited Sir Hugh Greene, then director general, for a drink on his way home from a BBC studio. In an interview recorded in 1981, Wilson explained: 'A lot of our people – my people, working in Liverpool, long journey out, perhaps then a high tea and so on, it was getting late, especially if they wanted to have a pint first . . . I said I didn't want a popular programme between 8 and 9 o'clock.' When asked what he would prefer in the final hour before the polls closed, he suggested 'Greek drama, preferably in the original'. Sir Hugh said that he discussed the matter the next day with the controller of BBC One and agreed that the programme, which attracted audiences of 26 million, should be moved to 9 p.m. 'I rang up Harold Wilson and told him about this decision,' Sir Hugh said, 'and he said to me he was very grateful – it might make a difference of about twenty seats to him. He won, I think by four, and I've sometimes wondered what effect my decision had on British political history.'[3]

Joe Haines covered the 1964 election for the newly launched *Sun* newspaper, which then supported Labour. He was a Labour man himself, a former councillor and chair of his local party, who worked for several papers before becoming a political correspondent for the *Daily Mail*. He resigned when the paper declared its support for the Tories. Five years after the election, he would become Wilson's press secretary and one of his closest political advisers. When I met Haines recently he was in his nineties, but still as sharp as a pin and writing regular political articles.

For a man who spent so much time working on both sides of the Lobby system, Haines's low opinion of the institution is remarkable. It was a secret society then, he told me, its members running 'their own little political mafia'. In his memoirs he describes his fellow Westminster journalists as 'impossibly stuffy and full of their own importance' – a view that was reinforced from his first day as a Lobby correspondent in the late 1950s, when he managed to breach an unwritten part of its obscure code. He was taken aside by one of its elders and given a stern warning about his attire. He was told that if he wanted to continue in his role, he should never again wear Hush Puppies – a brand of suede shoes, later to become the hallmark of the Tory grandee Kenneth Clarke. It wasn't long before Haines received another reprimand. As he sat chatting with a Scottish MP on a narrow bench just outside the Members' Lobby, the Speaker passed by at the head of his formal procession, a tradition that is still part of the daily ritual when the Commons is sitting. Haines was given a written warning, stating that if he failed to stand up, to show his respect on such occasions in future, his pass would be withdrawn.

Haines's frustration with the system increased when he realised the constraints it placed on journalists. As MPs headed away from Westminster at the start of the 1964 election campaign, he ran into William Whitelaw, later Margaret Thatcher's deputy

and the Conservative chief whip at the time. 'Off to your constituency?' Haines asked. 'Yes,' Whitelaw replied, 'it's going to
be bloody disastrous old boy. We're going to lose by a mile.'
Such comments, by a senior party figure, were potentially a big
story that would almost certainly be reported today. Haines,
however, realised that this was a conversation 'on Lobby terms'
and under its rules he would only be able to report Whitelaw's
words anonymously. Without explaining who had uttered them,
the story would be meaningless. He decided it was not worth
reporting at all.

As Opposition leader, Wilson had often briefed Westminster
journalists in person and he was supportive of the Lobby system, despite the continuing arguments over its workings. In a
speech the year before becoming prime minister he declared:
'This unique phrase of only three words, unknown in any other
country, more binding than any legal contract, these three words
"on Lobby terms" are an essential thread of precious metal in our
British parliamentary democracy.'[4] It was a thread that would be
stretched to breaking point over his time in power.

Nevertheless, in his early days at Downing Street, Wilson
wanted to charm the media and was well aware of the importance of establishing a media team he could trust. He appointed
a journalist he knew from his constituency in Merseyside, Trevor
Lloyd-Hughes of the *Liverpool Daily Post*, as his first press secretary. When Wilson arrived in Downing Street there were as
many as three Lobby briefings a day, some of them given by
the prime minister himself. Lloyd-Hughes helped to modernise the
communications team at No. 10, installing more news agency
feeds to keep them updated on the latest stories, and winning
a battle with Whitehall to have televisions in his and the prime
minister's office. Critically, Lloyd-Hughes had (at least at first) a
cordial relationship with Marcia Williams, later Lady Falkender,

who became Wilson's private secretary and a highly controversial member of his so-called 'Kitchen cabinet' of key advisers.

While Wilson continued to dominate the airwaves and enjoyed reasonably favourable coverage in his early months, he was already convinced that any critical stories were the result of journalists and editors conspiring with his political rivals to undermine his position. Wilson arranged to have all the newspapers delivered to Downing Street, so he could read them as soon as they came off the presses. He noted which reporters were writing critical accounts and immediately lodged complaints when they reported speeches and comments from his opponents.

It was always going to be a struggle to govern with such a slender majority and in 1966 the prime minister called another election. Edward Heath had become leader of the Conservative Party but could not compete with Wilson's popularity in a campaign that focused on the personalities of the rival contenders for power. Despite the faltering economy, with rising inflation and huge debts, Wilson won a majority of ninety-six, the second largest in his party's history. Yet although the prime minister had established a more stable government, his problems were piling up. The country was facing a sterling crisis, as ministers grappled with a significant trade deficit, low productivity and rising inflation. Yet Wilson regarded the pound as a symbol of national status and not only resisted devaluation, but tried to prevent speculation that he was planning such a move.

His strategy was derailed by his own press secretary. At a Lobby briefing, Trevor Lloyd-Hughes was asked directly if the government would intervene to defend its value. His response was blunt and unequivocal: 'No.' As soon as his remarks were reported there was a run on the pound and its value tumbled as traders scrambled to sell sterling. His briefing would cost the

Bank of England £240 million in gold reserves. Lloyd-Hughes clearly felt he could not give advance warning of sensitive financial decisions, but many of the political correspondents who had been at his briefing were furious, believing they had been misled.

On Saturday, 18 November 1967 the government announced that the pound would be devalued by 14 per cent to a rate of $2.40. Recently released cabinet papers reveal how the chancellor acknowledged that 'it marked the end of the economic strategy which the Government had been pursuing hitherto'.[5] Wilson sought to limit the damage with his famous television broadcast, declaring that 'it does not mean that the pound here in Britain, in your pocket or purse or in your bank, has been devalued'.[6] This may have been strictly true, but the prime minister's unwillingness to admit to any failure or change of policy brought more unfavourable press comment. 'Can Wilson survive?' was the headline in the *London Evening News* on the Monday after the announcement. The London Stock Exchange and the banks were closed for a day, leaving brokers and traders milling around outside on what was described by Pathé News as a 'black moneyless Monday'.

As the economy and his reputation suffered, Wilson devoted much time and energy to trying to work out the source of hostile stories. He did not accept that they were often accurate accounts of the political wrangling within his government. One particular target was David Wood, political correspondent of *The Times*. He had annoyed the prime minister with his suggestion that he should have one of the health checks that had been proposed for MPs, as he was troubled by a stye in one of his eyes. Wilson invited newspaper proprietors and editors to a weekend at Chequers, but then used the occasion to launch into a series of highly personal attacks on senior Lobby journalists. One of

his guests was Lord Thomson, who was in the process of trying to add *The Times* to his media empire. James Margach, who
was political correspondent of *The Sunday Times*, was present
and described how Thomson asked the prime minister what
he should do for the future of *The Times* if his bid succeeded.
Wilson's answer was abrupt: 'Well you can start by giving a
golden handshake to four people on your staff, starting with
the political correspondent David Wood. Get rid of him first.'[7]
Wilson went on to claim that Wood was biased against him
and had planted stories favouring rivals within his cabinet. The
prime minister went on to list what he saw as the shortcomings
of other senior members of the Lobby, describing one as 'past it,
tippling too much' and another as 'a shorthand slave, not a political writer'.[8] At subsequent lunches at *The Times*, Wilson kept
up the attacks on Wood. In a move of admirable defiance, Wood
was promoted to become the paper's political editor in 1968.

Nora Beloff of the *Observer*, the doyenne of the Lobby, who
had spent many years as a foreign correspondent before joining
the political team, was Wilson's next target. He was incensed by
her reports on his 'Kitchen cabinet' and on the power and influence of his political secretary, Marcia Williams. His employment
minister, Barbara Castle, described an 'astonishing outburst' from
the prime minister at a cabinet meeting in May 1967, when he
'spat out that it was time some members of the cabinet stopped
talking to our enemies like Nora Beloff and feeding them with
material designed to destroy him'.[9]

Wilson's suggestion that his ministers should refuse to talk to
Beloff and other journalists whom he accused of siding with his
enemies did not impress his cabinet colleagues, who questioned
the wisdom of ignoring senior correspondents. Castle herself
was appalled, writing: 'I think Harold is getting quite pathologi-
cal about the press.'[10] His tirade was ignored. Indeed, Beloff's

reports on Wilson's reliance on this close circle of non-elected advisers were a direct reflection of the concerns of some of those around the cabinet table. Beloff was subsequently summoned to No. 10 for a ticking-off from one of Wilson's aides, but the *Observer* was fiercely proud of its independence from political interference and the indomitable Beloff continued her work undeterred.

When word of all this reached the *Observer*'s editor, Lord Astor, he arranged to meet Wilson at his office in the Commons. Taking a bulky file out of a cabinet, the prime minister produced a collection of newspaper cuttings containing numerous reports written by Beloff. Astor was astonished as Wilson began to go through them, pointing to phrases that had been underlined or circled as wrong, inaccurate and malicious. He tried to defuse the situation, but Wilson would not be calmed. 'That woman hates me, she hates me,' he said. 'She's always slanting things against me; she repeats in your paper all the gossip she picks up from my enemies. She's no good as a journalist; she peddles gossip only; she can't deal with serious politics and policies; everything she writes is riddled with lies and half-truths, lending herself as a gossip columnist.'[11] To Astor's amazement, Wilson then told him that he had people 'keeping an eye' on Beloff and revealed a list of dates and addresses, apparently confirming she was under surveillance.

Throughout my years at Westminster, it was clear that every government had its favoured correspondents, those rewarded with early tip-offs of the latest initiatives, and those who are kept at arm's length. Wilson's government, though, appears to have taken this to the extreme. The Labour leader's once-cordial approach to the media swung to one of outright mistrust and hostility. Lord Hennessy told me how Wilson tried to ban him from working as a Whitehall correspondent seeking stories about the civil service as well as politicians. When word of Hennessy's new role, operating outside the tight Lobby system, reached the prime minister he was deeply suspicious. Wilson told the cabinet secretary, the head of the civil service, to write to all Whitehall staff instructing them not to have any dealings whatsoever with the young journalist. *The Times* took a robust view of the attempt to curtail Hennessy's endeavours and urged him to pursue them as hard as possible. Another eminent journalist, Anthony Howard, was greeted with a similarly hostile response when he began working as Whitehall correspondent of *The Sunday Times*. Wilson denounced him as a dangerous man and ordered his ministers not to have anything to do with him.

The prime minister, who had been so keen to appear on television in the early days, had become convinced the BBC was also part of the wider media conspiracy against him. Wilson sought to exert pressure on the corporation, complaining about lines in news reports and jokes on satirical programmes and threatening to prevent any increase in the licence fee. When the BBC chairman Lord Normanbrook died in office in 1967, Wilson installed Lord Hill as his successor. As chairman of the Independent Television Authority, Hill had been critical of the BBC and his appointment did nothing to ease the government's difficult relationship with the broadcaster.

In an attempt to find a way through the animosity between his government and the media, Wilson took to inviting a select group of senior Lobby correspondents to Downing Street for drinks. Over lengthy and informal discussions, frequently in a room called the 'White Boudoir', the prime minister would regale them with his thinking on the politics of the day. Yet this privileged group, which came to be known as the 'White Commonwealth', often left frustrated at the lack of any actual stories. Furthermore, there was inevitably resentment among those who were not invited. Fifty years before Boris Johnson's aides sparked a huge row with a similar attempt to restrict their briefings to just a few journalists of their choosing, the move was seen as part of an attempt to 'divide and rule' the media. Those left out of Wilson's select soirées included Joe Haines, then still at the *Sun*. Haines told me the exclusive gatherings merely increased the suspicions that the government was trying to manipulate journalists. When the *Daily Express*, which was also excluded, reported what was happening, the cosy chats swiftly came to an end.

Haines had already turned down one offer to join the Downing Street press team, partly because he did not want to work under Trevor Lloyd-Hughes. 'I thought he was a bumptious, arrogant and fairly stupid man,' he told me with characteristic bluntness. The two men had already clashed on several occasions. Then, in December 1968, Haines received a call from No. 10 saying the prime minister wanted to see him. At their meeting in his Commons office, Wilson told Haines that he wanted him to replace Lloyd-Hughes – after a few months as his deputy to learn the ropes. Haines accepted and, as promised, soon took over as press secretary. Haines had been brought in to try to bolster Wilson's image in the run-up to the 1970 general election, but, as he told me, 'there's only so much a press secretary can do'.

Haines believes he was taken on because Wilson wanted somebody who was prepared to stand up to the powerful media. He saw his role as a political adviser, serving the prime minister, not the press. He certainly earned a reputation as a forthright and pugnacious spokesman, but it was not an easy job, with crises coming thick and fast and senior ministers increasingly ready to defy their leader. Even before he started, he reflected that the government he was about to join was 'divided, bitter, conspiratorial, jealous and rebellious, and 23 points behind in the polls'.

Haines defied the tendency of most press secretaries to centralise government communications and decided he would no longer be responsible for briefing on the business of all departments. He'd had enough of being showered with documents from every element of government, including embassies around the world, a system he believed was wrong from the outset. 'No one took a decision on anything without referring it to me,' he wrote in his memoirs, 'but most of every morning each day was taken up by my staff ringing round government departments to ask questions of their press officers which might be asked of the press secretary when he held his first Lobby meeting of the day at 11 o'clock.'[12] Haines stopped chairing the weekly meeting of press officers from across Whitehall, and when Lobby reporters asked him about proposals on a particular policy, he told them to check with the relevant department. Haines disliked the entire Lobby system, believed it encouraged lazy journalism and did not see why he should have to provide information that reporters could find out for themselves. He also decided he would not answer any questions on financial, military or security issues, a move partly intended to avoid the costly mistakes of his predecessor, but which led to further frustration among journalists seeking a steer on vitally important matters.

Haines told me he would have liked to put his Lobby briefings on the record, to be named as the official source, but Wilson opposed the idea. Haines believed that if he had been named as press secretary and quoted openly, it would have provided greater 'transparency and honesty', pointing out 'you can always misreport an anonymous or unnamed source'. The prime minister, with his eye on his reputation as ever, did not want to hand so much control over the government's message to his aide, so the briefings continued as before, off the record and unattributable.

Haines undoubtedly wielded considerable influence behind the scenes. He would spend long evenings with the prime minister in Downing Street, discussing politics and policies over glasses of wine or whisky. He told me their relationship was such that he could say what he thought in private, even if it meant disagreeing with his boss. Haines says he convinced the prime minister to hold back from announcing a compulsory wage policy, which would have allowed the government to control the pay of millions of workers, and to support a voluntary cap instead. The *Mail* later called Haines 'The Original Prince of Darkness',[13] to underline the significance of the role he played in the shadows, thirty years before Peter Mandelson earned the title for his part in the New Labour project.

Haines was just as influential in the timing of the election and, despite his criticism of the exclusive, secretive nature of the Lobby, he was quite prepared to brief journalists selectively when it suited him. In 1970, with speculation growing over when the government would go to the country, Wilson wanted to choose a date in June. 'I began the softening up,' Haines wrote in his autobiography, 'by suggesting to Rowley Summerscales of the *Daily Telegraph* that an early election was worth speculating on, provided he didn't tell anyone it came from me. Leaking it to the *Mirror* would have been a hint stronger than Wilson wanted to give.'[14]

The date was duly set for 18 June and, when it came to the campaign, Wilson broke new ground with the first walkabouts, shaking hands with people out on the streets. He sought to portray his Conservative opponent, Edward Heath, as aloof and out of touch, but the public mood had swung against the Labour leader. Wilson had been worn down by years of political infighting and his reputation suffered a further blow when poor trading and unemployment figures were published just before polling day. Heath won an unexpected victory with a respectable majority, leaving the Labour Party in shock.

Overnight, the relationship with the media changed as Heath moved into Downing Street with a very different attitude to the whole process of communication. The Conservative leader came to power promising a new style of government, focusing on 'deeds, not words'. He was unmarried, with few close friends, a man who loved playing his piano and sailing his yacht, *Morning Cloud*. Heath was more interested in delivering his policies and using the power of civil servants than trying to win favour with journalists. He did, though, seek a more transparent relationship with the media and sought to change the way the Lobby worked. In Opposition he had declared: 'It is only when the opaque windows of Whitehall and around our working lives are opened that we shall find ourselves braced to make the immense efforts which are required in Britain today.'[15]

In a further sign of change, Heath appointed a diplomat named Donald Maitland as his press secretary. He was a courageous and skilful negotiator who had been British ambassador to Libya and head of news at the Foreign Office, but he did not have any journalistic experience, in marked contrast to the combative former tabloid reporter he'd replaced. Thus he found some Lobby conventions – including its entirely 'off-the-record' nature – frankly puzzling.

The strict rule of non-attribution meant that the government could not provide its journalists with direct statements or quotes, even when it wanted to do so. Maitland wrote to the Lobby chairman, Keith Renshaw, to point out that this meant they were getting an 'inferior service' to other reporters. 'If a non-lobby correspondent who makes an enquiry by telephone asks for the answer to be put on the record, we may well agree. However, this same answer may normally only be given to a lobby correspondent non-attributably.' Maitland proposed a change to the rules, so that 'Lobby briefings might, on appropriate occasions, include a statement "on the record", provided that a clear dividing line could be drawn between this and the non-attributable part of the briefing.'[16] Maitland argued that this arrangement would 'safeguard the lobby correspondent against deception and the press office against distortion', thus benefiting both sides. It may seem like a modest suggestion by today's standards, but the Lobby records reveal that it prompted such a heated and lengthy dispute that the matter was eventually put to a special meeting of all its members.

One of the strongest opponents of change in 1970 was Leslie Way of the *Western Morning News*, who argued that the proposal was all about 'news management' from a government that 'wanted to go on the record when it suited themselves, for their own convenience and advantage, and in their own good time'. He said it would 'erode the very foundations of the basis on which the Lobby worked', demoting Lobby correspondents to the role of general reporters. Way put down an amendment, warning that 'unless the Lobby wanted to commit suicide it had better throw the proposal out altogether'.[17] When it came to the vote on 2 December 1970, Way's amendment was passed by twenty-five votes to twenty-one and the Lobby briefings continued as before. Though the arguments resurfaced frequently, it was almost thirty years before Tony Blair's chief spin doctor, Alastair Campbell, finally put all the meetings on the record.

Donald Maitland tried another tactic, distributing press releases that could be quoted directly and were handed out at his briefings. Next he created uproar by suggesting the morning Lobby meetings should be moved out of No. 10. Maitland believed it was amateurish and ridiculous to have journalists crowding into his office, where they perched on the arms of settees and leaned their notebooks on the fireplace. He suggested holding his briefings in the old Welsh Office building nearby. While some correspondents did not mind going a few extra yards along Whitehall, others were incensed at the symbolism of being kept out of Downing Street. It was a remarkable forerunner of the row Boris Johnson's advisers provoked when they changed the location of some Lobby briefings, at a time when they were already adopting a hostile approach to parts of the media.

The Lobby Committee again objected strongly to Maitland's proposal and lengthy negotiations ensued. Various different locations were suggested for different days. Eventually, a compromise was reached whereby the morning briefings on Mondays, Tuesdays and Thursdays would be held at the government whips' office at No. 12 Downing Street, adjacent to the prime minister's abode, and the Wednesday briefings would still take place at No. 10. This may all seem rather trivial, but the changes were part of wider moves to formalise the gatherings. They also reflected the reality that the once-cosy chats were increasingly confrontational exchanges between a government seeking to put across its case and journalists trying to extract a phrase that would signal a good story.

Heath then tried holding on-the-record news conferences himself. The prime minister held forth in the grandeur of Lancaster House, wanting to recreate the impact he'd made with similar events on overseas trips. He was keen to explain what he believed was a notable achievement: his successful negotiation of Britain's entry into the European Economic Community, later the European Union. His confident performance worked well on television, but there were immediate complaints that he was bypassing Parliament and newspaper correspondents were not at all happy that their control of the news agenda was being eroded.

Yet after the novelty of the first such occasion, Heath's lengthy speeches and presidential style were less well received, and just four news conferences were held before the idea was dropped. Heath then came up with the idea of prime ministerial 'fireside chats', to be aired on both the BBC and ITV. When the broadcasters pointed out that they would have to offer Harold Wilson the same opportunity, for the sake of political balance, that plan was also abandoned.

Like Wilson, Heath became increasingly preoccupied by the coverage of his premiership, seeing every unfavourable story as a malicious, personal attack. In May 1973, the *Financial Times* carried an article by the respected columnist Joe Rogaly entitled 'A Government of Little Stature' which was scathing in its criticism of Heath's administration, concluding: 'There will be no true solutions while we continue to be governed by pygmies.' It was published the day before Heath was due to have lunch with the paper's chairman and senior editorial team. Heath was incensed at the article, and not only cancelled his lunch appointment but ordered his staff to tell his hosts he considered their behaviour despicable. His mistrust of journalists grew and even Peregrine Worsthorne, then deputy editor of the *Sunday Telegraph*, described an atmosphere of 'impatient formality' when he was granted an on-the-record interview, after which he was 'hustled out . . . no jokes or private confidences, not a trace of the charm or bonhomie with which these rather gaunt occasions are usually enlivened'.[18]

As unemployment rose and industrial strife intensified, Heath struggled to convince the public that he had the solutions and leadership the country needed. When the miners went on strike, power cuts plunged households into darkness and the prime minister announced the three-day week to conserve fuel supplies. To add to the sense of crisis, violence was escalating in Northern Ireland and British troops there were struggling to maintain order.

The February 1974 general election, under the cloud of a state of emergency, resulted in a hung Parliament, with Labour the largest party by the slimmest of margins. After Heath's attempts to forge a coalition failed, Wilson returned to Downing Street. Alongside efforts to tackle the immense economic and industrial problems facing the country came a renewed determination to take on those he saw as his enemies. Journalists were left in no doubt that the mood had swung against them once more.

Even before he moved back into No. 10, Wilson told Barbara Castle: 'No more lobby briefings, just the *Mirror*, the *Sunday Mirror* and the *People* will have access to me . . . There will be no more of those off-the record discussions of what the Government is going to do. Instead, Government decisions will all be on the record – preferably announced in the evening before the 9 p.m. news.' Castle was relieved at the time, 'so long as he does not renew that vendetta with the press'.[19] In fact, while the regular off-the-record sessions with Lobby journalists did continue for a while, the vendetta had resumed.

As Joe Haines put it: 'Wilson's particular paranoias were about the press and the belief that someone, somewhere was determined to do him down, and showed most in his paranoia about defending Marcia against all comers and all the evidence.'[20] Marcia Williams was still the prime minister's powerful political secretary, and his readiness to stand by her was tested within weeks of the election. The *Daily Mail* broke what became known as the 'slag heaps scandal', revealing that Williams and other members of her family had invested in some Lancashire slag heaps, in a deal that could prove lucrative if the sites were cleared and permission granted for development. Wilson had frequently denounced land speculation and the story gathered pace when a businessman involved in the arrangement forged the prime minister's signature on a letter, in an attempt to link him directly to the scandal. The businessman, Ronald Milhench, was eventually jailed for fraud.

The media focused on the role of Marcia Williams and besieged her elegant London home in a bid for comment and photographs. Despite his differences with Williams, Haines not only supported her but was sympathetic to her plight; he and his colleagues spent time with her, providing support as she faced what he called 'harassment of an intimidating kind'. His Lobby briefings were almost as confrontational. They were, he said, 'consumed by questions about the affair and reached the depths when Ian Waller of the *Sunday Telegraph*, who had lunched too fluidly, drunkenly made absurd insinuations against Marcia and I walked out'.[21] Haines said relations between Downing Street and the Lobby had never been worse, though he did continue to deliver his briefings for a while.

The prime minister's next move was to make Marcia Williams a baroness, despite the objections of Haines and other close advisers. For Wilson it was a gesture of defiance to the press and of generous support to his closest aide, who was desperate to regain some respectability after the media storm she had faced. The *News of the World* got the story of her peerage before the official announcement, infuriating the prime minister, who dismissed the scoop as a 'pack of lies' and told Haines to brief the Lobby accordingly. There was no apology when Marcia Williams did indeed become Lady Falkender shortly afterwards.

It is hardly surprising that Wilson had a rough ride in the run-up to the second election of 1974, held on 10 October.

The miners' dispute had been settled but there was continuing industrial strife, with strikes by rubbish collectors, dockworkers and bakers, and senior Labour figures were facing allegations of sleaze. Far from trying to woo the media, as he had done before his first election, the prime minister delivered a speech attacking their behaviour, claiming that a cohort of journalists had been scouring the country trying to uncover scandals about his government. Despite all this, Wilson hoped to win a clear majority and the polls suggested he had a comfortable lead over Heath's Conservatives. The result, though, was a majority of just three seats. The turmoil and instability continued.

The strain on Wilson had by this time affected his health and his appetite for power. He told his closest aides he intended to serve only another two years. Just a few months after fighting his fourth election, the prime minister felt a flutter in his heart as he left the Élysée Palace in Paris, after talks with President Valéry Giscard d'Estaing. He headed immediately for the British Embassy and summoned his doctor, Sir Joseph Stone. After a medical examination Stone said Wilson was exhausted, but should make a full recovery as long as he did absolutely nothing for a week. The prime minister went to Chequers for the prescribed rest.

Haines, who was with him on the trip, told journalists Wilson was suffering from the flu. The economy was going through perilous times and Haines told me that if he had said the prime minister was suffering from heart trouble 'the markets would have gone crazy . . . and the bloody queue of would-be prime ministers would be forming in front of me in the Lobby'. Haines said it was the only time he lied to the Lobby and, despite all their rows, the journalists swallowed his explanation for Wilson's absence. Nevertheless, relations between Haines and the Lobby were so bad that some of its reporters were calling him the 'anti-press officer'. He had stopped taking journalists on the prime minister's plane on foreign trips, a practice he believed made life easier for the journalists but did not help the government.

Then, in June 1975, Haines wrote to the chairman of the Lobby Committee to say that he had decided to end his daily briefings altogether. The move was triggered partly by the behaviour of reporters towards Marcia Falkender, and partly because he believed some of them had passed information from a Lobby briefing about a forthcoming vote to the Conservative whips. In his letter, Haines said the fundamental question was whether the system of daily meetings was good for government, good for the press and good for the general public. 'In my firm opinion, and in the view of the prime minister it is not.' He wrote: 'Many people rightly suspect the validity of stories which lean heavily upon thin air,' and announced that if a statement needed to be made on behalf of the prime minister, it would be made on the record. Haines said this would 'eliminate the kind of extreme absurdity where, under the rules governing the present meetings, even the name of the annual poppy-day seller who calls on the prime minister is given unattributably'.[22]

Though his decision came without warning it was no great surprise, and the chairman of the Lobby, John Egan, noted that many colleagues were 'far from unhappy about the cessation of a system which, in practice had become an almost empty charade'. He warned against 'too much talk about the incompetence, laziness or hostility of those who are not here to speak for themselves', reflecting the anger of some correspondents at Haines's attitude towards them. Egan reminded Lobby members that their task was 'to inform their readers as rapidly and as fully as possible about what is in the mind of the prime minister . . . We must overcome any barrier put in our way by individuals who, deliberately or otherwise, find this task beyond their will or their talent.'[23]

In practice, the suspension of face-to-face meetings with Haines was no great loss to Westminster journalists. His belligerent attitude meant the gatherings had already ceased to provide much genuine insight. Thus the correspondents continued to work as they had always done, speaking to as many different sources as possible to find out what was happening and explain it to their readers and listeners.

The stand-off continued for the rest of Wilson's time in power, with no formal Lobby briefings, although Haines did speak to some journalists individually and off the record. The economic crisis continued, with crippling inflation fuelling further industrial unrest, but Wilson did win plaudits for his handling of the thorny issue of Europe, on which his party and his government were divided. He renegotiated the terms of our membership of the European Economic Community, and allowed his cabinet the freedom to express differing views during the referendum on the issue. It was an approach David Cameron would follow some forty years later, though, of course the result in 2016 reversed the original vote on the matter. In 1975, when the country voted by a two-thirds majority to stay in the EEC, even the *Daily Telegraph* described it as 'quite frankly a triumph' for the prime minister.

Yet Wilson would spend his final months in Downing Street convinced that both the media and the security services were out to get him, threatening legal action over articles he considered unfair. The announcement of his resignation on 16 March 1976 was a political sensation, taking the media by surprise and prompting much speculation over the reasons for his departure. Lobby journalists had no advance warning of the dramatic announcement, nor did the cabinet, who were only informed after the prime minister had been to Buckingham Palace to inform the Queen of his decision. It was five days after his sixtieth birthday; he had been Labour leader for thirteen years and had told his inner circle of his intentions two years earlier. Yet conspiracy theories over the reason for the abrupt end to his premiership continued to circulate for many years. There were suggestions that he could have been the victim of a plot by the security services, who were said to be concerned he had communist sympathies, and questions as to whether the onset of dementia had already started to affect his judgement. None of the rumours has ever been proved. At the time, the coverage of the end of the Wilson era was remarkably sympathetic, given his endless rows with the media. The *Sun*'s tribute was headed 'Thank you from all of us', writing that he 'towers head and shoulders above any other parliamentarian of his own or any other party', though it went on to suggest he had given too much power to the trade unions. Even the *Daily Telegraph* described him as 'the man who came near to making Labour a natural party of government', but it added, witheringly, that he'd been 'the ideal leader to guide Britain on her long slide down into mediocrity'.

Haines turned down Wilson's offer of a peerage, telling him he wanted to abolish the House of Lords. He added: 'The truth was that there was no way I was going to be associated with this shabby betrayal of what I thought we all stood for.'[24] Haines left government when Wilson stood down and wrote a revelatory book describing his time in Downing Street. He subsequently resumed working as a journalist, becoming a leader writer and then political editor of the *Daily Mirror*, returning once again to the Westminster Lobby which he had so frequently disparaged.

During Wilson's time in office his government's relationship with the media had swung from the warm embrace of their early encounters to an arrangement where the two sides were barely on speaking terms. It swung back to a more amicable footing when Jim Callaghan won the leadership election to succeed Wilson and became prime minister.

Callaghan was an avuncular figure with long years of experience in senior cabinet posts, and was far less preoccupied with what the papers were saying. He set out from the beginning to restrict his media appearances, deliberately adopting a lower profile than that of his predecessor, while seeking to cultivate his image as 'Sunny Jim', as he was described by the tabloids, a positive and straightforward leader. It was an approach he tried to sustain in the face of daunting challenges – an economy continuing to falter, crippling strikes, high unemployment and the lack of a parliamentary majority.

Callaghan appointed as press secretary Tom McCaffrey, a civil servant who had been his head of information at the Home Office and Foreign Office. McCaffrey's first move was to phone the chairman of the Lobby and inform him that the regular briefings would resume the next day. The resumption of normal service to the Lobby came as great relief to its journalists, yet relations with the media were far from easy and it wasn't long before the first big row.

Sir Peter Ramsbotham, a distinguished diplomat, had been appointed to the plum post of British ambassador to Washington in 1974 and had worked to build relationships with three different US presidents – Nixon, Ford and Carter. In 1977 the foreign secretary, Anthony Crosland, died suddenly and was replaced by Dr David Owen, then a dashing young rising star keen to make his mark at the Foreign Office. Owen decided to replace Ramsbotham with his friend Peter Jay, economics editor of *The Times* and Callaghan's son-in-law.

Jay had no diplomatic experience and when the move was announced, there were roars of laughter at the news conference.

Owen was taken aback at the reaction and questions were, of course, raised at subsequent Lobby briefings. In an attempt to explain why he was being moved on, McCaffrey described Ramsbotham as 'snobbish' and a 'fuddy-duddy' to the assembled journalists, comments that made the headlines of some tabloids. Ramsbotham himself later said the episode was 'silly', and believed he was 'smeared' by press teams in London who had panicked. 'I didn't mind that at all because I knew I wasn't a fuddy-duddy, but I did object when they started saying I was professionally not very good. I know when I'm good and when I'm bad in my career, and I know that I was good in Washington. It was just my cup of tea.'[25]

Ramsbotham was given the post of governor of Bermuda as a consolation, but the remarks made about him by the prime minister's spokesman continued to reverberate. Callaghan made a statement to the Commons, denying there had been a deliberate smear campaign against the ousted ambassador and declaring his son-in-law's new position as an 'imaginative appointment'. He batted away questions about his spokesman's comments but declared to the House that he was attracted to the idea of public rather than private briefings.

The result was a further round of arguments about the terms of McCaffrey's briefing, as well as the controversial Washington appointment. The Lobby Committee's annual report for that year said the row had left 'strains and bruising from which neither side has yet fully recovered'. It added that: 'McCaffrey felt that he had been deprived of the protection normally provided by the conventions of Lobby reporting. The prime minister wondered aloud to MPs whether the Lobby system stood up to this sort of strain. The Lobby resented being used as a whipping boy.'[26] There were further discussions over whether the prime minister's spokesman could be quoted and how his words should be reported. There was another brief trial of on-the-record meetings, for at least part of the time, but McCaffrey was so cautious about what he would say that the arrangement did not last long.

There were far bigger battles looming for Callaghan's government as it grappled with continuing industrial unrest and a precarious economy, with an overwhelmingly right-wing press increasingly critical of his approach. While his aides sought to portray him as calm and unflappable, Callaghan faced accusations of complacency and a failure to get a grip on the nation's problems. In January 1979, the prime minister attended a summit on nuclear arms control with the leaders of the USA, France and Germany. It was held in Guadeloupe in the West Indies, a remote location intended to allow world leaders to pursue their discussions away from the press. Undeterred, the media despatched teams to cover the talks and the *Mail* managed to get a shot of Callaghan in his swimming trunks. The photo did not look good back at home, where Britain faced freezing temperatures in what became known as the 'winter of discontent', with key public services, including rubbish collections, fuel deliveries and some ambulance services, disrupted by strikes.

The prime minister decided to speak to journalists at Heathrow on his return, against the advice of his press secretary. What he actually said was: 'I don't think other people in the world will share the view that there is mounting chaos.'[27] The *Sun* reported the story with the famous headline 'Crisis? What Crisis?', three words that would help to bring about Callaghan's downfall. He lost a vote of confidence and was forced to call a general election. Lobby briefings become largely redundant once an election is called as the government spokesperson is not supposed to get involved in party matters.

As the country prepared to go to the polls in 1979, the media focus was on the new Opposition leader, Margaret Thatcher. The first woman to rise to the top of her party, Thatcher was already wooing key figures in the papers as she sought to reach out to a broad swathe of voters, including those who had traditionally supported Labour. The editor of the *Sun*, Larry Lamb, would visit her at home to dispense advice and encouragement. He was, she said, 'a valued friend and ally'.[28] David English, his counterpart on the *Daily Mail*, was another confidant. In a personal letter, she described him as 'a wonderful friend in recent years, especially in lean times when friendship matters most'.[29]

At the same time, she set out to charm the broadcasters and bolster her image as a leader who understood the everyday concerns of the people. During the five-week campaign, she happily posed for pictures as she filled her shopping basket, drank tea in a factory and famously cuddled a calf. Helped by a team of advertising experts, the Conservatives sought to blame Labour for the disastrous state of the economy with the famous 'Labour Isn't Working' poster, evoking the long queues of the unemployed.

The result was a swing to the Conservatives of more than 5 per cent, the biggest in any election since the end of the war. Margaret Thatcher became the country's first woman prime minister, with a substantial majority, a victory undoubtedly helped by the support of much of the popular press. 'Our Maggie', as she was described by the tabloids, fought and won a highly professional campaign, combining the down-to-earth appeal of a housewife with the crusading zeal of a leader determined to forge a new, free-market approach to the economy. It was the start of an intense new relationship with the media that helped to establish her grip on power and her reputation around the world, but which came under immense strain during the many battles she fought over more than a decade in Downing Street.

4 BERNARD AND THE BOYCOTT

'It is with great admiration and heartfelt thanks that Denis and I say goodbye to you and to No. 10 – for the two are almost inseparable in our minds.'

Margaret Thatcher's farewell letter to Bernard Ingham,
28 November 1990

A Bernard Ingham briefing was an unmissable occasion for any political journalist in the Thatcher era, and not just because attendance was required under the Lobby rules unless there were good reasons for absence. The saying at the time was that what Bernard said today, Thatcher would be thinking tomorrow. The Westminster news corps swiftly realised that the new press secretary was so close to the prime minister that he could speak for her, without actually discussing each specific issue with Thatcher herself. Furthermore, every Ingham briefing carried the tantalising prospect of a good story.

'Rumbustious' is the word frequently used to describe his regular meetings with the Lobby, which would begin with the usual formal rundown of the diary for the day and announcements of government business. Then the questions, and the fun, would begin. He would be asked his views on a minister who had stepped out of line or a certain trade union leader. He'd give a straightforward but diplomatic answer, which would prompt a series of additional queries as the journalists pressed him to go further. 'Does the prime minister agree with everything the minister has said?', they would ask, or 'does she think the union leader is acting irresponsibly?'. Ingham's favourite phrase for dismissing suggestions he considered unworthy of more serious consideration was 'bunkum and balderdash'. Elinor Goodman, former political editor of Channel 4 News, believes he often used that catchphrase to defuse a confrontation and to try to deflect the focus of the meeting. She described him as an 'ebullient, big character' who would fight back if anyone criticised the government, but she also found him 'pretty fair, as long as you didn't mind him going for you occasionally'. And there was always the chance that he might lose his patience and utter another colourful phrase or a comment that would make the morning headlines.

Robert Harris, Ingham's unofficial biographer, said he embodied the Thatcherite spirit, 'embattled, aggressive, often brutally frank', and created a vicious circle: 'He would brief the Lobby, emphasizing her toughness and determination; the following morning, he would relay the resulting headlines to the prime minister in his press summary; this would fire her up to be still more tough and determined, giving him more ammunition for his next Lobby briefing.'[1] For Andrew Thomson, Thatcher's former constituency agent, 'Listening to Ingham gave the media the certain impression that there was a ferocious tigress on the loose in Whitehall.'[2]

It was not enough just to listen to those briefings. Correspondents learned to keep a close eye on his famous eyebrows, which, according to Robert Harris, would 'writhe and heave like a pair of lovesick squirrels'.[3] Trevor Kavanagh, who was political editor of the *Sun* for more than twenty years, recalls: 'His face was very mobile and sort of broadcast a language of its own.' If Ingham wanted to emphasise a point, he would twitch those eyebrows in an alarming manner. 'Sometimes you knew that he was trying to say something without necessarily saying it in words and on occasions whole stories could be written on the basis of the signals that were transmitted that way.'

Ingham remains as divisive a figure as the prime minister whom he served for more than a decade. Kavanagh says he was trusted by Lobby journalists, whichever political line their papers took. 'They felt that what they were getting from him was the truth,' he told me, 'that he would not mislead you, and that was a very precious commodity.' Others, however, believe he abused his position. Andrew Marr, a political reporter during the Thatcher years, told me Ingham played a critical role in 'a high-handed government regime' using a Lobby system that, he says, was at its most iniquitous and most powerful. According to Marr, Ingham was frequently 'doing over' cabinet ministers who didn't agree with the prime minister through his unattributable briefings. 'They would mysteriously find their reputations being trashed in the papers,' he told me. 'Margaret Thatcher was using Bernard Ingham and using the Lobby system to strengthen her own position in cabinet and to exclude or downgrade opponents at the top of the Conservative Party.'

Although Ingham is frequently described as the original spin doctor, it is a description he rejects strongly. 'It isn't a game, it's a serious mission, trying to communicate and to represent the views of the government and of the prime minister.' He admits he could be 'quite brutal' with journalists who crossed him, but also likes to stress that he was a civil servant, rather than a political adviser, despite the many instances when he strayed into political territory. Julia Langdon, doyenne of the Lobby and a former political editor of the *Daily Mirror* and the *Sunday Telegraph*, says there were numerous occasions when Ingham was pushed to the point of 'imploding'. 'He is an irascible character,' she told me. 'He got irritated very easily, but he was extremely fair. I could not fault him on that, ever.'

Sir Bernard Ingham received his knighthood in Thatcher's resignation honours list. Now in his late eighties, the robust, outspoken Yorkshireman still peppers his answers with the colourful phrases for which he is renowned. He told me that during his eleven years as press secretary he conducted some 5,000 formal Lobby briefings and around 30,000 meetings with journalists on overseas trips, over lunch, drinks or on the phone.

Ingham undoubtedly shared many of Thatcher's core beliefs: her readiness to stand up to the Establishment, to take on the unions and reduce the role of the state. Yet he was originally a Labour man and once stood for the party as a council candidate. He's proud of his roots, growing up in Hebden Bridge and working as a journalist on the *Yorkshire Evening Post* and *Yorkshire Post*. Ingham became labour correspondent at the *Guardian* at a time when many British businesses were beset with strikes and industrial action. He left the Labour Party when he began working as a government press officer in 1967 and handled media relations for Labour ministers including Barbara Castle and Tony Benn, as well as senior Conservatives including Lord Carrington.

Ingham never expected to end up working for the prime minister, and before he was offered the job as her press secretary had only met her for fifteen seconds during a visit to his department. The scale of the challenge was immediately clear. According to Ingham, Thatcher 'wilfully refused' to read the newspapers. When the writer and broadcaster Iain Dale asked her if she read them, she exclaimed: 'Oh no! . . . they make such hurtful and damaging remarks about me and my family, that if I read the papers every day, I could never get on with the job I am here to do.'[4]

However, this left her vulnerable to appearing out of touch, an issue that would recur during her leadership. So Ingham began providing a digest of relevant stories that they would discuss every morning. It was this daily conversation that would help form the close bond between the prime minister and her chief press secretary, enabling him to speak with authority on her behalf. He told me they did not agree specific lines: 'I would just absorb her reaction . . . the plain fact is I think we thought alike . . . or came to think alike.'

Ingham also shared Thatcher's capacity for work, arriving at the office by 6.30 a.m. every morning to prepare his press digest before their 9 a.m. meeting. He briefed the Lobby at 11 a.m. and 4 p.m. most days, the Foreign Press Association on Mondays, a group of European reporters on Tuesdays, American correspondents on Wednesdays, regional UK journalists on Thursdays and those from the Sunday newspapers on Fridays. He chaired a weekly meeting of government press officers, had lunches with journalists and frequently attended evening receptions. Ingham often accepted the prime minister's invitation for a chat over a glass of whisky at the end of a long day, though he tried to be home by 9 p.m. for what was then the main BBC evening news bulletin.

Even Ingham's formidable stamina was tested when news broke on 2 April 1982 that Argentine forces had invaded the Falkland Islands and seized other British territories in the South Atlantic, including South Georgia. Recently released government documents show that, although there had been some contingency planning, the prime minister was taken by surprise by the offensive. 'I never, never expected the Argentines to invade the

Falklands head-on. It was such a stupid thing to do, as events happened, such a stupid thing even to contemplate.'[5] The prime minister's response was swift, and a task force was despatched within days. It was an arduous and controversial mission in which 255 British servicemen were killed, but within ten weeks it would succeed in forcing the surrender of the Argentine troops and recapturing the Falkland Islands.

It was a defining episode for Margaret Thatcher, securing her image as the conquering hero – 'Our Maggie' – in the popular press, though there was criticism of the way the military campaign was conducted and the attempts to silence dissenting voices. For Bernard Ingham, who was head of the Government Information Service as well as the prime minister's chief press secretary, it was the most difficult and nerve-wracking challenge in his time at No. 10. He had to deal with the military's desire for secrecy over its operations, rivalry between the three armed services, hostility towards the media from parts of the Royal Navy and the government's need to maintain public support for its conduct of the war. 'I sometimes felt that there was more unarmed combat both between Government and journalists and within Whitehall than was ever seen in Port Stanley,' he said.[6]

Initially, navy commanders did not want to take any journalists with them to the South Atlantic at all, a stance Ingham saw as politically impossible to accept, particularly as coverage and pictures were already emerging from the Argentine side. Ingham was bombarded with calls from the newspapers and broadcasters and fought hard on their behalf. There were rows over how many reporters and camera crews could be accommodated, but eventually the military was persuaded to provide sufficient places for representatives of most national newspapers, broadcasters and news agencies to cover the campaign. Their reports were, however, censored and often delayed.

The news correspondents who were 'embedded' with the British military became household names – Brian Hanrahan of the BBC, Michael Nicholson of ITN and John Witherow of *The Times*, who went on to become the paper's editor. The Lobby correspondents back at Westminster provided the political context to the unfolding drama.

The Ministry of Defence wanted to ensure that all information was strictly controlled and came from a single source. They decided that public updates would be given by their own deputy director of public relations, Ian McDonald, an identikit civil servant with no media experience whatsoever. It showed. He stuck meticulously to carefully worded scripts and there was no opportunity for journalists to ask questions.

Bernard Ingham was not impressed by the arrangement, which he said was 'dreamt up by a misguided mandarin in the MOD'. He believed the information should have been delivered by a minister in the Commons who could then be questioned by MPs and thought this should have been demanded by Parliament itself. Yet McDonald's deadpan tone, devoid of all emotion, enunciated at slow-dictation speed, made him an unlikely star of the war and millions tuned in to watch the bespectacled man from the ministry deliver his televised statements.

With the MOD wanting full control over the release of any information, Bernard Ingham was also told to stop his off-the-record briefings to Lobby journalists. Ingham refused to give way and clashed with Sir Frank Cooper, the MOD's most senior civil servant: 'I said, well, you've got a problem. I am playing to full houses; there isn't a square foot of carpet not occupied in my room. And may I remind you that the prime minister's running this. In other words, get lost.' Critically, Ingham had the backing of Mrs Thatcher and continued his meetings and private chats with Lobby correspondents, despite continuing battles to get details from the MOD. Furthermore, Thatcher despatched her ally the party chairman, Cecil Parkinson, a member of the war cabinet, to provide his own background briefings for Lobby reporters, to reinforce the political messages of the campaign.

These off-the-record sessions with Lobby journalists were an important part of Thatcher's efforts to counter the pressure from within her own cabinet from ministers, such as her foreign secretary, Francis Pym, who wanted to pursue the option of negotiations to end the hostilities. As the British task force approached the Falklands, Pym travelled to Washington for talks with his US counterpart. The Americans opposed the war and Pym returned with a draft agreement for an intensified push for a diplomatic settlement. Thatcher was furious at the idea of compromising with the enemy. The recently released documents show she rejected Pym's plan as 'totally unacceptable' and a 'total retreat' that would have betrayed the Falkland Islanders. Thatcher herself wrote: 'We were at loggerheads.'[7]

John Cole, who had just been appointed the BBC's political editor, believed it was important to reflect these disagreements, however unpopular it made the BBC in the eyes of No. 10. He reported on the turmoil in the Commons lobbies, as a number of Conservatives supported negotiations rather than force, although many were reluctant to express their views openly. When a senior Tory, Sir David Crouch, did so at a backbench committee he was booed and hissed. Cole said: 'The best way for me to find out the balance of opinion was to talk to as many MPs as possible myself, on Lobby terms – that is, on the understanding that their names would not be used – and then to form a judgement.' He estimated that up to one-fifth of Conservative MPs wanted a diplomatic settlement on the best conditions that Francis Pym could negotiate.[8] Supporters of Thatcher's view – that the Argentines had to be defeated militarily – were far more vocal and put down a motion in the Commons warning the government against a 'sell-out'.

When reports of the differences within the cabinet emerged on the BBC and elsewhere, Ingham made a rare statement on the record, dismissing the stories as 'bunkum', and Thatcher herself publicly denied the rift, even though she knew that Pym and others were unhappy with her determination to go all-out for a military victory.

The most contentious attack of the Falklands War was the sinking of the Argentine ship *Belgrano* on 2 May, with the loss of 323 of those on board. The vessel was outside the exclusion zone and apparently sailing away from the islands. Its sinking became a cause célèbre for anti-war campaigners, who believed the use of force could have been avoided. Thatcher, who was famously challenged over the episode on the BBC's *Nationwide* programme, insisted the *Belgrano* posed a threat to British forces and that the attack was justified.

Mrs Thatcher's battles with the BBC are well documented. She summed up her 'trouble' with the way the conflict was reported, saying: 'Many of the public, including me, did not like the attitude particularly of the BBC and I was very worried about it. They were sometimes reporting as if they were neutral between Britain and Argentina.' I am sure that on this last point the BBC would entirely accept her view. Indeed, the corporation was keen to uphold its reputation for impartiality and warned staff not to use terms such as 'our boys' or even 'our troops', which would imply their support for one side in the war. Thatcher added that she 'felt strongly that they were assisting the enemy by open discussions with experts on the next likely steps in the campaign'.[9]

Despite the rows with the broadcasters, it is notable that during the conflict the prime minister did not spend much time considering the newspapers' coverage. Documents in the Margaret Thatcher Foundation show that Ingham's press digests from this period went mostly unread. However, even without studying them in any detail, Thatcher would have been aware that most of the tabloids were cheering her on, with the *Sun* proclaiming – in a notorious headline – 'Gotcha' on the day of the sinking of the *Belgrano*.

The fact that the conflict was fought almost 8,000 miles away from the UK, with the censored media embedded with the British military, meant it was easier for the government to control the flow of information on what was actually happening. When the Argentine forces surrendered, after the loss of 649 of their personnel, the government imposed a news blackout that would be almost impossible today, much to the annoyance of reporters who accompanied British soldiers as they marched into Port Stanley. It meant the prime minister herself could announce the victory to a packed House of Commons.

At 10 p.m. on 14 June, an hour after she had received a call from Fleet Command confirming the surrender, Mrs Thatcher made a brief statement to MPs. 'Our forces reached the outskirts of Port Stanley. Large numbers of Argentine soldiers threw down their weapons. They are reported to be flying white flags over Port Stanley.' The news was greeted by cheers in the Commons and crowds gathered outside Downing Street. Thatcher's popularity soared, and from that moment she was able to evoke the Falklands spirit to reinforce her image as a patriotic leader prepared to fight for her principles.

Of course, there were many with huge misgivings over the conduct of the war, and there was further controversy over the government's handling of Lord Franks's inquiry into the conflict. Its key finding, though, was that Thatcher's administration should not be blamed for failing to foresee the invasion of the Falkland

Islands. Buoyed by her victory and some encouraging economic figures, Thatcher decided to go to the polls. The result was a landslide Conservative victory and Thatcher returned to Downing Street, with Ingham at her side, in a stronger position than ever, ready for the next big battle – with the powerful trade unions.

Industrial action by the miners had been central to the chaos that had brought down the previous Conservative prime minister, Edward Heath. Thatcher was determined not to suffer the same fate. Two years after she became prime minister she had backed down from plans for pit closures in order to avert a threatened national miners' strike, but by 1984, strengthened by her victories in the Falklands and at the general election, she was in no mood to compromise. The National Coal Board announced plans to close twenty pits with the loss of 20,000 jobs and Arthur Scargill, leader of the National Union of Mineworkers, announced a nationwide walkout. The bitter dispute would last a year, with violent clashes between police and pickets, thousands of arrests, hardship and divisions within mining communities. The miners were forced to return to work and the pit closure programme went ahead. It was a defining drama in Margaret Thatcher's struggle to curb the strength of the unions, reinforcing her image as an unbending leader who would not shrink from confrontation.

The dispute was the focus of an intense propaganda battle and, from the outset, the government had the majority of the newspapers on its side. 'Pit War' was the headline in the *Sun* as clashes between miners and police broke out on picket lines at the start of the strike. The prime minister famously spoke of 'the enemy within' as she addressed the 1922 Committee of Conservative parliamentarians in the summer of 1984, telling them: 'We had to fight the enemy without in the Falklands. We always have to be aware of the enemy within, which is much more difficult to fight and more dangerous to liberty.' Her words were seen as inflammatory at the time, and recently released documents reveal fascinating detail of how Bernard Ingham explained this phrase in his Lobby briefings. His message was that 'militancy and intimidation was a challenge to our form of democracy'. He told journalists that while some reports had equated 'the enemy within' with the miners, 'this was not the case – she was referring to the minority of militants. The PM was in favour of the workers who wanted to work and in favour of the constructive elements in the trade unions.'[10]

It later emerged that Thatcher at one stage planned to use a similar phrase to describe left-wing figures in the Labour Party and it still has deep resonance for many in the Labour movement. Seumas Milne, who became a senior aide to Jeremy Corbyn when he was Labour leader, has suggested that 'the chilling catchphrase embodied her government's scorched earth onslaught on Britain's mining communities – and gave the green light for the entire state to treat the miners' union as outlaws'.[11]

Nick Jones worked as a political correspondent for *The Times* before he became industrial correspondent for the BBC and a key figure in its coverage of the miners' strike. He told me the government went into 'maximum propaganda mode' in a bid to mobilise the country against the strikers and their leaders. Jones says the power of the Downing Street machine was directed at Lobby correspondents, seen by No. 10 as 'their clients' who could be trusted with confidential briefings, while he and other industrial correspondents were kept out of the loop. 'They thought we would be unreliable because we were too close to the trade union movement,' he told me. 'They would not want to feed us lines.' The government's objective was to get at least half of the miners back to work and Jones found himself under pressure to report the growing tally of so-called 'new faces' who crossed the picket lines. Jones, who has written several books about relations between politicians and the media, notes that 'it was the moment for me when I began to realise how, as a journalist, you can get swept along by the government's agenda of the day'. He says that he was not alone in this, claiming 'the BBC coverage went along with that agenda', though the corporation has always insisted it remained impartial.

Downing Street, meanwhile, sought to position itself on the side of the workers against the union barons. The recently released notes of Ingham's briefings to the Lobby at the time show how he seized on the failure of the NUM to hold a national strike ballot. He told Lobby journalists that the government's controversial legislation, requiring ballots to authorise industrial action, 'sought to put power into the hands of the Trade Union members, and distance it from the Trade Union militants to use for their own ends'. He said that the measures on balloting had been 'toughened up' and claimed the moves were targeted at union leaders rather than their wider membership, adding: 'There seemed to be a feeling of revulsion in society at attempts to usurp the democratic procedures. It would be important to help arm the moderates with the power of public opinion.'[12] The message was reflected in the coverage of the dispute, particularly in the tabloids, with the NUM president Arthur Scargill described in the *Daily Express* as an 'army general' and the *Sun* calling him a 'dictator', though there is no suggestion that Ingham had used such words himself.

When Nick Jones returned to Westminster as a BBC political correspondent in 1988, after a decade as an industrial reporter, he was in no doubt that No. 10 had manipulated coverage of the miners' strike and other disputes. Jones, in turn, was treated with deep suspicion by Bernard Ingham and others in his team. 'I was a marked man,' he told me. Jones said there were several occasions when Ingham 'took the mickey' out of him during Lobby briefings or sought to undermine his credentials. After a dispute over an incident involving the IRA, Jones was attempting to ask Ingham a series of questions at a Lobby briefing when the press secretary turned on him, saying: 'It's about time you decided whether you are part of society or apart from society, laddie.' It was a response that had the rest of the room laughing and made it impossible for Jones to pursue his quest for answers. On another occasion, when he was trying to establish the status of a leaked document, he was labelled a troublemaker, with Ingham warning him, 'the BBC's job is not trouble'. Though some might have found this intimidating, Jones calmly assessed that it was all part of the press secretary's game: 'He's avoided my question, he's got the whole of the Lobby cackling and he's taken the wind out of my sails and it's very difficult to come back and argue.'

Journalists were not the only ones who found themselves undermined by the prime minister's closest aide. There were several infamous occasions when Ingham's briefings to the Lobby, all unattributable of course, derailed the careers of senior cabinet ministers who were deemed to have stepped out of line.

Francis Pym's differences with the prime minister were evident even before the Falklands War. In 1982, when he was Leader of the Commons, he delivered a speech to the Allied Brewery Trades Association that was notably pessimistic, even for a man not known for his upbeat demeanour. Pym said that while the government was committed to a long-term economic recovery, 'this cannot lead to an early return to full or nearly full employment, or an early improvement in living standards generally'. He said it would be a long time before new industries could replace the jobs lost by the demise of old ones and spoke of a 'very painful period of transition'. He concluded that in the short run, 'living standards generally can only fall'. Pym's comments not only undermined Thatcher's more upbeat message on the economy, they were a marked contrast to the assessment of the chancellor just a few days earlier, who had stressed the signs of recovery.

The following day, with newspapers full of stories of Pym's bleak view of the economic prospects, Thatcher faced the Opposition leader, Michael Foot, at Prime Minister's Questions. She was irritated at Pym's intervention, but she could not disown one of her own ministers on the floor of the House, so resorted to quoting his words and, when pressed, said 'it was a very good speech'. Half an hour later, when her press secretary held his usual off-the-record Lobby briefing, he struck a markedly different tone. After numerous questions, Ingham sought to explain Pym's remarks by pointing to his reputation as a 'somewhat gloomy chap'. He then added, 'Come off it, you know as well as I do it's being so cheerful as keeps him going' – the lugubrious catchphrase of a glum character in a wartime radio show. Of course it was Ingham's colourful turn of phrase, rather than the prime minister's words in the Commons, that made the headlines the next day: 'Maggie sends grim Pym to the doghouse' said the *Sun*; 'Fury over Pym's bleak warning of gloom' was the *Daily Mail*'s version.

Pym survived this episode but was deemed to have stepped out of line again during the run-up to the 1983 election, when he said a Conservative landslide would not be good for the country because there would be no need for the government to seek consensus. Thatcher was furious and pointedly told a news conference the next day: 'I think I could handle a landslide majority all right.' Lobby journalists were then treated to a lively round of briefing and counter-briefing. They reported 'authoritative sources', who were in fact Thatcher's inner circle including Cecil Parkinson, suggesting that Pym was no good. Then there were 'friends of the foreign secretary', which meant Pym himself, making it clear that he would walk out if he were to be moved from the Foreign Office. He kept his job until Thatcher did indeed win her landslide election victory, when he was promptly sacked.

He was not the only cabinet casualty to be wounded in an off-the-record Lobby briefing. John Biffen, an intellectual Thatcherite who replaced Pym as Leader of the Commons, had a difficult relationship with Bernard Ingham, once jokingly describing him as a 'rough-spoken Yorkshire Rasputin'. By 1986 Thatcher's popularity had slumped after a series of political setbacks and the Conservatives suffered heavy losses in local elections. Biffen went on London Weekend Television's *Weekend World* and suggested that the party should fight the next general election on a 'balanced ticket', with a team that had 'a spread of views'. After all, he remarked, 'nobody seriously supposes that the prime minister would be prime minister throughout the entire period of the next Parliament'.

Thatcher did indeed seriously suppose she would serve another full term and was furious. Yet, once again, she played down the remarks when questioned in the Commons, saying that Biffen had 'made many robust policy points on Sunday with which I wholly agree'. Ingham told me that at his next briefing the Lobby 'came at me in waves', questioning whether Biffen could keep his job. Ingham eventually said: 'I really am surprised at you lot. You all know as well as I do that John Biffen is that well-known semi-detached member of the cabinet.' That phrase 'semi-detached' was splashed across the next day's newspapers and it was clear that Biffen's ministerial career was hanging by a thread. When Thatcher won her third election victory the following year, Biffen was dismissed.

Ingham told me he was attempting to defend a minister under fire, to give a convincing explanation. In his autobiography he admits: 'I make no bones about it: I should not have made such remarks and I wish I never had. But I did.'[13] Trevor Kavanagh of the *Sun* said he saw it as the press secretary being blunt but frank. 'The idea that John Biffen was semi-detached didn't seem to be like a dagger in his back, it just seemed to be an observation.' Years after the event, Biffen acknowledged the significance of Ingham's description of his position at the time, calling his autobiography *Semi-Detached*.

Much later in Thatcher's premiership, another senior minister, Sir Geoffrey Howe, found himself at the wrong end of an Ingham briefing to the Lobby. In a complex and controversial reshuffle in 1989, Howe lost his job as foreign secretary and was made Leader of the House, but with the added role of deputy prime minister. The title was clearly intended to compensate for what would otherwise have been a demotion. When the Lobby gathered, the BBC's political editor at the time, John Cole, asked for more details of the role: whether it would entail Howe deputising for the prime minister on overseas trips and chairing key cabinet committees. Far from confirming these responsibilities, Ingham said that Howe had been given 'a courtesy title with no constitutional status'. It clearly undermined Howe's position and he took his revenge the following year, resigning from the government with a famously devastating attack on the prime minister. The politician known for his quiet, understated demeanour had fallen out with Thatcher over her approach to Europe and accused her of undermining his own position during negotiations on the future relationship. He told a hushed Commons: 'It is rather like sending your opening batsmen to the crease, only for them to find that their bats have been broken before the game by the team captain.' Ingham was unrepentant over his remarks about Howe, saying that he had not intended to diminish his new role but simply to explain the position. He remarked to me that the former deputy prime minister was 'so sensitive it's amazing he didn't die of a pinprick'.

Ingham insists he never intended to hound any ministers out of office and says it is unfair to judge him on a handful of comments about certain members of the government, given the thousands of conversations he had with journalists, collectively and individually, over the course of eleven years. He has calculated that such incidents amount to one per 6,000 briefings and said that from his perspective, facing the Lobby was sometimes like a fox hunt: 'Picture the lobby, all foregathered, in its afternoon eyrie all scenting trouble. It is not a pretty sight. The lobby in full tally-ho cry after a minister – which happened roughly once every full moon – never was, though sometimes they could be painfully funny when they almost parodied themselves.'[14]

I have certainly attended numerous briefings when the Lobby pack scents that a minister is in trouble and sets off in pursuit of a telling line. The usual opener is whether the prime minister has full confidence in whoever is at the centre of the latest controversy. Any wavering or qualification in the press secretary's response is a clear signal that he or she is on the way out. The follow-up questions will inevitably press the spokesperson on whether the prime minister supports the views or comments expressed by the imperilled politician. Of course, both sides have learned from Ingham's experiences that anything less than a full-throated defence of a minister will trigger headlines declaring that their days in office are numbered.

Nonetheless, Robin Oakley, former political editor of *The Times* and the BBC, told me that he believed the occasions when Ingham undermined elected politicians amounted to 'skulduggery' by the prime minister and her press team. He said they were also the result of the extraordinarily close relationship between Ingham and Thatcher, where they would have conversations in private and Ingham would then 'freelance to a considerable degree'. The dangers of such an approach were laid bare when Ingham strayed into sensitive economic territory early in 1985.

The value of sterling had been falling and the prime minister disagreed with her chancellor, Nigel Lawson, on what the government's response should be. She shared the view of her economic adviser, Sir Alan Walters, that the pound should be allowed to find its own level. With the pound in danger of falling to the psychologically significant level of parity with the dollar, Lawson came to the view that intervention was needed. On 11 January 1985 he decided that interest rates should be raised to try to stop the slide.

Ingham was not fully informed of the Treasury's plans, though he had discussed the issue with Thatcher, who told him that you could not buck the market and there was no point in throwing good money after bad. When he came to brief the Lobby of Sunday newspaper journalists on the Friday afternoon he faced a barrage of questions. He admitted it was an extremely difficult occasion. 'I vehemently stated that the government was not going to waste its reserves on supporting the pound,' he told me. Of course, his words made the headlines in most of the Sunday papers. 'You can be absolutely certain that we are not going to throw money at the pound' was the quote in the *Sunday Telegraph* from 'authoritative government sources'. Other newspapers had similar stories, *The Sunday Times*'s headline declaring: 'Thatcher ready to let £1 equal $1'.

Though the Treasury had briefed a very different story to the *Observer*, explaining the measures it would take to bolster sterling, the duty press officer at Downing Street steered the BBC to follow Ingham's briefing, which it duly reported. The result was economic and political turmoil. The Bank of England intervened on the Hong Kong markets that evening and interest rates were hiked to 12 per cent. Lawson told the Commons the next day: 'There was a feeling in the markets that the government had lost their willingness and ability to control their affairs.'[15] It is estimated that the episode cost the country £100 million in foreign reserves.

Ingham admitted to me, 'of course I had made a mistake,' but explained that he had believed he was accurately conveying Thatcher's approach to the issue. Despite the huge cost, both financially and to the reputation of the government, the prime minister made it clear that Ingham should not take the blame. At a party in the Commons a few days later, attended by many political journalists, she circulated the room with her press secretary, telling everyone: 'Bernard's marvellous. He's great. He's the greatest.' It was a sign of how indispensable Ingham had become. Though the arguments over economic policy continued, his position was secure. Indeed, Ingham's role had been enhanced to enable him to co-ordinate the work of different departments and try to ensure a more coherent message. He installed a new computer system and insisted that all planned announcements, speeches and media interviews from ministers across Whitehall were agreed through No. 10. It was a forerunner of the so-called 'grid' set up by Alastair Campbell to control and plan the Blair government's agenda, a version of which still operates today.

There were limits to Ingham's power, though. Lord Whitelaw, deputy prime minister and Thatcher's close confidant, was put in overall charge of the Government Information Service. It earned him the nickname of 'Minister for Banana Skins' – the voice of the government in times of crisis. As Leader of the House of Lords, Whitelaw also had his own briefings for Lobby journalists, which were held over drinks in his resplendent room in Parliament.

This weekly gathering on a Friday in the Lords was another of the secrets of the Lobby, which had lapsed, sadly, by the time I joined. Michael White, former political editor of the *Guardian*, recalls a large mahogany table with an ample array of whiskies, brandies and sodas and the trembling hand of one of the Lobby stalwarts reaching for the first Scotch of the day at 12 noon. Things have certainly changed since then. These convivial gatherings, hosted by the genial and courteous Whitelaw, were very different from the cut and thrust of the more formal briefings from No. 10, but discerning journalists came to realise that the relaxed atmosphere meant that they could be a valuable source of gossip and stories. It was all too good to last. When Bernard Ingham learned how these reports were emerging, he decided he would attend himself and sat at the back to ensure Whitelaw's remarks were all on-message. The Friday engagements were never the same again, to the regret of many who had attended over the years.

Although the business of government communication was changing, the Lobby continued to operate under the code that had been in place for decades. It did, however, relax its strict rules of secrecy for its centenary celebrations in 1984. There was a reception, a party and a lunch at the Savoy, addressed by the prime minister, where the cameras were allowed in, despite the misgivings of some long-standing members. In her speech Thatcher acknowledged the significance of the occasion, 'the first time that the Fourth Estate has avowed its Secret Service'. Until this moment, it was supposedly only Lobby members who knew that 'Celestial Blue' was code for the prime minister. Yet Thatcher stood before the television crews and declared: 'Celestial Blue is on the record.' She knew all the other obscure rules too, as she spoke of 'the organisation that never was . . . is after a century without a notebook at worst, very discreetly and unobtrusively using the back of an order paper; never running after a minister; never joining a conversation with a minister, MP or peer unless invited to do so; never in any circumstance making use of anything accidentally overheard in any part of the Palace of Westminster.' Despite gently mocking the arrangements, the prime minister had some qualified praise for the system. 'I myself, I must tell you, am not lost in uncritical admiration of the Lobby, a feeling which I judge to be warmly reciprocated. But whatever else, I may think of you as a mirror which holds up the political process to the people; I do not find you tame or cosy, or gullible, or even wet. But then, come to think of it, not often dry either.'[16] Thatcher said she expected the Lobby to return to the shadows for another 100 years.

It was just two years later, however, in the summer of 1986 that a concerted effort was made to modernise and open up the Lobby. The *Independent* was launched, out to challenge the established newspapers with a fresh approach, free from any party-political allegiance. Its first political editor was Anthony Bevins, a fiercely independent-minded journalist, who had arrived at Westminster in 1967 as Lobby correspondent of the *Liverpool Post*. He was the son of Reggie Bevins, who had been the only working-class Tory minister in Harold Macmillan's cabinet. Anthony Bevins had built a reputation for digging out uncomfortable truths, asking awkward questions and scorning the tendency of some journalists to club together to corroborate stories. He had worked at the *Sun* and *Daily Mail* before becoming chief political correspondent of *The Times*.

Bevins had long believed that Lobby briefings were an attempt by No. 10 to 'bottle-feed' the media and decided that the *Independent* would boycott them. Andrew Marr, who had joined the paper as a junior political correspondent, supported the view that it was time to take a stand against a system which, he said, allowed Margaret Thatcher to use unattributable briefings to 'trash the reputations' of cabinet ministers who did not agree with her. Marr told me the idea was to be an 'insurgent newspaper, no longer playing by the old rules'; but 'it was more than boycotting, we really wanted to get to create as much trouble as possible'. By this measure they certainly succeeded.

Sir Bernard Ingham said that when Bevins told him of the move, 'the thought of not having the sneering Bevins looking at me every day was enormously attractive'. Yet Ingham realised the real intention was to break open the Lobby system and put his briefings on the record, something he was determined to resist. He was scathing about Bevins's approach, pointing out that the *Independent* team still intended to use their Lobby passes to access the corridors of Parliament, to talk to ministers off the record and to receive embargoed copies of reports and legislation. Ingham told me his attitude to Bevins was: 'What you're saying is you'll talk to anybody on Lobby terms but me – get lost.' Digging in his heels, Ingham made it clear that if Bevins and his colleagues were refusing to attend his briefings, they could not expect the benefit of his guidance on the prime minister's views through other means. There would be no lunches, drinks or phone conversations to provide the *Independent*'s political correspondents with the background chats that Lobby members would usually seek on a regular basis.

Ingham did make an exception, however, when he was invited to dinner at the Garrick Club to discuss the whole issue with Bevins and his newspaper's editor, Andreas Whittam Smith. It resulted in what he described as a 'right set-to'. After a stormy meal, where it was clear neither side was prepared to compromise, battle lines were drawn.

Yet the paper found ways around the difficulties thrown up by the stand-off. Andrew Marr describes how the *Independent* discovered what Ingham was saying, despite the boycott. 'We had narks, people who agreed with us privately inside the Lobby, who gave us the wink about what was going on.' On other occasions the *Independent* would simply read copy from other newspapers and instead of saying 'sources close to the prime minister', it would name Bernard Ingham and print his words as direct quotes. The paper was reporting stories provided at briefings it refused to attend and breaching all the Lobby rules, an approach that infuriated both Downing Street and many other journalists. 'It drove a lot of my colleagues absolutely spare with anger, they were very, very cross,' Marr told me. He was accused of behaving like a hooligan, destroying what other political reporters regarded as highly valuable. 'There were a lot of raised voices, and a lot of very, very angry arguments around Westminster and around the Press Gallery at that time.'

Trevor Kavanagh of the *Sun*, who was chairman of the Lobby for much of this uneasy episode, was not impressed by what he saw as 'two-faced' tactics. He was amazed to watch as those he described as the *Independent*'s 'tame lackeys' from other news organisations went into Lobby briefings, then sat on a bench in a Commons corridor to debrief Bevins or one of his colleagues. Kavanagh saw it as 'cheating' to duck out of the Lobby system but then get the same briefing, second-hand. He also dismissed as 'rubbish' the arguments against anonymous briefings, telling me they were a 'light-touch process of exchange of information, access and an opportunity to ask questions'.

Philip Webster of *The Times* was a friend of Bevins and was one of those who helped him occasionally, passing on some of what he had been told at briefings. Yet Webster made it plain that he too had doubts about the *Independent*'s tactics. 'I'd often say, look, this is what they're saying, but are you sure you really want to know, Tony? You're supposed not to be interested in these briefings any more.'

The *Guardian* and the *Scotsman* later joined the boycott, but Ingham made it plain he was determined to see off what he called 'The Stupid Tendency'. In an effort to resolve the ongoing row, Lobby reporters decided to hold a series of votes. Proposals to put the briefings on the record, attributable to a Downing Street spokesperson, were rejected, with journalists voting by sixty-seven to fifty-five to continue the meetings on the same basis. They also voted against a suggestion that anyone attending a briefing should pledge to abide by the rules but did decide to hold an inquiry to clarify how the Lobby would operate in future.

In a written submission, Ingham argued that the prime source of information from the government should continue to be on-the-record statements in Parliament by ministers and published documents, but that the Lobby system should supplement this. He wrote:

The Government notes that journalists who seek to end unattributable briefings of the lobby as a group by the chief press secretary are in no way opposed to his (or others including ministers and MPs) briefing them individually on an unattributable basis, and seek such briefings as a matter of course. Indeed, journalists apparently consider it would be entirely impractical – and undesirable – to end the well-tried system of unattributable briefing in favour of an exclusively on-the-record relationship between informant and correspondent. The Government cannot accept that the lobby should seek to treat differently collective briefings with the chief press secretary . . . . The Government considers that, properly operated according to the conventions, the lobby system can serve a useful purpose in our democracy and for that practical reason would wish to see it continue.

Despite the boycott, the heated arguments and the review of the system, Thatcher's press secretary won the day. The result was that almost nothing changed and his briefings continued as before, with the journalists who attended them referring to Ingham as a 'government source' or 'sources close to the prime minister'. Ingham told me he got a certain 'grim pleasure' from excluding those who continued their boycott from accompanying the prime minister on foreign trips. He also ensured that his team of press officers 'gave them the run-around' as they pursued more mundane enquiries. All of this he saw as a significant victory and he described the whole episode as 'The Great Lobby Revolt that Flopped'.[17]

Trevor Kavanagh, with the backing of colleagues from other papers, had written a letter to *The Times* declaring his support for Ingham. Yet Kavanagh told me that after the row and the inquiry: 'Things were never quite the quite the same again, trust had disappeared.' Lobby briefings became far more limited, and he had to ring Bernard Ingham separately to get the off-the-record guidance he needed. Philip Webster said the boycott did not work for the simple reason that the briefings were 'an amazing source of news' and political journalists needed to be inside the meetings to know what was going on.

Even some of the journalists on newspapers that maintained the boycott were not convinced it was worthwhile. Michael White, who returned from a stint in Washington to become the *Guardian*'s political editor, saw it as little more than 'gesture politics'. He was one of those who ended up talking to reporters from other publications who had been at the briefings, a situation he saw as 'absurd'. Relations between his paper and No. 10 were difficult, 'like two countries where diplomatic relations have been broken off'. White did not even agree with the objective, as in his view: 'Most briefing on the record is by definition useless. The good stuff is always off the record.'

Chris Moncrieff, who spent nearly forty years covering politics for the Press Association, dismissed all the controversy around the Lobby system at the time as 'a lot of rot'. He said it was fascinating and a privilege to be at the hub of political life. 'Without being an actual member of government, you couldn't be closer to what was happening,' he said. 'You knew more about what was going on than your average MP.' Moncrieff viewed Ingham's years at No. 10 as a 'golden era' for Lobby journalists. 'Getting a story was all that I was interested in.' He certainly delivered plenty of those over the years, many of them through his close relationship with Ingham, a rapport bolstered by the fact that, as an agency, the PA reported news and direct quotes without any political commentary. In the pre-Twitter era, the PA was a prime source of breaking news and Moncrieff personally landed some of the biggest political stories of recent history, being the first to report the resignation of Sir Geoffrey Howe as deputy prime minister and the departure of Nigel Lawson from the government. When Thatcher finally decided to stand down, Ingham rang Moncrieff, telling him: 'You might want to snap this.' A snap was a PA alert signifying an important story to newsrooms across the land. This one had just two words: 'Thatcher resigns.'

Thatcher's downfall has been well documented and Ingham remained loyal as, one by one, her cabinet turned against her. She told him, with tears in her eyes, that they were all deserting her. He replied, 'We aren't,' though he knew it was all over.[18]

Ingham was at the funeral of his brother-in-law on the day of Margaret Thatcher's emotional departure from Downing Street, but returned to No. 10 for the briefest of handovers to his successor, Gus O'Donnell. Just as Thatcher's resignation divided opinion, so Bernard Ingham's retirement provoked some widely differing reactions. Lobby journalists arranged a farewell lunch, Sunday newspaper reporters lined up to shake his hand and government press officers gave him a round of applause. There were also some highly critical profiles published, prompted in part by Robert Harris's unauthorised biography of him. *The Sunday Times* wrote a feature entitled 'The Hard Man of No. 10' and the writer Christopher Hitchens, in typically forthright style, described him as 'a bulldog-visaged, anti-intellectual, aggressive, insecure, class-conscious reactionary tyke'.[19]

In response Trevor Kavanagh of the *Sun* wrote a letter to *The Times*, saying that very few Lobby journalists saw Ingham as the manipulative character portrayed by Harris and other critics. He said it was important to understand that Ingham's first duty was towards the prime minister, not the media. Kavanagh wrote that, while there were times that Ingham could not tell them the whole truth, he was 'unfailingly straight, honest and fair'. He added that more senior members of the Lobby, with experience of earlier Downing Street press secretaries, rated him as 'the best'.

Ingham has always been remarkably frank about his own shortcomings. 'I find it curious that no one has suggested over the last eleven years that I was temperamentally unsuited to the job of chief press secretary,' he wrote in his account of his time at No. 10. 'Not even my severest critics – those who would kill the messenger on sight if they thought they could get away with it – have advanced that theory. Yet there is at least a case to be made that no one with my temper (which is as quick down as it is up) and robust approach to the would-be bullies of this world should never be allowed within a mile of Number 10

– except, perhaps to represent that similarly straightforward person, Mrs Thatcher.'[20]

For all the rows, there were undoubtedly many Lobby journalists who look with affection on Ingham's time at No. 10, and indeed it was his temper that often provided them with stories. At a reception for the Lobby centenary, where the cameras were not present, Julia Langdon, then at the *Sunday Telegraph*, with colleagues from other papers, performed a cabaret tribute to the chief press secretary – to the tune of 'Hello Dolly':

> Hello Bernard,
> Well hello Bernard,
> It's so great to see you there at four o'clock.
>
> You're looking swell Bernard,
> We can tell, Bernard,
> That the Lady's had a fit, you're in a state of shock.
>
> So, we feel the room swaying
> So, we keep praying
> That you'll lose your temper like you always do.
>
> So, (altogether now), hold the front-page, fellas,
> Bernard's in a rage, fellas,
> That means we got a front-page lead for you . . .

It seems unlikely that our current cohort of political editors and correspondents would ever have delivered a similar tribute to Dominic Cummings.

5 A MAJOR MAULING

'A sound bite never buttered any parsnips.'
John Major, the *Guardian*, 31 January 1998

obby journalists who had covered every twist and turn of the
dramatic events leading to Margaret Thatcher's downfall had
mixed emotions as they turned their attention to the new political
landscape and a relatively unknown prime minister. Whatever
their views on Britain's first female leader, Thatcher had provided
an almost ceaseless flow of gripping stories for more than a
decade, and her successor was certainly a very different character. Few had expected John Major to win the battle of the big
beasts in the Conservative Party to succeed her. Indeed, Major
famously opened his first cabinet meeting in November 1990
with the words, 'Well, who would have thought it?' Similarly, Gus
O'Donnell never expected to find himself at No. 10 as the prime
minister's press secretary. He was an economist who worked at
the Treasury, where he became press secretary to Nigel Lawson
when he was chancellor and then to John Major, who succeeded
him. A year later, Major asked O'Donnell to come with him as

he entered Downing Street. He is often known as GOD, thanks to his initials, and was later given a peerage after a high-flying career that would see him become cabinet secretary and head of the civil service.

Though he has faced numerous huge challenges, working for successive governments, O'Donnell has described his time as Major's press secretary as the hardest job he's done, advising and speaking on behalf of a prime minister obsessed with his portrayal in the media. While Thatcher often had no time for the press digest prepared for her, Major had the first editions of the papers delivered to No. 10 after they were printed late at night. They were not a relaxing bedtime read for a leader so sensitive to criticism. Major was frequently characterised as weak, dull and indecisive, with the *Guardian* cartoonist Steve Bell depicting him as a pathetic Superman wearing Y-fronts over a grey suit.

O'Donnell's first task was to try to resolve the rift with the Lobby, to end the boycott of the system by the *Guardian*, *Independent* and *Scotsman* while bringing greater transparency to the role. He discussed the issue with the cabinet secretary, Robin Butler (now Lord Butler), who raised the idea of putting his briefings on camera. O'Donnell insisted he did not want to become a public figure, competing for airtime with elected politicians. He believed that as press secretary he should not become the story. 'I just think it's really important that as civil servants, we avoid the cult of personality. We are not standing for office,' he told me. The suggestion went no further.

O'Donnell did agree, however, that his words in the regular briefings to the Lobby could be quoted and that they could be attributed to 'a Downing Street source', instead of journalists saying, 'I understand the prime minister believes . . .' or 'my sources suggest . . .'. While this still sounds like an obscure arrangement for an official briefing, it was a significant change, given the heated arguments over the decades. This time the modest reform was agreed swiftly and eight months later the boycott was over. O'Donnell saw this as 'a big success'. He wanted to make his role less political, to have an inclusive system where he could brief all the political correspondents at the same time and avoid accusations of favouritism. It is a mark of his integrity that he was liked and respected by many journalists across the board, despite the almost impossible job that he undertook.

Today, O'Donnell conveys an air of calm, down-to-earth pragmatism after being at the heart of some of our biggest political crises over the decades. Yet thirty years ago, he found his first experience of briefing the Lobby quite a challenge. 'I wouldn't say daunting; the word I'd use is terrifying,' he told me. He'd been comfortable chatting to economic correspondents about taxation and statistics, but found he was expected to give instant answers to questions about every aspect of government policy: 'And you knew that if you got it wrong, it wouldn't be a minor error, it would be emblazoned across the news.' Adding to the pressure was the knowledge that his boss fretted over every unfavourable headline.

O'Donnell spent four years battling to defend a prime minister struggling to cope with economic turmoil, deep divisions over Europe and allegations of sleaze. Whereas Bernard Ingham had confronted journalists, erupting with colourful phrases when he did not like their questions, O'Donnell would seek consensus and try to explain the reasons for Major's approach to the issue of the day.

Despite, or perhaps because of, his amiable manner and conciliatory approach, O'Donnell did not get an easy ride from a press corps that had honed its skills during the regular jousting sessions with Ingham over the previous decade. The BBC's Carolyn Quinn welcomed the arrival of a press secretary who was more approachable, but told me: 'His niceness became his worst enemy, because people took advantage of him a bit more and, as time went on, he had to toughen up his act.' Trevor Kavanagh of the *Sun* described O'Donnell as 'a very amiable guy, easy to like, easy to get on with'. He admitted that some of the experienced hands in the Lobby took advantage of O'Donnell's honesty, and knew when to press for more answers: 'Being a devout Catholic, it was always clearly difficult for him to tell anything even approaching a lie. And you could see his eyes rotating as he started to dissemble. So you knew when you were on the right track.'

O'Donnell told me that lying is something he would never do. 'If I had not told the truth, well then my credibility would be gone. That credibility is to die for, that's what makes people want to listen to you and you have got to keep that.'

O'Donnell says Major always wanted to play straight with the media too, to be honest with them and the British people, but the former prime minister has since admitted that he was too preoccupied with his portrayal in the press. 'Absolutely!' he told Julia Langdon, 'I was wrong. I shouldn't have read the papers so much.' He describes the stories of him staying up all night, awaiting the first editions as 'overdone', but he clearly did feel he had to be aware of the endless reports of dissent among his own MPs. 'The most extraordinary stories were appearing daily and one did need to know what they were. That said, I should have ignored them more than I did.' In his defence, he added that they had not, however, affected his policies.[1]

While Major has admitted that he did not handle the press very well, others around him in the early years of his premiership are more damning. Judith Chaplin, who was Major's political secretary and special adviser at the time, thought he was 'a nice man', but one who had been 'pitchforked in with no clear principles about what he is trying to achieve'. As her diaries make clear, she quickly became frustrated with the amount of time he spent dealing with what the media had been saying about him. 'He cannot bear to be criticised and takes it as a personal slight: he is obsessed by his image and will have to get a tougher skin.'[2]

Langdon described how, as political editor of the *Sunday Telegraph*, she received a call from O'Donnell asking her to explain why a Conservative newspaper was being so beastly to a Conservative prime minister. She had written a front-page story reporting that Margaret Thatcher had been raging about the mistake she had made in supporting Major as her successor, quoting her as saying: 'He is grey. He has no ideas.' Langdon calmly replied that she was accurately reporting Thatcher's words.[3]

Despite all this, when Major called a general election in April 1992 most of the right-wing newspapers swung behind the man they had so brutally caricatured, turning their vitriol on the Labour leader, Neil Kinnock. For all his efforts to modernise his party, they feared Labour was still in the grip of the unions and wanted a Conservative government, despite their reservations about the Tory leader. Major sought to make a virtue of his ordinary background, campaigning from his soapbox as the boy from Brixton who'd never been to university and liked to eat at Little Chef. Once again, he defied the pollsters and the pundits and emerged victorious with a slim twenty-one-seat majority. 'It's the Sun Wot Won It' was the paper's famous headline on the day he secured a fourth term for the Conservatives. The *Sun*'s owner Rupert Murdoch has since said the much-disputed claim was 'tasteless and wrong', and insisted the media do not have such power, but there is no doubt that the support of his papers had made a difference. That support did not last long.

Within months of his unexpected election victory, John Major faced a political and media onslaught as the disastrous events of

'Black Wednesday' unfolded. Britain crashed out of the Exchange Rate Mechanism, which had tied the value of the pound to that of other European currencies. Interest rates soared and recently released documents show the government spent almost £27 billion trying to prop up the pound. It was an episode that destroyed the Conservatives' record for economic competence, the moment when the right-wing media turned against Major. He was vilified for his personal role in persuading Thatcher to join the ERM when he was chancellor two years earlier, and for insisting it was the right decision just a week before the Black Wednesday debacle.

Fearing how the dreadful day would be reported, Major decided to call newspaper editors himself. It did not go well. Kelvin MacKenzie, the colourful editor of the *Sun*, told him: 'Prime Minister, I have in front of me a very large bucket of shit which I am just about to pour all over you.' Major has since disputed what was said in this conversation, but MacKenzie has stood by his account, stating he had a witness.[4] The *Sun*'s headline the next day was: 'Now we've all been screwed by the cabinet'.

There was a new and confrontational mood in the Lobby briefings as O'Donnell struggled to explain the government's handling of the crisis. 'He had a very, very rough time,' the BBC's Nick Jones told me. He said Lobby correspondents would 'work as a pack', sharing information, sensing that O'Donnell was on the back foot. Jones explained how it worked: 'Journalist A asks a question, and journalists B, C, D and E have got supplementary questions and we're all chasing the same thing, and we hope that one of us is going to get the actual answer which tells us what is really going on.' It was a very powerful way of attacking the weaknesses of the government, he said, and O'Donnell 'just wasn't a street fighter'.

During his statement to the Commons on the economic crash, the prime minister was repeatedly challenged by Eurosceptics in his party who believed the ERM disaster showed the danger of handing too much power to Europe. He insisted it was in Britain's interests to play a leading role in what was then the European Community. Over the next year, Major fought a series of bitter battles with members of his own party over the Maastricht Treaty, which created the European Union and Single Market. Tory MPs who opposed the treaty voted repeatedly against the government, forcing a series of knife-edge votes. Major's slim majority had already been whittled down and, when the rebels inflicted defeat on a crucial part of the legislation to enshrine the Maastricht provisions into UK law, Major called a vote of confidence. He won by a comfortable margin of forty votes and celebrated with champagne for his staff in his parliamentary office. Yet his fight with the Eurosceptics was far from over and the divisions over Europe continued for decades.

When Theresa May fought and won a similar confidence vote after suffering defeat on her Brexit deal more than twenty-five years later, I spent many long hours on the small patch of grass opposite Parliament, trying to explain the unfolding drama above the noise of rival groups of demonstrators. In 1993 the place to be was the Members' Lobby, where Maastricht rebels were all too eager to catch a word with reporters. With all conversations supposedly off the record, there were plenty of other senior Conservatives, including ministers, who were ready to deliver choice phrases on the performance and future prospects of the prime minister. The rebels would claim that Major was betraying British sovereignty, handing power to unelected bureaucrats, and should not be leading the country down such a disastrous path.

Elinor Goodman, who was then political editor of Channel 4, told me it was a 'glorious place to be' for political journalists as rival factions delivered their views, fuelling tales of divisions within the government. Jon Sopel, now the BBC's North America editor, was then a political correspondent for the corporation and describes it in less flattering terms. He told me there were times when it felt 'like a meat market', with certain MPs keen to catch the eye of reporters for liaisons that could lead to profile-raising media appearances. 'They were sort of hookers touting for business,' he told me, offering quotes and contributions to spice up the daily stories of Tory in-fighting. A few became known as 'rent-a-quote' MPs, always available to comment on the latest twists and turns, rarely helpful to the beleaguered prime minister.

When the prime minister ordered his cabinet to show some discipline, his words were in the papers by the next morning. After various enquiries to find the culprits were launched and abandoned, Major consulted the cabinet secretary, Robin Butler, over the scale of the leaks from his ministerial team. Butler set out a long list of reasons for all the unauthorised stories, including the jockeying for position of rival cabinet ministers, a note that was also leaked. Somehow, Butler seemed to think all of this could be handled by better news management. 'We need to stop the agenda being set by the press,' he argued, and suggested putting the daily Lobby briefings entirely on the record with a summary sent to cabinet ministers.[5] The plan was never implemented, and it is hard to imagine it would have had much effect on the 'big beasts' around the cabinet table such as Michael Heseltine, Kenneth Clarke and Michael Portillo. It certainly would not have stopped the rival ministers privately sharing their views of the embattled prime minister with journalists. It is a scenario that dogged Theresa May's time in office. Lobby correspondents develop their contacts with senior ministers, who know when it is in their interests to let their views be known, off the record, without publicly breaching the requirement to stick to the collective view of the cabinet. Journalists will always be keen to find a way of reporting dissent among those around the prime minister, without revealing their sources.

John Major's frustration was laid bare when he was recorded chatting to ITN's political editor Michael Brunson after an interview, when they both believed the microphones were switched off. In fact, the line was being monitored by BBC technical staff who were waiting for their own interview and made a recording of the conversation. In it Major discussed his options for dealing with the Eurosceptic members of his cabinet who had threatened to resign if he gave Brussels greater power over social and employment policy. He warned of the difficulties he'd face from others in his party if the ministers did walk out: 'I could bring in other people,' he said, 'but where do you think most of this poison is coming from? From the dispossessed and the never-possessed. You can think of ex-ministers who are going around causing all sorts of trouble. We don't want another three more of the bastards out there.'[6]

He did not name the ministers he had in mind, but the prime suspects were Michael Howard, Peter Lilley and Michael Portillo, and his use of the word 'bastards' to describe senior figures within his own party sparked a huge furore. In the Lobby briefings there was little that Gus O'Donnell could say to mitigate the damage. Philip Webster of *The Times* said O'Donnell was 'almost too nice to be in that role, where he was being mauled by the animals of the Lobby'.

After four years of intense pressure, O'Donnell was replaced by Christopher (now Sir Christopher) Meyer, who went on to become British ambassador to the USA and was deputy head of mission in Washington at the time. When Meyer was persuaded to come to London for an interview for the role, Major's first question to him was along the lines of 'Why on earth do you want this awful job?' Meyer realised he was, in fact, the only candidate. Within weeks he had taken over from O'Donnell, who was longing to move on.

Meyer is a very different character from his predecessor, more flamboyant, outgoing and with a disarming charm that was undoubtedly an important factor in his highly successful diplomatic career. Meyer enjoyed engaging with journalists, approaching the confrontations at Lobby briefings as a performance. It was, perhaps, the only way to defend a prime minister in such a precarious position. Meyer told me that the biggest difficulty was 'treading a tightrope' over the position on Europe when rival factions within the cabinet were telling journalists very different things. Weekends were a 'dangerous time': ministers would appear on the television sofas, contradicting one another and the prime minister. At the Monday morning Lobby, Meyer would face a barrage of questions from reporters. 'The only way I could deal with this was by the loud assertion that there was absolutely no difference whatsoever between these four different positions.' He would describe them as 'four facets of the same diamond . . . an entirely consistent position', adding: 'Of course I had to say this with a kind of twinkle in the eye.' Meyer developed a technique of training his gaze on one of the journalists in the room, often Nick Jones, who became something of a lightning conductor. 'I would let off steam, fixing him with a beady eye, and conduct the briefing almost as if I was just talking to him and nobody else.' Jones himself recalls that whenever he asked a potentially awkward question, Meyer would respond by saying, 'Ah, your eyes were flashing when you asked that question, excellent question,' and would thus defuse the situation while avoiding a direct answer.

Meyer would not have wanted his briefings to have been on-camera, but if they had they would have been box-office hits. I was struck by his flair for an engaging turn of phrase and his ability to use humour to defuse a tense confrontation. Nevertheless, the idea of televising them was never actively considered at the time. The prevailing view in Downing Street was that ministers should be setting out policies in Parliament and it would not be right for officials or special advisers to compete with them for airtime. Indeed, Meyer told me that John Major was often so frustrated with the coverage of his tenure that he would suggest abolishing the Lobby altogether, although these were never serious proposals. Major was well aware that he needed the system in place to get the government's message across.

Meyer was happy with the arrangement whereby his words were attributed to a 'Downing Street source' and believed on-camera briefings would only have increased the demands on his time. He told me: 'The key thing to bear in mind is the more the spokesman goes on the record, the more you increase the appetite and the need for off-the-record briefings where some of the deep and dark stories are discussed.' He added: 'You can't get rid of unattributable briefing.'

Meyer said one of the most difficult aspects of the job was dealing with Major himself, who became very bitter and edgy when he read critical articles written by journalists whom he had considered friends. Meyer tried to ease him away from his constant preoccupation with the frequently hostile coverage and offered to prepare a news digest, as Bernard Ingham had done for Margaret Thatcher, but Major refused. He continued to read the papers when they arrived late at night and grabbed the *London Evening Standard* as soon as it was delivered in the afternoon. He would then put pressure on his press secretary to complain, often about trivial issues.

Meyer would meet the prime minister at about 7 a.m., usually when he was having breakfast with his wife Norma, to discuss what lines to take on the issues of the moment. Often Meyer would find that Major's view shifted during the day as the news agenda moved on, making it almost impossible to establish a consistent position. At the suggestion of the prime minister's political secretary, Howell James, Meyer agreed that it was better not to keep consulting their boss. 'The thing was to start out with what you thought was a position which could last the day, and a day was a long time in politics at that time.'

Meyer was confident that he could accurately reflect the government's overriding objectives, yet there were moments when it was a struggle to establish how the prime minister intended to approach a specific issue. One such occasion came at a summit in the summer of 1994, when European leaders were deciding who should replace Mrs Thatcher's bête noir, Jacques Delors, as president of the European Commission. Lobby journalists covering the gathering wanted to know if Major was going to veto the appointment of the Belgian prime minister Jean-Luc Dehaene, who was viewed with hostility by Eurosceptics. Meyer was unable to speak to Major himself, who was engaged in discussions, and none of his senior political team knew what he was going to do. Meyer knew he could not let on that he had no idea what the plan was. 'I tried to suggest that the prime minister was playing a deep game and there was no way in which I could tell them what he would do,' he told me. The tactic worked and the prime minister did eventually block Dehaene, to the delight of many in the Conservative Party and the right-wing press.

The moment of triumph was all too brief. Major had created a whole new set of problems when he launched his disastrous 'Back to Basics' campaign at his party conference in the autumn of 1993. In a highly personal speech, he said it was time to return to 'the old values of neighbourliness, decency and courtesy'. He went on: 'It is time to return to core values, time to get back to basics, to self-discipline and respect for the law, to consideration for others, to accepting responsibility for yourself and your family – and not shuffling it off on other people and the state.'[7]

The trouble was that many of his colleagues did not appear to live up to the prime minister's ideals. David Mellor had already had to resign as heritage minister after a stream of revelations of his affair with the actress Antonia de Sancha. Tim Yeo later resigned as environment minister after it emerged that he had fathered a child outside his marriage. The tales of misdemeanours by senior Tories came thick and fast.

Major made things even worse when he was asked at a news conference whether his Back to Basics principles applied to personal morality, and he said that it did. Meyer said the prime minister's reply 'fired the starting pistol for every newspaper in the country to hunt down instances of improper behaviour by anybody in the Tory Party'. He told me how a ritual developed, which would start with a phone call on a Saturday afternoon from the *News of the World* or the *Mail on Sunday* outlining the latest tale of dubious behaviour involving a Conservative MP or minister and asking whether this breached the Back to Basics mantra. Meyer would ring the prime minister and hear a sharp intake of breath as he explained the latest incident. Meyer would then consult senior party figures, including the chief whip, and advise them to get rid of the individual in question, removing them from any government or advisory posts to limit the damage.

Even so, the Lobby briefings on a Monday morning were far from easy. Meyer told me his one fundamental rule was that he would never tell a lie, but he would resort to the technique of bold assertions, with what he hoped was a fierce look in his eye, while trying to avoid getting drawn into any details: 'The Back to Basics campaign is in wonderful form, absolutely blazing away, and it appeals to the public. And yes, the prime minister is utterly committed to the policy, you should have no doubt whatsoever about this.' Meyer recognised the strength of the Lobby in the unerring pursuit of a story by senior political journalists such as Trevor Kavanagh of the *Sun* and Charles Reiss of the *London Evening Standard*, who knew how to exploit any weakness in the government's case. 'I had to admire their astonishing sense for where the jugular was and how to go for it,' he told me.

Defending the government became harder still when the tide of allegations took a more serious turn. Two parliamentary aides were caught by *The Sunday Times* taking money to ask parliamentary questions. Cash-for-questions became an even bigger story when a Northern Ireland minister, Tim Smith, stood down over claims that he had accepted money from Harrods owner Mohammed Al-Fayed to ask questions in the Commons. Sleaze became an immensely damaging charge as the polls showed that Major's government was one of the most unpopular in recent history.

Jonathan Haslam, who had been deputy press secretary, became director of communications during the final year of John Major's premiership. It was, he told me, a very tough time indeed, with an unstoppable tide of scandals and resignations. 'I think we lost one minister in the course of the twenty-yard walk from the cabinet room to the front door of No. 10 with the prime minister and his political secretary.' That was Patrick Nicholls, who was sacked as a deputy chairman of the party. Other cases took longer to resolve, and Haslam says it was not always easy to get hold of the prime minister or his political team in time to strike the right note at the next Lobby briefing. Yet it was important to avoid defending an individual, only to find them removed a few hours or days later: Haslam knew he had to maintain his integrity in the eyes of the assembled journalists. 'There's a lot of showing you're on top of the game that's important in the Downing Street communications team . . . showing that you know what's going on,' he told me.

While Haslam prepared meticulously for his briefings and tried to talk about the government's successes, everything was moving towards preparations for the election of 1997 and Conservative Party HQ was taking the lead, rather than No. 10. Haslam said that during the final few months of Major's time in power he felt like the nightwatchman at the tail end of a long day's cricket, defending his side against ceaseless hostile bowling.

I had arrived at Westminster early in 1996, switching from foreign reporting to become a political correspondent for the BBC. It was quite a time to join the Lobby corps. Though it was not easy to build my own contacts from scratch and get to grips with the unique way of working, there was certainly no shortage of news as the Conservatives headed towards the election, riven with factional fighting and battered by allegations of sleaze. The almost total lack of discipline within the Tory Party was wonderful for a newly arrived journalist on the hunt for stories, as MPs and ministers happily revealed their views on the colleagues they blamed for the party's woes.

I would venture, with some trepidation, into the Members' Lobby and wait for an opportunity to introduce myself to one of the figures who had been all over our television screens in recent months. It was a strange dance, as you were not allowed to approach an MP who was already in conversation with another journalist, yet it was extraordinarily rewarding for a newcomer trying to get a sense of the political mood. Most Conservative MPs were more than willing to share their opinions on the latest developments, their leader and any issue that might improve their standing in the eyes of their constituents. Labour MPs tended to be more cautious, clearly aware of the need to stay on-message as the election loomed, though they were usually ready with the agreed line of attack on the government.

Then there were my first briefings from Christopher Meyer. He was elegant, composed and had clearly learned how to deal with questions that would begin politely enough, but become increasingly challenging as the assembled journalists took up the quest for a newsworthy comment on the latest Tory MP to be caught out misbehaving. It became apparent that there was a strict hierarchy, with the political editors from the broadcasters and national papers always first to ask their questions and representatives from regional organisations only venturing to raise their hands when everyone else had finished. I attended several sessions before I dared to put a question myself, which of course was answered with polished respect and sincerity. My biggest concern was ensuring I did not miss a quote, as my shorthand was decidedly rusty and there was no question of recording the proceedings. I soon realised that I was not alone in this and found that most reporters were happy to check the words of any choice remarks afterwards. Indeed, it became clear that in the Lobby system, as in other fields of journalism, despite all the rivalry between different news organisations, reporters do like to compare notes. They do so not only to ensure accuracy, but also to discuss the potential significance of particular comments that might signal a change of policy or give a clue to the fate of a certain minister. Hacks would frequently huddle together to try to work out the best lines, although as a new arrival I hesitated to join the discreet gatherings.

One of the biggest criticisms of the Lobby has always been that it has tended to work as a pack, but I have come to the view that the dangers of this are overstated. In my experience, these moments when reporters gather to compare notes generally happen after collective briefings, where no one wants to miss an important line spotted by colleagues and there is no question of anyone having an exclusive story anyway. The sharing of information is limited; each of the journalists will also be speaking to their other contacts to get the wider picture and anyone who has a scoop will certainly go to great lengths to keep it from others. Each Lobby member will have their own take on a story, their own way of conveying a narrative and, in some cases, will be reflecting the political stance of their paper.

While it was the left-leaning *Guardian* that first broke the allegations that Conservative MPs had taken cash to ask parliamentary questions, most of the tales of improper behaviour by Tories were revealed by tabloid reporters rather than Lobby journalists. Yet all these stories shaped the political battles and undoubtedly contributed to the demise of John Major's government, with even the *Daily Telegraph* describing his administration as 'mired in sleaze'.

As the story-rich disarray of the final months of John Major's premiership unfolded, the briefings from the Opposition became increasingly important. Under the fresh-faced leadership of Tony Blair and Gordon Brown, New Labour were providing immediate responses and lines of attack on each of Major's misfortunes. Their communications teams were already building relationships with Lobby reporters and briefing their own stories.

Eighteen years of Conservative rule were coming to an end. Lobby journalists turned their attention to the rapid stream of new initiatives and policy announcements from New Labour. Yet before long they would find themselves at the centre of the rows over spin and media manipulation that would rock the era of New Labour.

6 NEW LABOUR, NEW LOBBY

'The fear of missing out means today's media, more than ever before, hunts in a pack. In these modes it is like a feral beast, just tearing people and reputations to bits.'

Tony Blair speech, 12 June 2007

On 1 April 1997 I was squashed alongside my cameraman in a tightly packed media pen as Tony Blair strode down the steps of his battle bus and wave to the cheering crowds. He bounded on to a small square box, apparently called the 'People's Platform', and seized the microphone. 'Hello Northampton! The sun's out – and in a few weeks, with your help, the Tories will be out too!' There was a rock star-style wave to the fans on the balconies, although in fact there were no balconies, and there was ample space down on the High Street for any local voters keen to catch a glimpse of the Labour leader that Tuesday morning. He delivered a short stump speech promising a New Britain, run 'for the many not the few'. Then he waded into the knot of supporters and shook a few hands before disappearing back on to the bus bearing the slogan 'New Labour, New Britain'.

It was the first of many similar stops on Tony Blair's general election tour in 1997, a campaign that would set his party on course for a landslide victory, changing the British political landscape and returning Labour to power after eighteen years. It was a tour that also gave me first-hand experience of the communications strategy that would become such a significant factor in Blair's decade in power. At the outset it focused on his party's five key commitments, summarised on a pledge card, which included promises to cut class sizes, reduce NHS waiting times and get more young people off benefits and into work. I spent the entire six-week campaign on Blair's battle bus, covering his every move for the BBC.

The relentless tour took in more than seventy locations. At each meticulously planned visit Blair would be greeted by a small knot of cheering Labour fans waving red New Labour flags. There would always be at least enough people to fill the shot as he smiled for the cameras and that wave to the balconies looked great on television, providing just the right image for the evening bulletins.

A few of us were invited to join Alastair and Tony, as we knew them, for informal chats over cups of tea on certain legs of the journey. These are moments to treasure as a political journalist, unrehearsed conversations about family and lack of sleep with the man who would shortly be leading the country and his closest adviser and confidant. At the time their key concern was to downplay expectations of an overwhelming Labour victory, fearing some of their supporters might not bother to turn out to vote. They need not have worried. Tony Blair became the century's youngest prime minister, winning the largest number of seats in his party's history, leaving the Conservatives in tatters.

At the outset, the new government's Lobby briefings were a heady mix of new policies, neat sound bites and banter.

Alastair Campbell and his team worked hard to set the agenda and ensured journalists had no shortage of material, as they raced from Downing Street with fresh lines and announcements. In the first few days the chancellor, Gordon Brown, gave the Bank of England power to control interest rates. Over the next few weeks plans were unveiled for measures that included a windfall tax on the privatised utility companies, the New Deal to get young people off the dole and referendums on devolving more powers to Scotland and Wales. Yet by the time the government revealed its checklist of '100 achievements in 100 days', journalists spotted that many of the items listed amounted to further declarations of intentions rather than the attainment of objectives. Yes, new legislation had been introduced in line with some of those early pledges, but the government had not, at this stage, delivered significant changes. And some of the items included were hard to measure, such as the foreign secretary's announcement of a mission statement or the Northern Ireland secretary's claim to have 'taken decisive steps to improve the prospects for lasting peace'.

Alastair Campbell would later admit that, in government, New Labour carried on for too long with the tactics that had proved so successful in Opposition. Spin – efforts by No. 10 to control or manipulate the media – undoubtedly became a hugely damaging issue, clouding much of Tony Blair's decade in power. Campbell told me he did not immediately appreciate how serious a problem it would become: 'I definitely underestimated the way that I would be seen, and our media operation would be seen, as newsworthy in its own right, and that was incredibly irritating.' He is unapologetic, however, about the attempts to 'change the terms of debate' as he tried to ensure that Blair did not suffer from the sustained, brutal treatment from the press that did so much to undermine previous Labour leaders.

Peter Mandelson, one of the original architects of the New Labour project, had embarked on the long battle to change the party and its portrayal by the media when he was appointed director of communications in 1985 by Neil Kinnock. It was a process, he told me, of retrieving the Labour Party from what he described as 'its near-death experience' after the miners' strike and reintroducing it to the public under a leadership prepared to confront the hard left. Mandelson told me that the 'core mechanism' in this endeavour was the Lobby of political journalists, shaping media coverage and public perceptions. He said that it was a rough ride initially, with almost three-quarters of the newspapers in the hands of right-wing proprietors and editors.

Mandelson would go over to the Commons every afternoon to talk to Lobby journalists at their offices along what is known as the Burma Road, a corridor above the Press Gallery. His mission was to try to convince them to give the Labour Party a sympathetic hearing. 'They were the intermediary,' he told me. 'They were the interface with the public, almost literally.' Despite all his efforts, on polling day in April 1992 the *Sun*'s front page depicted Neil Kinnock's face in a light bulb, with the headline: 'If Kinnock wins today will the last person to leave Britain please turn out the lights'. Though Labour was defeated, Mandelson won his first parliamentary seat and became a key figure in Tony Blair's successful leadership campaign two years later. Mandelson was keen to be recognised as a politician in his own right, but he continued to play a significant role in communicating the New Labour message and was instrumental in the appointment of Alastair Campbell as Blair's press secretary.

As political editor of the *Daily Mirror*, Campbell had been supportive of the efforts to modernise the Labour Party and a cheerleader for Neil Kinnock, in marked contrast to his counterparts on most of the other papers. Campbell's distaste for the behaviour of many of his Lobby colleagues was laid bare when he wrote an article for the *New Statesman* in 1987 entitled 'You Guys are the Pits'. It was prompted by the scathing coverage of Kinnock's visit to the USA, when the Labour leader had the briefest of meetings with President Ronald Reagan and senior figures in the US administration made it clear the White House had serious concerns about Labour's policy of unilateral nuclear disarmament. The *Daily Mail*'s headline was 'The Revenge of Reagan'. Campbell's article, accusing his fellow journalists of working collectively to undermine Kinnock, understandably did not go down well with his Lobby contemporaries. 'I did not much like them,' he admitted later. 'They hated me over the secrets of their freemasonry being exposed.'[1]

When Campbell became Blair's press secretary in 1994, he too began daily tours of the press corridors in the Commons, where he'd worked for many years. It was, he told me, an important part of the job, talking to Lobby journalists who were getting their daily briefings from John Major's team at No. 10 and ensuring they also reflected Labour's lines. 'We had to get into that the whole time,' he told me, 'picking up intelligence, finding out what they were writing, how we could feed into narratives that were being developed.' He knew many of the Westminster reporters personally from his time as a political correspondent and some considered themselves his friends. Those relationships changed the moment Campbell crossed the line from journalist to spin doctor and underwent a further dramatic shift when Labour seized the reins of power.

I remember the transformation in the atmosphere of the lobbies and corridors of Westminster. After those chaotic times before the Tories lost power, when disgruntled MPs and ambitious ministers would freely reveal their dissent to Lobby members, suddenly the new government was imposing strict discipline on its ranks. Its MPs were discouraged from the ad hoc chats that are such an essential part of the job of a political reporter. Many newly elected Labour MPs were reluctant to talk to us at all or stuck closely to the party's agreed lines. For Westminster's journalists, it was not a welcome development. Channel 4's Elinor Goodman recalls Trevor Kavanagh of the *Sun* telling her how terrible it was going to be: 'We've dined on the red blood of John Major for the last two years and now we're going to be fed pet food by Alastair Campbell.' 'He was right,' she told me. 'We went to this situation where Alastair rewarded those who were nice to the Labour Party with little morsels.' Goodman said favoured reporters almost had stories dictated to them, which they were happy to accept because it allowed them to claim 'scoops' on up-and-coming announcements. 'You could argue that they weren't worth having,' she said, 'but try telling that to your news desk.'

In this new, tightly controlled environment, ministers were told they had to take a press officer with them if they were having lunch with a journalist. I remember one such painful occasion with a middle-ranking minister and his adviser, where the only subject of discussion was the latest figures for getting people off benefits and into work. While this was, of course, an important issue, I learned nothing that I could not have found in a departmental press release. I presume my Labour guests thought it a great success.

Alastair Campbell's diaries provide a compelling insight into his years at No. 10 and it is hard to think of another political adviser who has been the subject of so much comment and criticism, although Dominic Cummings, Boris Johnson's former chief adviser, certainly came close. Every Westminster journalist has their own story of what it was like to deal with Blair's closest ally and spokesman, with Campbell often described at the time as the second most powerful man in Britain. Fiercely committed to the New Labour project, the Cambridge graduate, who'd made money writing sex stories for the men's magazine *Forum* and had battled alcoholism and mental issues, became almost as well known as his boss. Just as Blair's huge popularity was eroded by the stark reality of governing, so Campbell's talent for casting his party's endeavours in the best possible terms became a problem when critics began to question the accuracy of his assertions.

Campbell, however, did not hold back when it came to challenging stories he considered to be inaccurate or unfair. Less than a year after Blair became prime minister, an Italian newspaper reported that the country's leader, Romano Prodi, during a phone call with Blair had discussed a bid by the media magnate Rupert Murdoch for Mediaset, an Italian television and publishing company. The story was picked up in the British press, and some commentators suggested that Blair had promoted the Murdoch bid. When the issue was raised at a Lobby briefing Alastair Campbell dismissed the tale as 'baloney'. He did not deny that the conversation between the two leaders had taken place, but he spelled out his point: 'It's balls that the prime minister intervened over some deal with Murdoch. That's C-R-A-P.'[2]

Shortly after his outburst *The Times*, which is part of Murdoch's media group, reported that its proprietor had spoken to Blair a week before the much-discussed phone call and that information from the prime minister had informed Murdoch's business decisions. The row escalated, with the Conservatives raising the issue in the Commons and the shadow culture secretary, Francis Maude, calling on the prime minister to explain why his official spokesman had given out information that was 'at best misleading and at worst deliberately false'. Campbell stood his ground, insisting that Blair had not intervened on Murdoch's behalf. 'There is not a single person in this room who can say I have lied on this story. If there is, I would like them to say it now because it is not true.'[3] Journalists whose stories he had criticised, including Robert Peston, then political editor of the *Financial Times*, insisted their accounts were justified, given the public interest in Blair's relationship with Murdoch. The controversy fed into the growing mistrust between Lobby journalists and No. 10.

I had got to know Campbell on the campaign trail, when everything was going right for Blair and his team and he had a stream of positive initiatives, which he was keen for the BBC to reflect. His attitude inevitably hardened when the government hit turbulence and it became more difficult for No. 10 to control the agenda. Campbell's approach was undoubtedly direct and uncompromising, and he would not hesitate to get on the phone within moments of one of my reports going on-air if he did not agree with my assessment of the latest events. Yet he also had great charisma, charm and a readiness to provide insight into the thinking behind a particular proposal, which was enormously useful to a broadcast journalist preparing to explain and ana-lyse what was happening. He knew this, of course, and I was well aware it was all part of the spin operation, to be treated warily. As a BBC political correspondent I would always regard Campbell's words as one element to be taken into account, along with many others, and it did not mean I would be cowed from reporting the government's shortcomings and misjudgements when they occurred.

On one occasion, during a Labour Party conference, I was standing on the sea front for a live appearance on the *Breakfast* programme, explaining the stories of the day. When I finished I heard a voice shouting, 'That's about right – but you left out some good new figures.' It was Campbell, leaning from the window of his hotel suite above me, who had been listening to my broadcast. I was slightly concerned that he approved of so much of what I'd said.

Campbell knew how to deploy his influence beyond the routine briefings and conversations with Lobby correspondents, often phoning the editors of specific programmes or more senior BBC bosses to make his point. They would be overseeing entire programmes and deciding on the priorities of the day, whereas I was providing just one of many reports.

Just as Bernard Ingham's relationship with Margaret Thatcher gave him the authority to speak on her behalf, so Alastair Campbell's power came from the fact that he was so close to Tony Blair. Campbell sat in on all the key meetings, which meant that we always knew that he was giving us a real sense of Blair's views. Philip Webster, political editor of *The Times* and a stalwart of the Lobby, told me that 'you had a sense that you were getting "His Master's Voice" most of the time' because Campbell would come to the daily Lobby meetings fresh from discussions with Blair. Webster said that Campbell's background as a newspaper man meant that he knew 'which buttons to press' to get positive coverage. 'He would sell a story to *The Times* in a completely different way than he would sell the same story to the *Daily Mail*,' aware of the different market for different publications. While journalists were well aware of such techniques, they also knew the strategy could work to their advantage, allowing them to get stories ahead of their rivals.

The *Sun*'s decision to back Blair at the 1997 election, after more than twenty years of loyalty to the Conservatives, was seen as a hugely significant move in widening Labour's support. The *Sun* had more than 10 million readers per day at the time and it is no surprise that Campbell went to great lengths to keep the paper on side. Trevor Kavanagh, its political editor, has often been described as Britain's most influential political journalist and was not happy with his paper's decision to support Blair, though he accepted it with good grace and the *Sun* did not waver from its staunchly Eurosceptic stance. Kavanagh believes Labour's spin operation led to a breach of trust between government and the media. He told me it was an 'absolute negative almost from the beginning' and that it changed the Lobby system even before the reforms to its rules and structure: 'It meant that nobody trusted anything that the government said.' Kavanagh drew on the infamous comments of the former *Newsnight* presenter Jeremy Paxman, who said that when he interviewed politicians his attitude was: 'Why is this lying bastard lying to me?' Kavanagh told me: 'That became our approach to everything that emanated from Downing Street, nothing could be taken at face value.'

That wariness, combined with Campbell's notoriously combative approach, brought a new adversarial edge to the Lobby briefings. Kavanagh told me that though he liked Campbell personally, they clashed frequently over the years: 'Alastair was a bully. He's a forceful personality and I can understand why the Conservatives were constantly looking for someone who could do an Alastair Campbell job for them. He was an impossible act to follow.' Others were more forthright in their criticism. Charles Moore, editor of the *Daily Telegraph* when Campbell was at Blair's side, described Campbell as 'the most pointlessly combative person in human history'.[4]

Nick Jones, whom I worked alongside for several years when he was a BBC political correspondent, was frequently the target for such mocking attacks from Alastair Campbell. As an author of several books on government communications, Jones would assiduously note down every detail of the Lobby briefings he attended. His behaviour infuriated Campbell, who once referred to him as 'that tick, Nick Jones, meaning that nasty little insect that gets under your skin and sucks your blood'. Jones recalls one Lobby briefing when Campbell was being asked about a feature in the *New Musical Express* on why musicians, who had once been happy to attend the so-called 'Cool Britannia' receptions in Downing Street, were distancing themselves from the Blair government. Campbell was joking about Labour's 'post euphoria, pre-delivery stage' when he suddenly halted proceedings. 'Hang on a minute,' he said. 'The only person who's taking any notice of this answer is that Nick Jones. Look, can you see him over in the corner, he's having an orgasm on spin.' Jones recalls that while this was all a 'tremendous hoot' for everyone else, Campbell had successfully deflected attention from an awkward question.

Campbell frequently accused Jones of focusing on process rather than policies. Jones's defence is that the democratic process does matter, and spin and manipulation are an important part of it. He was a former industrial correspondent and believes another reason he was so frequently taunted by Campbell was that he still had good contacts within the unions, who resisted some of Blair's reforms: 'The New Labour machine hated the fact that there were old industrial hacks like me who could get information from the union movement.'

His brother George Jones was political editor of the *Daily Telegraph* for many years and has been even more scathing, once writing an article entitled 'Alastair Campbell stops me from doing my job'. Three years into Blair's time in power, Campbell launched a typically outspoken attack on the media for 'the scale of distortion and misrepresentation' in its coverage of disagreements within the Labour Party over Europe, which he said was 'a joke'. George Jones responded by accusing Campbell and others in his team of treating reporters with contempt. 'Mr Campbell makes no attempt to disguise his dislike of briefing the press – and he often uses his sharp wit to humiliate in front of their colleagues those correspondents who have reported stories unfavourable to the Government.'[5] He warned that 'The whole argument over spin suddenly seems about to consume its creators, like some deranged Frankenstein's monster.' Jones concluded: 'There is now an air of mutual suspicion between Mr Campbell and the Lobby that is making his job impossible and is damaging the Government's legitimate efforts to get its message across.'

Campbell himself has been frank about his attitude to the briefings, particularly when he objected to the line of questioning. In his diaries he describes how Lobby journalists had 'worked themselves into a mini-frenzy' over a story in *The Times*, in May 1998, that the Duke of Edinburgh had opposed a decision to award the Order of the Garter to the Emperor of Japan, who was due to visit Britain later that month. Buckingham Palace had taken the rare step of issuing a statement denying that the Duke had expressed any view, privately or publicly, on the award, but British survivors of Japanese prisoner-of-war camps had condemned the move to honour the Emperor and were demanding an urgent meeting with the prime minister. Campbell spoke to the Queen's private secretary and agreed on a robust denial of the story. In his diaries he described how he delivered this line at the morning briefing, but the journalists 'kept coming at me on it and I got totally fed up with it and started really going at them', adding that he was 'in total "fuck it" mode'. He wrote: 'I went for Liam Halligan [*Financial Times* political correspondent], totally over the top, was horrible to Patrick Wintour [*Guardian* political editor] – so horrible I later apologised – then took a pop at George Jones [*Daily Telegraph*].' When the BBC's political editor, Robin Oakley, pointed out that he was there to answer questions, Campbell's reply was, 'If they didn't like the answers, tough.' When Donald Macintyre, political editor of the *Independent*, took him for a cup of tea afterwards and said he should calm down, Campbell told him he was 'sick of dealing with wankers', adding, 'why should I pretend to respect them when I didn't'.[6]

When I talked to Campbell about his reputation and his approach to the briefings he was unapologetic about his stance. 'I took the decision fairly early on that I was going to be quite robust in terms of dealing with stuff that I thought was made up or inaccurate or unfair,' he told me. 'I would call it out and I think sometimes I went over the top.' He did, though, often apologise to individuals afterwards. Campbell said he was particularly exasperated at some of the speculation about cabinet reshuffles. On one occasion, when a new ministerial line-up was completed after days of conjecture, he handed out prizes at his Lobby briefing for what he saw as the most ridiculous stories. 'I quite enjoyed calling them out when they wrote absolute shit,' he told me. 'I was definitely combative, and I didn't step back if somebody had a go . . . and I probably did swear too much.'

Campbell is believed to have been the inspiration for Malcolm Tucker in the television satire *The Thick of It*, a swearing Scot, bawling and cursing at colleagues and correspondents. When I asked him what he made of the programme, he said: 'I think it was really funny and there's a germ of truth in it. I was a control freak and I was trying to control the media agenda, trying to control the government agenda because that was my job.' He added that some years ago his daughter came home from school and asked him if he was Malcolm Tucker – 'Please say it's you, I so want it to be you.' Campbell clearly enjoyed his children's pride at their father's connection to the cult comedy.

There was also a more subtle and informative side to our most famous spin doctor, however. One of Blair's most notable achievements was his role in the negotiations that led to the Good Friday Agreement, the political settlement ending decades of conflict in Northern Ireland. Campbell told me that during the months of talks leading to the agreement he would frequently deal with senior broadcasters, such as Robin Oakley and Denis Murray of the BBC and Michael Brunson of ITN, who were on location to cover developments. Campbell said these conversations were very different from the mass briefings for the entire Lobby, as he tried to point out the need for balance, to reflect all aspects of proposals, because of the risks of the whole process collapsing. 'I wasn't manipulating them, I wasn't misleading them, on the contrary I was actually being utterly frank about why certain phrases were included.' He said he wanted to point out the potentially serious ramifications if journalists focused on one aspect without also including others. Oakley believes such briefings certainly meant he was better informed on the government's approach and says these conversations had to be off the record. He does, though, stress that Campbell's remarks would only ever be one of his sources and he would have been talking to all the other parties involved.

Campbell had less patience when dealing with the constant drip of alternative briefings from his nearest neighbour, Gordon Brown. The complex and difficult relationship between the prime minister and his chancellor was a source of many rows and the undercurrent to numerous stories throughout Blair's years in No. 10. While in the formal Lobby briefings we were given endless assurances that the two were working closely together, Brown's team operated as a separate rival camp, often setting out their own agenda.

In the autumn of 1997, just months after Labour's victory, the government was rocked by an indiscreet briefing on the crucial issue of whether Britain would join the European single currency. Gordon Brown's ebullient spin doctor Charlie Whelan was enjoying a pint at the Red Lion pub in Whitehall, conveniently close to both Downing Street and the Treasury. Outside the crowded pub, he was overheard by two Liberal Democrat press officers while he was briefing journalists on the phone. 'Yes, Gordon is ruling out British membership of the single currency for the whole of this Parliament. No, he doesn't say it in the interview, but Gordon is effectively ruling out joining in this Parliament.'[7] The chancellor had given an interview to Philip Webster of *The Times* in which he hinted at the government's decision without explicitly spelling it out, but Whelan's words allowed *The Times*, and its allied paper the *Sun*, to trumpet 'Brown says no to the Euro'. The two papers that got the scoop, which were both owned by Rupert Murdoch and strongly supported the decision, were delighted. Their rivals were furious. So were many MPs, who demanded that Parliament be recalled so that the chancellor could make a statement to the Commons on a policy with such far-reaching consequences. The prime minister was likewise angry and bewildered as to how it had happened.

On this occasion Alastair Campbell and Charlie Whelan had been co-operating closely. In his diaries, Campbell says the Treasury had drafted the words that would be briefed to Webster and he had made a couple of changes to tone down the pro-Europeanism. He wrote: 'I spoke to Webster and agreed that the intro was that he was effectively ruling it out for this Parliament while saying it would be folly to close options. God knows how we had got to this, or to the headline at the end of the day, "Blair Rules out Single Currency for this Parliament",[8] because while CW [Whelan] and I both believed we were doing what TB and GB wanted us to, they having discussed it earlier, it seemed they had not really gone over the line in any detail.'

He added, 'the words went to Webster, the spin was applied, and away we went'.[9]

The story erupted late on a Friday evening and dominated the news coverage over what Campbell has described as 'pretty much a weekend from hell', adding: 'I was beating myself up too because I knew I had screwed up.' When the chancellor went to the Stock Exchange on the Monday morning for a long-planned photocall to switch on a new electronic trading system, the screens behind him showed billions of pounds being wiped off share values. It was another week before Brown made a statement to the Commons, setting out five tests on which the Treasury would judge whether it was in the national interest for the UK to join what was then known as Economic and Monetary Union.

The disarray over a key economic policy was hugely damaging and exposed the flaws in the government's system of communications. Campbell admitted in his diaries at the time that it had been a 'cock-up', but sought to repair some of the damage. He declared that he wanted to ensure that important guidance on government policy was given to the Lobby on the record and to establish a clear system of attribution.

Campbell launched a review, carried out by Sir Robin Mountfield, a senior civil servant, which concluded: 'A lobby system which relies on non-attribution tends to give an unwarranted credibility to those unnamed sources who are always "senior" and invariably "close" to whichever minister is the prime subject of the story. In these circumstances, it becomes ever more important to ensure that authentic government statements, especially from the centre, carry due authority.'[10] He recommended that Lobby briefings should in future be attributed to the prime minister's official spokesperson, the PMOS.

The government accepted the Mountfield report – hardly surprising given that Campbell himself was a member of one of its key working groups. On the day it was published, he arrived at the afternoon Lobby briefing with a microphone and tape recorder, which he placed on the table in front of him. It represented a significant change from the days when even to admit that such meetings took place was forbidden. Campbell confirmed that he should now be described as the PMOS. He told the Lobby: 'We think this will achieve greater clarity and avoid the position where one anonymous source denies another anonymous source. It will also draw attention to the fact that there are journalists who make up quotes and try to suggest they are coming from ministers' friends or advisors.'[11]

Despite his disparaging remarks and all the long years of arguments over every previous proposal to bring greater openness to Lobby proceedings, the decision was accepted with barely a murmur of opposition. Journalists soon began bringing in their own voice recorders, in the days before mobile phones were routinely used for such tasks, a change which certainly came as a relief to me. At last I had a back-up for my scribbled notes. The official recordings of Campbell's briefings were not made public at this stage, but they were circulated to other government departments.

The Mountfield report also recommended wider changes, to give 'strategic coherence' to government communications. It resulted in No. 10 having greater control over the media operations of other departments across Whitehall, ensuring they knew the lines to take on the issues of the day and were ready with 'rapid rebuttal' of negative stories. A new strategic communications unit was also established under Alastair Campbell to work on advance planning and establish a 'grid' of major announcements, speeches and visits.

It was the first of many changes, as the Blair government struggled to shake off its reputation for spin by opening up parts of its media operation. The morning Lobby briefings were moved across St James's Park to the Foreign Press Association and journalists from overseas publications were allowed to attend. Summaries of the meetings were posted on the Downing Street website. The prime minister himself held regular on-the-record news conferences. After years of negotiations, the BBC documentary-maker Michael Cockerell was allowed to film some of the Lobby briefings for a behind-the-scenes programme called *News from Number 10*.

Cockerell told me that most of the resistance to letting the cameras into the once-secretive meetings came from the journalists rather than from Downing Street, as they jealously guarded their exclusive access. He said he was struck by 'the state of combat between Her Majesty's press corps and No. 10'. His film showed Alastair Campbell pointing his finger at reporters, telling them 'You guys are the spin doctors', as he tried to turn the tables on journalists. He accused them of blurring news and comment, putting their own interpretation on events. Cockerell's programme also showed the correspondents challenging Campbell on his stance. 'It was good for democracy,' Cockerell said. 'You saw that these journalists were not being spoon-fed, not taking dictation. In fact, because New Labour had been so good at the art of news management, news manipulation and all the rest of those things, the journalists always went in with a much more sceptical approach than they'd had before.' It was the first time any Lobby proceedings had ever been televised.

During the filming of Cockerell's programme, Campbell announced he would take a step back from the front line, spending less time holding the daily briefings so he could focus on longer-term strategy. 'I had got myself into a situation where combat was the only language that was really being spoken and that's not terribly sensible either way,' he said. Blair told Cockerell it was he who had made the decision, partly because of the sheer pressure on Campbell, and because he wanted his key adviser to be looking at the broader challenge of how to put across the government's message. Blair said it did not make sense for Campbell to be 'doing his own equivalent of Prime Minister's Questions twice a day'.

Campbell told me the media focus on him had reached the point where it was getting in the way of what he was trying to do. In one month, the media monitoring unit showed he had been the subject of more coverage than Iain Duncan Smith, who was Opposition leader at the time. 'The briefings themselves had become way too newsworthy,' he said. The tipping point came after the prime minister launched an overhaul of the secondary school system to allow more specialist schools. During a Lobby briefing, Campbell said the reforms would mean the end of the 'bog-standard comprehensive'. The phrase sparked a furious reaction from teaching unions and some Labour MPs and still reverberates today. David Blunkett, education secretary at the time, said he did not recognise the term. Yet Campbell told me he had only used the words 'bog-standard' because the prime minister himself had included the phrase in a speech a few days earlier, when nobody had batted an eyelid. 'That's when I said we have to find a new way of doing the briefings,' he told me, and a strategy was established to try to take the heat out of the regular sessions with journalists.

The task of delivering that strategy was handed to Godric Smith, Campbell's deputy and a figure who could hardly have provided a greater contrast in character or approach. Smith was a quiet, unassuming civil servant who was liked and respected by Lobby journalists, but some of those who had complained about Campbell's aggressive tactics had a new grievance. As

Robin Oakley of the BBC said: 'If Alastair is not there with the kind of access he has to the prime minister, reflecting the prime minister's instincts and personality as well as policy lines, then we simply don't believe we are getting the voice of Downing Street.' Trevor Kavanagh said that Campbell's absence from regular briefings would leave a 'vacuum in the relationship between the press and Downing Street', though he believed that this was dangerous for the government rather than the media.

I certainly remember that attending the Lobby briefings became much less interesting and newsworthy without the unpredictable dramas that were a frequent feature when Campbell addressed the room. Godric Smith shared the task with Tom Kelly, a former senior BBC journalist who had been head of the press team at the Northern Ireland Office. Smith was under no illusions over why he was given the job. 'A judgement was made that, effectively, the Lobby had become too big a part of the political discourse,' he told me. His job was 'to try to tone it down'. As Kelly said: 'Compared to Alastair, I was a boring civil servant.'

The general election of 2001 returned Blair to Downing Street with a powerful mandate to continue his programme of changes to the public services. Alastair Campbell, though, was clearly feeling tired and disillusioned. He wrote: 'I felt like I had some kind of post-natal depression. We'd won the election but every day since it had felt like swimming through shit.'[12] The prime minister did not want to lose such a close and trusted adviser and a new role was created for Campbell as director of strategy and communications. He was given his own office at No. 12 Downing Street, connected to No. 10, symbolically evicting the chief whip, who oversees party discipline.

None of this made much difference to the mood of confrontation and mistrust between the press and Downing Street, however. Lance Price, a former BBC political correspondent whom I had worked alongside at Westminster, joined the Downing Street press team in 1998. He said: 'Far from improving, relations swiftly deteriorated further and within a year Number 10 was engaged in the biggest battle it had ever fought with the media.'[13]

The prime minister was preparing to deliver a speech to the TUC in Brighton when news of the 9/11 attacks on New York's Twin Towers came through. He cut short the event to return to London and lead the emergency response. In a statement to the nation later he said there was a battle between 'the free and democratic world and terrorism'. He pledged that Britain would 'stand shoulder to shoulder with our American friends in this hour of tragedy and we, like them, will not rest until this evil is driven from our world'.

His words established Blair's approach to the events that would unfold over the coming months and years, as British troops were deployed to Afghanistan and then Iraq alongside those of the USA and other allies. I do not intend to consider in detail the conflict, or the controversial decisions during the run-up to the war, which have been the subject of several in-depth inquiries, numerous books, academic studies and debates. It is, however, worth recalling aspects of the way the government dealt with journalists over this period, a time of huge tension and uncertainty.

Having reported directly from Iraq during the first Gulf War in 1990/91, it was a very different experience to be covering developments at Westminster during the second Iraq War, which began in 2003 and dragged on for so many years. We did, at times, feel that we were on the political front line.

Relations between government and media are always strained during wartime. For Tony Blair, the rows over spin and manipulation meant that his statements making the case for war were inevitably treated with suspicion. It was on 24 September 2002 that the government set out its analysis of Iraq's weapons of mass destruction (WMD). In his foreword to the dossier entitled 'Iraq's Weapons of Mass Destruction – The Assessment of the British Government', the prime minister said: 'I believe the assessed intelligence has established beyond doubt that Saddam has continued to produce chemical and biological weapons, that he continues in his efforts to produce chemical and biological weapons.' He went on: 'I am in no doubt that the threat is serious and current, that he has made progress on WMD, and that he has to be stopped.' He then added: 'The document discloses that his military planning allows for some of the WMD to be ready within 45 minutes of an order to use them.' The claim made headlines around the world.

The document was followed, on 30 January 2003, by a second dossier, which was slipped under the hotel doors of Lobby correspondents accompanying the prime minister on a trip to the USA. It was entitled 'Iraq: Its Infrastructure of Concealment, Deception and Intimidation'. Once again, many British newspapers reported this as a further indication of the threat posed by Saddam Hussein. Yet its credibility was called into question within a week, when Channel 4 News reported that some of its contents had been lifted from an academic report on the internet. It became known as the 'Dodgy Dossier' and Campbell himself admitted it was a 'bad own goal'.[14] It added to the ongoing questions at Westminster and beyond over the government's case for going to war.

Nevertheless, most of the papers were still backing the prime minister on his approach to Iraq and on 19 March 2003 he won the support of the Commons to send British forces into action, despite a rebellion by 139 Labour MPs. The military offensive was launched two days later with the 'shock and awe' campaign of aerial bombardment and, within weeks, Baghdad fell as US troops entered the capital. Saddam Hussein had fled into hiding. It was when UN weapons inspectors failed to find evidence of Saddam's WMD that the government's judgement and its justification for the war were seriously called into doubt.

As the weeks and months passed after the fall of Saddam Hussein, more and more questions were raised at the regular Lobby briefings over the government's claims of the former dictator's WMD. Initially, the response was that the inspectors' work was ongoing, that it would take a while to complete the process. The spokesman, usually either Godric Smith or Tom Kelly, would explain that the judgements were based on the intelligence at the time. Their replies were cautious and measured, insisting that Saddam Hussein had posed a threat to his own country and to the wider region.

On 29 May 2003, Tony Blair, accompanied by Alastair Campbell, was on his first visit to Iraq, to thank British troops for their service. Shortly after 6 a.m. that morning, the BBC *Today* programme's defence correspondent, Andrew Gilligan, who was not a member of the Lobby, was on-air down the line from his home with the latest on the dossier. He told the presenter, John Humphrys: 'What we've been told by one of the senior officials in charge of drawing up that dossier was that actually the government probably knew that that forty-five-minute figure was wrong, even before it decided to put it in.' He went on to say that, a week before publication, Downing Street had ordered that the document should be 'sexed up, to be made more exciting and ordered more facts to be, to be discovered'. Campbell, at the British base in Iraq, spoke to the accompanying media about what he called 'a ghastly Gilligan story claiming that the spooks were not happy with the dossier'; his initial reaction was to dismiss it as 'a repeat of the stories at the time'. Downing Street, though, put out an immediate rebuttal, telling the *Today* programme: 'Not one word of the dossier was not entirely the work of the intelligence agencies.'

The prime minister believed that 'there could hardly have been a more inflammatory or severe charge. Mistaken intelligence is one thing. Intelligence known to be mistaken but nonetheless still published is a wholly different matter. That is not a mistake but misconduct. What's more, directly attributed to Number 10.'[15] Blair has acknowledged that his integrity probably never recovered from this allegation. He also believes it had further consequences: 'As a result of it, something else happened: the division over the war became not a disagreement but a rather vicious dispute about the honesty of those involved. A difficult situation became and remains an ugly one.'[16]

The row escalated, with neither side prepared to back down and Andrew Gilligan naming Alastair Campbell as the person who wanted the dossier 'sexed up'. In June Campbell appeared before the Commons Foreign Affairs Select Committee. The prime minister had urged him to remain calm, but, although Campbell was composed throughout, his anger was clear as he set out his objections to Gilligan's report: 'Let's get to the heart of what the allegation is, that the prime minister, the cabinet, the intelligence agencies, people like myself, connived to persuade Parliament to send British forces into action on a lie.' He said the BBC should admit its mistakes and apologise: 'Until the BBC acknowledges that that is a lie, I will keep banging on.'[17] The BBC responded by accusing Campbell of conducting a vendetta against Gilligan. This prompted Campbell to go live on to Channel 4 News to launch a further onslaught against the BBC.

It was a deeply uncomfortable time to be a BBC political correspondent, reporting day and night on the twists and turns of the row. Every Lobby briefing was dominated by questions on the dossier and the basis for the claims of Saddam's WMDs. Downing Street repeatedly, categorically denied putting pressure on the security services and attacked the BBC for its coverage. Our task was to try to report each new development fairly and impartially, to stick to the unbiased and factual approach that was fundamental to the way we worked. Indeed, I attended Lobby briefings where the BBC was strongly criticised and went on-air to report the comments on the corporation's own coverage. The sense of being at the centre of an all-out battle, with the integrity and reputation of our own organisation at stake, as well as that of the government, put a huge strain on all of us as we continued to report the unfolding events.

I did not know Andrew Gilligan, nor the basis for his claims, until it emerged that his source was Dr David Kelly, a government scientist and weapons expert. Dr Kelly appeared before MPs on the Foreign Affairs Committee and confirmed he had spoken to Gilligan before his highly controversial broadcast. Two days later, when Blair was flying to Japan on a tour of the Far East, he received a call telling him that Dr Kelly's body had been found and it appeared he had taken his own life. Blair was clearly under huge emotional strain when he spoke to reporters on arrival. He expressed his deep sorrow, calling for respect and restraint until the full circumstances were known, and announced an independent inquiry into the events leading to Dr Kelly's death.

Alastair Campbell, who was back in London, wept when he heard the news of the scientist's death. He had been trying to leave Downing Street for some time and wanted to resign immediately. The prime minister warned it would be a disaster for Campbell if he did and friends persuaded him not to go in the midst of the crisis. Campbell, Blair, Gilligan and other senior figures in the government and the BBC all gave evidence to the inquiry that was set up under Lord Hutton, a Law Lord who'd been Lord Chief Justice in Northern Ireland, to investigate the circumstances surrounding Dr Kelly's death.

When Hutton's report was published in January 2004 it delivered a damning verdict on the behaviour of the BBC. It said Gilligan's key allegation was unfounded, that the BBC's editorial and complaints processes were defective and the governors had not been diligent. The corporation's chairman, Gavyn Davies, and director general, Greg Dyke, both resigned. I remember all too clearly the deep sense of trauma in the BBC's Millbank office as we took in the weight of the damage to our organisation, even as I raced against deadlines to try to broadcast the key findings of the report in the balanced and impartial way that was then more important than ever.

The government emerged virtually unscathed. Blair said there was 'an audible collective sigh of relief' as he and his closest advisers read the conclusions.[18] The inquiry found there was no underhand strategy to leak Dr Kelly's name to the media, though it did say the Ministry of Defence was at fault in the way it dealt with the scientist once his name had been made public. Hutton concluded: 'No one involved could have contemplated that Dr Kelly would take his own life as a result of the pressures he felt.'

Several newspapers were not happy at the verdict. 'Whitewash' was the headline in the *Independent*, while in the *Mail*, hardly known for its support of the BBC, Max Hastings wrote: 'It has been Mr Campbell's function to serve as a professional deceiver in the service of Mr Blair.' He said that thanks to Lord Hutton, 'Mr Campbell bestrides the prostrate form of the corporation, humbled as never before in its history,' and added that although Blair and his colleagues had been acquitted, 'the accused leave the dock with stains on their character that no amount of judicial laundering can remove'.[19]

The Hutton inquiry was one of several investigations into various aspects of the Iraq War. The fundamental problem for No. 10 was that it had built its case for the mission on the threat posed by Saddam Hussein and his weapons of mass destruction, but no WMDs were ever found. Many of the newspapers who had supported the decision to go to war clearly felt their trust had been betrayed. 'I think we were utterly misled,' Trevor Kavanagh of the *Sun* told me, 'and I think we were gullible, and I think we were knowingly misled and the military intelligence was deliberately skewed.' Journalists and their editors were angry and mistrust of anything the government said was deeper than ever.

Campbell had finally left Downing Street on the day after the prime minister gave his evidence to the Hutton inquiry. Blair said he had not appreciated the strain his friend and close adviser had been under until that moment, and only really understood its full extent when he read his diaries. He described Campbell as 'an immensely able, fearless, loyal servant of the cause he believes in who was dedicated not only to that cause but to his country . . . he was, is, and will remain a good friend.'

Campbell's departure was given wall-to-wall coverage, with breaking news flashes and hours of rolling comment and discussion on the news channels. 'I suppose I knew it would go quite big, but it was ludicrous just how big it went,' Campbell observed.[20] He did a round of broadcast interviews with political editors from the Lobby before clearing his desk and leaving No. 10, ignoring the media scrum outside. As he left, Blair said: 'You do realise I will phone you every day, don't you?' Campbell's reply was: 'Yes and I hope you realise sometimes I won't be there.'[21]

Campbell had a unique place in the history of relations between the media and No. 10. No press secretary since has been as powerful, influential or as close to the prime minister. His force of character and abrasive style inevitably brought him into confrontation with the media and others. Yet, as *The Times*'s Philip Webster observed, his departure left many Lobby journalists yearning for him like jilted lovers. Their daily briefings had already changed significantly, and Downing Street was determined that Campbell's successors would ensure it could still get its message across without the dramas that had so often proved counterproductive to the government.

7 SPOKESPERSON, SPIN DOCTOR, SPAD

'An unexciting truth may be eclipsed by a thrilling falsehood.'

Aldous Huxley, *Brave New World Revisited*

I magine this is your task at work each morning: you will stand at the front of a room full of forty to fifty journalists. They will include the political editors of some of our national newspapers, experienced broadcasters with long experience of interviewing senior politicians and some up-and-coming reporters out to make a name for themselves. They can ask you anything they like and follow up their questions if they are not satisfied with your replies. There is no fixed time limit to the session, which may continue for an hour or more. When it does come to an end, your answers will be quoted in tweets and online stories within moments and may find their way on to newspaper front pages. They could prompt questions in the Commons. Your words can affect public perceptions of significant policies, prompt reactions around the world and bolster or undermine the reputation of your government. This is the task of the PMOS, whose role is to convey the views of the leader of our nation to the public and to explain and defend the government's position at regular appointments with the men and women of the Lobby. Their task is to seek clarification of Downing Street's line on the issues of the moment and to try to extract a telling phrase or more information than the spokesperson intended to impart.

No one taking on the role ever expects much sympathy. After all, spin doctors hardly have a great reputation. Their roles and methods became such a serious issue for Tony Blair's government that it was considered a significant story when Godric Smith replaced Alastair Campbell at the daily briefings, as part of the deliberate attempts to take the heat out of the relationship with the media. Smith acknowledges that his style is completely different from that of his predecessor. As he prepared to take his first Monday morning session, he found that someone at No. 10 had briefed the journalists: 'We're going to bore you with Godric, Godric and more Godric.' With characteristic understatement, he told me: 'I think it was strategically helpful for the government, but perhaps not the most morale-raising for me personally as I entered the room for the first time.'

Smith, a quietly spoken, unassuming former Whitehall press officer, was a civil servant, so did not comment on party political matters. Since his appointment, successive leaders have continued with the arrangement whereby the PMOS, who gives the regular briefings, is a non-political civil servant who works for the government. The spin doctors who give political context to a story are special advisers, known as SPADs, who often address what are known as 'huddles' of the Lobby after Prime Minister's Questions in the Commons or other big political events, and frequently speak to journalists individually. Alastair Campbell was the last person to combine both roles and also had the right to direct civil servants across other departments, giving him huge power and influence.

After Campbell's departure, Westminster journalists could no longer rely on the regular Lobby briefings for the political context to stories and needed more conversations with the relevant SPADS to understand the thinking behind government policies and initiatives. They also swiftly realised that Godric Smith's understated approach would not provide the choice phrases that so often resulted from Campbell's clashes with reporters and provided them with significant news lines. As Smith put it: 'I think I would normally err on the side of caution.' He acknowledged that his briefings were 'a bit drier and perhaps not quite as lively as some of the ones that went before'. His audience would certainly agree with that.

He found delivering the daily briefings an enormously demanding task – 'totally all-consuming' – every day of the week. He told me: 'You are very aware that you're going to be live on stage as it were, in twenty-four hours' time, and you're going to need to know what's going on, the contours of all the different debates. Your mind is constantly thinking about how you might answer questions, what are the areas of weakness and what are the issues that you need to make sure you're properly briefed on or need to speak to the prime minister about.' While Smith earned the respect of journalists for his integrity and commitment, there were times when they worked as a pack to try to push him further than he wanted to go. 'Sometimes you do feel you are the wildebeest,' he said 'and you've just got to keep running.'

Looking back on this period, Smith believes that some of the seeds of the controversy over spin were sown in the early years of the Labour government. 'I think we sometimes confused headlines with delivery,' he told me, 'so we would get fantastic coverage for our intention to, for example, reform childcare, but what we didn't do was enough expectation management in terms of the time it would take from people reading about it to people feeling the benefit.' He said that would lead to justifiable questions over when progress would be achieved.

Tom Kelly had been brought in to work alongside Smith, continuing in the role for four years when Smith moved on. Kelly is a tough Ulsterman who worked in Northern Ireland during the Troubles, yet even he admitted that addressing the assembled ranks of Lobby journalists was quite a challenge. 'Daunting is putting it mildly, terrifying is probably more apt,' he said, though with a grin that suggested he actually enjoyed the experience. 'Many of these people have been doing this for years and years. They know every nook and cranny, they know every game in town. I'd been a fairly experienced journalist in Northern Ireland, I'd dealt with the press in my role at the Northern Ireland office, but nothing quite prepares you for that Monday morning when twenty to thirty hacks are all trying to catch you out.' To add to the pressure, Kelly was well aware that he was stepping into the role at a time when many of the journalists were resentful that they would no longer have regular access to Campbell. 'Let's put it this way,' he said. 'I had a little bit to prove.'

Tom Kelly's worst mistake came shortly after Dr David Kelly (no relation) was revealed as the source of Andrew Gilligan's hugely controversial claims over the case made by the government for going to war in Iraq. In the course of a conversation with Paul Waugh, then political correspondent for the *Independent*, Tom Kelly used the phrase 'Walter Mitty' while talking about the weapons inspector who had taken his own life. Dr Kelly's bereaved family were furious at the suggestion that he may have exaggerated his own importance. Tom Kelly told me he thought he was having a private conversation with Waugh, though he said he should have known better than to think that was possible. He was discussing the potential questions the Hutton inquiry would consider and used the phrase in that context. 'I wasn't trying to smear Dr Kelly, I was simply thinking out loud,' he said, adding that he was completely horrified when his words became front-page news. Kelly issued an unreserved apology, but it was a damaging episode and he said it taught him a lesson about supposedly off-the-record conversations with journalists. There are no clear rules about the numerous individual phone calls and chats between advisers and correspondents, although it's not unusual for one or other to clarify whether or not a comment can be quoted or the source named. Waugh is a highly respected journalist and clearly believed he could report the phrase from the Downing Street spokesman, providing a further twist to the complex and emotional drama.

Looking back on the highly charged rows over the Iraq War, Tom Kelly told me how difficult it was to conduct the Lobby briefings at the time. He considered the accusation that No. 10 had deliberately misled the public to be false and considered it was right to challenge that, but he also thinks Blair's team lost sight of the bigger question, which was 'Where are the WMDs?' Kelly told me that he 'felt we would go in and find WMDs and suddenly they weren't there. As week after week went by, and all we could produce was sand, it became more difficult. You're trying to hold the line at the same time as the rational part of your brain suggests they've got a point.' Drawing on his experience in Northern Ireland, Kelly also accepts it was a mistake to drop the caveats in the case set out by the government that would have put the intelligence in a more balanced and more nuanced way. He adds, however, there was another problem: 'Equally on the other side, there was a sort of gotcha mentality, right, you can't produce WMD therefore you deliberately conspired to mislead the British public.' Kelly said that with the benefit of hindsight, he realised both sides were guilty of a 'loss of perspective'.

Kelly spent six years as PMOS from the summer of 2001 and became well aware of the mood of deep mistrust as he briefed Lobby journalists. He told me that listening was as important as speaking, especially when wanting to understand whether his message was landing. 'Part of the role of the spokesman is to go back into No. 10 and say that worked and that didn't, and we need to think about this.' It was, he told me, 'a two-way street'. A key part of Kelly's preparations was to sit in on all the important meetings. He would regularly lurk in the corner of what was known as the prime minister's 'den' to keep up to speed on Blair's approach to matters, rather than asking for a line. 'I always believed that if you worked from a script as a spokesman, you were dead before you started, you had to understand where he was coming from.' It was, he said, a 'process of osmosis'.

The Lobby journalists attending these briefings would themselves watch closely for early indications of difficulties ahead. Rob Hutton, until recently UK political correspondent for Bloomberg, recalls how he came up with what he described as 'a slightly snotty question' about the Blair government's proposals to allow the police to detain terror suspects for up to ninety days without charging them, a contentious issue when it was put forward in 2005. Hutton was relatively new to the Lobby and was somewhat taken aback when Tom Kelly 'got really grumpy . . . and flew off the handle with me'. The government subsequently lost the vote in the Commons on its plans. Hutton said that he realised how much you could learn from the reaction to a question: 'You poke him with a stick, and you find a soft spot.' Hutton likened the Lobby briefings to Test cricket, with long periods when not much happens and everyone carries on bowling very hard, hoping someone will make a mistake. He admits the analogy is imperfect because, in fact, the journalists just want the batsman to do something interesting, whether that is hitting a six or being clean-bowled.

For a civil servant, the toughest bowling to face is when the issues are personal as well as political. In late 2001, Tony and Cherie Blair had come under pressure to say whether their young son Leo had been given the MMR vaccine. The Department of Health had declared the jab against measles, mumps and rubella was safe, rejecting controversial claims linking it to autism and other health problems. For weeks, the Blairs refused to disclose whether Leo had been given the vaccine, on the grounds that it was a private family matter. The Conservatives called on the prime minister to make it clear whether he personally was supporting the government's policy to immunise all children. This was many years before the doctor at the centre of the claims linking MMR to autism was struck off the medical register for dishonesty and serious professional misconduct, and many newspapers were devoting significant coverage to the concerns he raised. *Daily Mail* headlines included 'MMR fears gain support', 'New evidence shows MMR link to autism' and 'MMR safe? Baloney. This is one scandal that's getting worse'.

Tom Kelly found himself facing endless questions on the Blairs' decision as Lobby briefings dragged on for up to an hour and a half. At the time, he stuck to the agreed line that this was a private matter on which he would not comment, but Kelly told me that, in fact, he was 'terribly conflicted', recognising the prime minister's right to privacy on such issues, but also aware of the legitimate public interest in whether Tony Blair had implemented his own public health policy. 'Suddenly, the boundaries between dealing with the media and private individuals and the government become a lot more blurred,' he said. 'That is when it becomes both professionally but also emotionally quite difficult.' Kelly told me at the time that he thought the questions were over-intrusive, but in retrospect he believes it would have been better if the prime minister had answered them directly. Years later Cherie Blair confirmed that her son had indeed been given the MMR jab.

While Kelly was conducting the Lobby briefings, Campbell's political role was filled by David Hill, who'd previously been director of communications for the Labour Party, where he'd built a reputation for honesty and unflappability. He was seen as a safe pair of hands, down to earth and with a straightforward approach, which was sorely needed if the government was to shake off its reputation for the dark arts of spin. He'd been chief of staff to Roy Hattersley when he was Labour's deputy leader, who praised the appointment. 'Hill finds it almost pathologically impossible to deceive or dissemble,' Hattersley said at the time, 'that is why he is the right man to re-establish a relationship of trust between Downing Street and the press.'[1] Certainly, Hill was viewed by the media as an experienced and straight-talking professional who was far less antagonistic than his predecessor. He said his main task was to calm the mood and build on the relationships he had developed with political journalists, after working with them for more than twenty years. He acknowledged there was only so much he could do, however, given the atmosphere at the time and not having the power to direct civil servants that his predecessor had wielded.

Hill's appointment, in September 2003, shortly after Campbell's much-publicised departure from Downing Street, had come about as part of a shake-up of government communications in response to another review. It was led this time by Sir Robert Phillis, a senior executive of the Guardian Media Group. He found 'a three-way breakdown in trust between government and politicians, the media and the general public'.[2]

Phillis said the adversarial relationship between No. 10 and the media had resulted in all information being mistrusted when it was believed to have come from 'political sources': 'The public now expects and believes the worst of politicians and government, even when there is strong objective evidence in favour of the government's position.' Phillis also strongly criticised the Lobby system, stating that it created an 'inner circle' among journalists with privileged access. The review found that it was not working effectively for either side, both of which had 'their credibility damaged by the impression that they are involved in a closed, secretive and opaque insider process'.

The Phillis review recommended that 'all major government media briefings should be on the record, live on television and radio and with full transcripts available promptly online'. He believed the briefings should be expanded to include politicians: 'Ministers should deliver announcements and briefings relevant to their department at the daily Lobby briefings, which should also be televised, and respond to questions of the day on behalf of the government.'[3]

Tom Kelly was a member of the review group and said it reached the conclusion that this was the modern way to address complaints about a lack of transparency. Kelly himself said he was 'completely agnostic' about the idea, but was happy to accept the majority view. He believed then, as now, that the most important issue was that the Lobby gatherings should be a proper dialogue about government policy and objectives, rather than being used as 'a PR exercise on one side and a game of Gotcha on the other'. He was also concerned about the 'celebrity question', warning that journalists would make life difficult for any spokesperson who seemed to be enjoying the limelight rather too much. 'You have to choose,' he told me. 'Do you want to be a celebrity or not? I very deliberately chose not.'

Kelly told me the prime minister did not have a particular view on the issue, except that he did not want the Lobby briefings to be a source of disputes and unwanted headlines, as they had been previously. Blair was well aware how damaging the accusations of spin had become and knew that any changes to the communications strategy would be seen in that context.

The government initially said it would accept all the key recommendations of the review. Ministers, though, raised objections that the role of Parliament and of elected politicians would be sidelined and MPs argued that announcements should be made in the Commons, where they would have a chance to raise points on behalf of their constituents. Lobby journalists were split, with those working for newspapers insisting that off-camera briefings should continue, while broadcast correspondents were understandably enthusiastic about the chance to grill a spokesperson or minister live on screen every day.

Nick Assinder, a BBC political journalist who was chairman of the Lobby at the time, said there was no approach from Downing Street to discuss or implement the proposals. He said the official position of the Lobby at the time was against televising the regular sessions with the prime minister's press secretary, explaining that 'Journalists are always happy to see ministers giving on-the-record, on-camera briefings, provided they are additional to, but not instead of, Lobby briefings, where more sensitive questions can be asked.'[4] By the autumn of 2003, with the arguments over the war with Iraq more intense than ever, the government quietly dropped the whole idea, unwilling to stoke an unnecessary battle with the media. As Kelly explained: 'Frankly, it just ran into the sand.'

The continuing row over spin was one of the reasons why Tony Blair was facing growing calls to declare when he would stand down as prime minister, with supporters of the chancellor,

Gordon Brown, becoming increasingly frustrated. The relation-ship between the two figures at the top of government was more hostile than ever as speculation over Blair's departure rose, only to be batted away as the prime minister made it clear, on several occasions, that he was not yet ready to relinquish the reins of power. Brown's team believed Blair was reneging on his pledge to hand over to his rival next door.

I remember it as a time when you got a much better sense of what was happening by chatting to advisers or MPs on either side of the growing divide than from the formal words of the PMOS. Rival supporters would talk about 'them' and 'us' as they disparaged the priorities and motivation of the other wing of their own party.

Andrew Marr, the BBC's political editor at the time, concurs. He told me that when talking to some of the players off the record or over a drink, 'you could just feel the throbbing anger of one camp for the other, and I got some of my best stories by playing one off against the other in a totally cynical way'. Yet in the Lobby briefings we were told repeatedly that the prime minister and the chancellor were working closely together on the issues of the day. Marr said the government did use the briefings to try to downplay something which was actually quite a serious problem: 'A lot of it was about trying to stop a story happening as much as to get a story running.'

Books from all the key players have exposed the real extent of the friction and manoeuvring between Blair and Brown through-out this era, and the hollowness of all the attempts in the formal Lobby briefings to dismiss the stories. It was in October 2004 that Blair announced he would not serve a fourth term in office, but, as the months and years went by with no sign of the promised smooth and orderly transition, dissent and frustration among Brown's supporters grew. Almost two years later, the so-called 'curry house coup' was launched by Tom Watson, one of Brown's closest allies and a defence minister at the time, at a restaurant in the West Midlands. It led to a wave of resignations from the government and a letter, signed by Labour MPs, openly calling for Blair to stand down. In May 2007 the prime minister finally announced he would leave No. 10 on 27 June. It is notable that in his memoirs he writes of the realisation that he had lost the support of much of the media, as well as many in his own party. 'My constituency in the media had evaporated. They admired the showmanship and political skills, but they had ceased listening to the political argument. They were bored. They were cynical. Iraq still caused too much bitterness and obstructed sensible analysis of the broader picture. They had bought the GB package, though I felt their motives were very mixed in doing so.'[5]

In one of his final speeches, the outgoing prime minister launched an outspoken critique of the media, accusing journalists of behaving like 'feral beasts' and suggesting tougher regulation was needed. He acknowledged that in the early days of New Labour he'd paid inordinate attention to 'courting, assuaging and persuading the media', but he said standards were bring driven down by the focus on 'impact journalism' in the twenty-four-hour news environment. He laid bare just how much effort was put into dealing with the press and broadcasters: 'A vast aspect of our jobs today – outside of the really major decisions, as big as anything else – is coping with the media, its sheer scale, weight and constant hyperactivity. At points, it literally overwhelms.' Blair concluded with a headline-grabbing warning: 'Today's media, more than ever before, hunts in a pack. In these modes it is like a feral beast, just tearing people and reputations to bits.'[6]

Blair said he knew his speech would be 'rubbished in certain quarters', and some did point out the irony of the attack from a politician who had put so much effort into courting the media. The *Economist* noted that for a leader whose 'administration will always be synonymous with spin, to question the system he has so often exploited seems a bit rich'. Trevor Kavanagh of the *Sun* called the speech 'ill advised' and 'very sad'.[7] Others, though, seized with glee on Blair's taunts. In *The Times*, the sketch-writer Ann Treneman replaced her photograph with a picture of a beast baring its teeth and pondered, 'Why bother with fiddly notebooks, when you can roam around, foaming at the mouth, mauling wildebeests and reputations?'[8] A new Facebook group was formed called 'Feral Beasts of the Media', and some journalists turned up to Lobby briefings wearing 'feral beast' badges.

The response demonstrated the complexity of the relationship between Labour's most successful leader and the journalists and commentators, whose appreciation of a skilled communicator turned to resentment at the attempts at media manipulation. Andrew Marr reflected that while 'spin' was never the most important thing, never the whole truth of the Blair years, 'it became a kind of grubby, smeared, opaque and distorting glass between Blair at his best and the rest of the country – just the opposite of the effective communication it had promised to be a dozen years before'.[9]

On the day of the long-awaited handover, Blair's last session of Prime Minister's Questions concluded to rare applause from all sides of the Commons. There was one last photocall in Downing Street with his family before his decade in power came to an end. For Gordon Brown, the many years of waiting were finally over. He'd been elected as Labour leader unopposed and stood on the steps of No. 10 with his wife Sarah to promise a 'new government with new priorities', one of which was to restore trust in politics.

At that morning's Lobby briefing, Tom Kelly said that Mr Blair would be preparing for questions in the House, then going to Buckingham Palace. 'The rest of the page is blank,' he said. By the afternoon briefing, Kelly had been replaced by Michael Ellam, a civil servant who'd got to know Brown while working as director of communications at the Treasury. Ellam had earned the respect of journalists for his calm, understated approach and his grasp of complex financial issues.

Michael Ellam told me that Gordon Brown had made it clear he wanted to address the lack of trust in politics, partly by making more announcements in Parliament, with less advance trailing to newspapers. He wanted the Lobby briefings to be 'functional, but relatively low-key'. I would say that Ellam undoubtedly achieved that. Indeed, I have struggled to recall anything dramatic in any of the numerous Lobby gatherings I attended while he was the prime minister's spokesman. In Test Match terms, he was a batsman who tended to dead-bat every ball. Yet while his approach was businesslike and, on occasions, pretty tedious, his political colleagues ensured there was no question of an end to the era of spin. Damian McBride, who'd been Brown's political adviser at the Treasury and already had a reputation for briefing against other ministers, was brought into Downing Street, where he would take the dark arts to new levels.

Gordon Brown experienced a turbulent start to his premiership, but he earned widespread praise for successfully steering the country through bungled terrorist attacks in London and Glasgow, serious flooding in Doncaster and Hull, and an outbreak of foot-and-mouth disease. Speculation of an early general election for Brown to establish his own mandate grew, not least because some of his inner circle were suggesting the idea to political journalists. Margaret Thatcher's favourite advertising agency, Saatchi and Saatchi, was appointed to work on the campaign, after coming up with the slogan 'Not Flash, Just Gordon'.

Every autumn Lobby journalists decamp en masse from Westminster to the party conferences. Civil servants remain back at base to ensure the wheels of government continue to turn, steering clear of the political gatherings. Labour's 2007 conference in Bournemouth could have been an opportunity for the new leader to set out his vision; instead, the forthcoming election was the only story in town. We all spoke to different members of Brown's political staff and allies on the Labour benches and reported the clear signals that momentum towards an election had become unstoppable. No one suggested the stories were wrong or overwritten. All the parties had begun gearing up for the campaign.

Then the Conservatives had an unexpectedly successful conference week, with Shadow Chancellor George Osborne's announcement of plans for a big cut in inheritance tax boosting his party's morale. Brown's visit to British troops in Iraq during the Tory conference was criticised as an electioneering stunt and the polls suggested Labour's popularity was sliding. After a breakfast meeting with his closest advisers, Brown decided the election should not go ahead after all. He caused further irritation by announcing his decision in a pre-recorded interview with the BBC's Andrew Marr, who went straight on-air to broadcast the news. Rival broadcasters and newspapers were furious that they were not informed before the story broke.

The prime minister immediately faced accusations that he had 'bottled it' and had misled journalists and voters over his intentions. David Cameron, the Tory Party's new leader, said it was a 'humiliating retreat' that showed 'great weakness and indecision'.[10] Even the *Guardian* said it was 'the biggest unforced political error in the history of New Labour',[11] one that decisively shaped the media prism through which Brown was seen. It certainly made a mockery of all the efforts to suggest Gordon Brown was a straight-talking leader who would not mislead the media or voters over his intentions.

Ellam swiftly learned that Brown expected him to be across all the developments and issues of the day before the meeting in Downing Street at 7.30 a.m. Brown was preoccupied by the desire to control the headlines day by day. He would stride into the press office, demanding to know what was happening. If he didn't like what he saw on the screens showing the twenty-four-hour news channels, he would order the team to get the coverage changed immediately. Stories emerged of his temper, though no serious complaints were ever upheld.

The *Guardian*'s Andrew Sparrow asked about these tales of Brown's temper at the routine Lobby briefing and was told: 'I think it is the sort of unsubstantiated, unsourced nonsense that you would expect to read in Sunday newspapers, not on the supposedly respectable financial wire services.' A colleague asked, 'But is it untrue, though?' When the laughter subsided, the spokesman said it was 'the sort of nonsense that you might expect to read in diary columns' and 'not an account that I recognise'.[12] It is a classic response from a spokesman keen to downplay a story but unable to say it was untrue. When I asked Michael Ellam recently about all this, he told me that Brown was 'a challenging boss . . . very passionate about what he did', adding, '95 per cent of the time he was angry with himself.'

By the summer of 2008, Gordon Brown's popularity had slumped, there was growing dissent within his party and the financial crisis was looming, with Northern Rock taken into public ownership. There were already tensions between Brown and his replacement at the Treasury, Alistair Darling, when the chancellor gave an interview to the *Guardian* from his remote croft in the Hebrides. Darling candidly declared 'people are pissed off with us' and said the prime minister needed to convey a clearer message of what the government stood for. He said the economic conditions were 'arguably the worst they've been in sixty years'.[13] Brown was furious at what he saw as a direct attack on his leadership, but Darling refused to back down and repeated his comments in television interviews. That was when Brown's 'attack dogs' were set loose. 'The forces of hell were unleashed', was how Darling put it in one later interview.[14] Charlie Whelan, Brown's former aide, was working for the Unite union, but was still informally spinning for his old boss. Lobby journalists fortunate enough to have been invited to a book launch party in Soho found they had a story on their hands when Whelan turned up and began laying into the chancellor. Darling's remarks were 'a gaffe', he told them, and 'a terrible thing to say'. Meanwhile, Damian McBride, Brown's key political aide, 'told every journalist who had access to a pencil that Alistair's interview was a disaster'.[15]

Several newspapers predicted Darling would soon be out of his job, but Brown was not in a strong enough position to remove him. By this time, the party discipline that had been such a significant feature of the early years of New Labour had almost completely broken down. I remember spending as much time as possible hanging around the lobbies and corridors of Westminster, where the dissent was evident. Labour MPs critical of the prime minister were all too keen to discuss his shortcomings, though most would only do so off the record, knowing they would be vulnerable to hostile counter-briefings from Brown's team. Some were wary of being spotted talking to me and would arrange to speak anonymously over the phone or in less conspicuous locations. Their complaints would be dismissed by MPs close to Brown as unhelpful interventions from disgruntled Blairites, thus adding to the stories of divisions within the party.

Gordon Brown's problems were compounded by the fact that various advisers and allies were spinning different lines to correspondents such as myself. It was far from clear who or what had been authorised. Paul Sinclair, a journalist who was brought into the Downing Street communications team, called it 'a shambles'. He said some colleagues 'had failed to make the mental leap from working for a chancellor who sought to be prime minister, to actually working for a prime minister' and did not realise the importance of working as a team. 'Some people thought that undermining certain other members of the cabinet was a way of defending Gordon, but those who sought to prove their loyalty and measured it in their own brutality were people who ultimately undermined Gordon Brown.'[16] He appeared to be taking aim at some of Brown's advisers, who were known for their efforts to disparage anyone whom they considered insufficiently loyal to their boss, including cabinet ministers.

The prime minister turned to the man who had been both a close political ally and, at times, a sworn enemy – Peter Mandelson. As part of a wider restructuring of the government, Mandelson was brought back from Brussels, where he was trade commissioner, to become business secretary. Mandelson had twice resigned from government previously; now he had been given a role at the heart of No. 10, where he became effectively Brown's deputy. He was one of the few figures who had the clout to give the prime minister frank advice and told him he needed to change his appearance: 'Anyone who looks as tired and exhausted and washed-out as he did would lead people to the conclusion that, even if they wanted to re-elect him for five more years, he was probably not up to it, he would run out of steam half-way through.' Mandelson also told Brown he needed to reconsider his approach to news conferences and interviews: 'Think of it as a conversation with people, not bellowing at them, not at war with them.'[17]

Mandelson's advice may have improved Brown's performance on some occasions, but the difficulties were mounting up. The financial crisis gathered pace, with the collapse of the American investment bank Lehman Brothers. Brown, who had frequently promised an end to 'boom and bust', came under pressure to apologise for his role at the helm of the economy for so many years. He was, though, widely praised for his role in chairing the summit of G20 nations in April 2009, where world leaders agreed a trillion-dollar deal to tackle the global financial turmoil.

Brown's success on the international stage did bring a brief upturn in his standing at home, but this came to an abrupt end when Damian McBride was forced to resign. In emails sent from a government computer, McBride made a series of false and obscene allegations about the Conservative leader, David Cameron, and shadow chancellor, George Osborne. He'd been asked by a Labour blogger, Derek Draper, if he had any gossip on the Tories that he could use on a website he was planning to launch. McBride offered various unsubstantiated smears against Cameron, Osborne and other senior Conservatives, which Draper admitted were in bad taste. The exchange was leaked by a rival Tory blog, Guido Fawkes. No. 10 sought to distance the prime minister from the behaviour of one of his closest advisers, saying that neither Brown nor anybody else in Downing Street knew about the emails and he believed there was 'no place in politics for the dissemination or publication of material of this kind'. McBride apologised for 'juvenile and inappropriate comments' and said no one else at No. 10 was involved, but his departure was swift.

McBride's departure prompted more Labour figures to tell of their own experiences of his practices. Stephen Byers, a former cabinet minister always seen as a leading Blairite, said he had been a victim of Mr McBride's 'aggressive and hostile media briefing' on a number of occasions. He told the *London Evening Standard*: 'As a result, I have to admit that I made little effort to suppress a smile when I heard about his enforced departure from Downing Street.' Frank Field, then a senior Labour MP, said the government information machine had been 'corrupted by a spin that seeks not to inform but control and, if needs be, destroy. And it has been in existence for over a decade.'[18]

Journalists were caught in the fallout. When McBride's memoirs were published, Helen Lewis in the *New Statesman* said he had revealed a 'brutal portrait' of Lobby journalists, 'like baby birds, constantly cheeping for regurgitated morsels of news or gossip; occasionally one stumbles on a proper story, only to kill it in exchange for something better from the spin doctor's back pocket', though she added that McBride had not mentioned how often the Brown spin machine had bullied political journalists who were deemed to be the enemy, or undermined them to their colleagues and employers.[19] Guido Fawkes, which had been at loggerheads with McBride for some time, condemned what it said was the 'cowardice and cronyism' that ran through the Lobby. Paul Staines, who runs the site, challenged correspondents: 'You all knew and said nothing.' Certainly, journalists who enjoyed briefings and beers with McBride knew he was a good source for a steer on Brown's views on both policies and personalities. Yet surely it was not unreasonable for them to write stories based on what they were told by a man who was employed to speak to them on behalf of the prime minister.

Michael Ellam admitted to the Lobby that there was 'huge frustration' at the way the prime minister's efforts to tackle the economic crisis had been overshadowed by the row. Brown himself wrote to those Conservatives who had been targeted in the emails, saying the scandal was a 'matter of deep regret', but he stopped short of an apology, insisting he had known nothing about the messages. He did order a tightening of the Code of Conduct, so that any special adviser could be sacked for preparing or disseminating inappropriate material.

The episode certainly undermined the reputation of the prime minister, but it was soon swept aside by a much bigger story, which did serious and lasting damage to public trust in all our politicians: the MPs' expenses scandal. The *Daily Telegraph* obtained an unredacted copy of all the claims for allowances and expenses made by MPs over five years, millions of documents that revealed how individuals had used the system to their advantage. For weeks to come, the paper's readers were regaled with stories of claims for duck houses, moat clearance and mower maintenance, along with the practice of MPs 'flipping' their designated main residence in order to maximise their eligible expenses. Dozens of MPs found their careers and reputations ruined; a handful ended up in court. It was a difficult time to be working as a political correspondent without access to the raw data that the *Telegraph* had bought. I remember the seemingly endless calls to individual MPs to ask for their responses, and the often long and complicated explanations. Some had clearly been milking the system, others believed they were simply lodging claims to which they were entitled. Many who had not technically broken any rules were still forced to repay thousands of pounds when their behaviour was deemed unacceptable. The public looked at the way their elected representatives had got away with claiming everything from chocolate biscuits to home cinema systems and was outraged.

It emerged that the disc containing the vast catalogue of explosive material had, in fact, been offered to other papers before its potential significance was spotted by Robert Winnett, deputy political editor of the *Daily Telegraph*, who had joined the Lobby after years as an investigative reporter. He played a key role in his paper's decision to publish the stories, which sent shockwaves through the political establishment. The expenses scandal not only damaged the reputation of parliamentarians, it also changed the relationship between politicians and the press.

Tom Newton Dunn, now chief political commentator at Times Radio, joined the Lobby as the *Sun*'s political editor at about this time and was struck by the divide between some of the old-school hacks, who'd been there for many years, and the new arrivals. There was, he told me, 'bad blood in the Lobby' about the *Daily Telegraph*'s decision to publish. Some established political journalists had not wanted to touch the story, he said, because they believed it was 'not the done thing to do' and 'breached some form of unwritten code of gentlemanly behaviour' whereby reporters did not probe too deeply into MPs' private matters, in return for tip-offs, quotes and stories. Indeed, there was a backlash, with some MPs reluctant to talk to journalists at all, particularly those from the *Telegraph*, who often found they were cold-shouldered for quite some time. Yet Newton Dunn believes the expenses row hastened the pace of change in what had still felt like 'an old boys' club' when he arrived in 2009.

It was a turbulent time for Simon Lewis to take on the role of director of communications in Downing Street, replacing Michael Ellam as the PMOS. He was warned it was the second-hardest job in government, after that of the prime minister himself. Lewis is a smooth-talking, unflappable public relations professional who had worked in corporate PR and spent two years as communications secretary at Buckingham Palace, helping to repair the image of the royal family after the death of Diana, Princess of Wales. He had no direct political experience and walked into his first Lobby briefing after an overnight flight back from Afghanistan, where he'd been on his first official visit with the prime minister. Lewis told me he was struck by the fact that the room was packed with almost exclusively male, white journalists and the mood was confrontational from the outset. Compared to the corporate world, he found it all rather old-fashioned and, he admitted, 'a terrifying experience', with the array of microphones and tape recorders a reminder that his every word could be reported within moments.

Lewis believed the adversarial nature of the Lobby system mirrored that of the House of Commons, so there was 'a working assumption that most of what you say should be challenged'. He quickly learned the techniques to use when under pressure, which we journalists had already come to recognise all too well: the refusal to discuss 'hypotheticals', the dismissal of a question as 'process' or 'process-ology', so not worth answering, and the suggestion that the matter under discussion was one for his political colleagues to address. The problem for Lewis was not just that he came from outside the political world, but that he was not part of Brown's inner team with access to the most important discussions. The journalists he was briefing quickly realised this and it undoubtedly undermined his authority. 'Nice chap, but we all knew more about what was going on in No. 10 than Simon did,' was how one of them put it.

Lewis thought that arrangements could and should be updated, and set up yet another working group with senior journalists to consider reforms. He believed the Lobby briefings should be televised, as they were at the White House. 'I always felt I was effectively live anyway, because everything I said was on the record,' he told me. 'The only difference was that the cameras were not there.' He did not see why it should be a huge problem, given the amount of resources and effort that already went into preparations for the daily briefings. Lewis believed it would be a way of 'rebalancing this inward-looking, old-fashioned club', allowing the public to find out more about what the government was doing. His proposal immediately ran into opposition, with familiar objections from all sides.

Print journalists feared it would completely change the nature of the Lobby briefings, with television correspondents 'grandstanding', making it impossible to have reasonable discussions. Others said the briefings would have to be conducted by a politician, prompting protests that this would hand the government the advantage of a daily platform to broadcast its own agenda. Lewis said the whole exercise revealed what he described as 'the tribal nature of journalism in the House of Commons'. He said some of the special advisers around at the time believed not only that the Lobby was an outdated institution, but that the daily briefings should be scrapped altogether. Once again, wiser heads prevailed, pointing out that such a move would hardly improve relations with an already hostile press. As Lewis put it, his suggestion was 'never really a runner'.

Lewis discussed various ideas with Gordon Brown and Peter Mandelson, who were said to be open-minded about modernising the arrangements. He then came up with what he saw as a compromise suggestion: that he would continue to brief the Lobby off-camera, but then record a podcast, summarising the main points, which could be posted on the No. 10 website. Pilots were recorded and circulated within the communications team, but never saw the light of day. I am not surprised. The idea of Downing Street giving its own Pravda-style summary would undoubtedly have been seen as an unacceptable form of spin. Would the official No. 10 version of a difficult Lobby confrontation provide an accurate picture of all the adversarial questioning? It would certainly be viewed with deep mistrust.

By this time the general election was looming, and the prime minister and his most senior advisers agreed that it was not the moment to proceed with changes that would further antagonise sections of the media which were already ruthlessly critical of Brown's leadership. Lewis acknowledges it would have been 'a bold step' at that stage of the electoral cycle.

In the run-up to the 2010 election, Gordon Brown did try broadcasting directly to the public, bypassing the media by posting videos on YouTube. It was not a success. His performance was widely mocked, with commentators suggesting his smile seemed either false or threatening or both. The former deputy prime minister John Prescott said it was 'the worst bloody smile in the world' and performed his own facial contortions to demonstrate the point, while the Labour MP Gordon Prentice said the footage was 'just too horrible to watch'.

Gordon Brown faced fundamental problems, beyond the need to modernise his communications strategy. In the summer of 2009, the work and pensions secretary, James Purnell, resigned, warning that Brown's leadership made a Conservative victory at the next election more likely. His dramatic departure was followed by further resignations and several Labour MPs questioned whether Brown could remain as leader. It was a time when Lobby journalists found that many of their contacts on the Labour benches were all too willing to voice their unhappiness at Brown's premiership both on and off the record. One senior MP, Barry Sheerman, told the *Guardian*'s political team there should be an immediate leadership contest. The paper had a detailed account of Brown's appearance at a supposedly private meeting of the Parliamentary Labour Party, where the former home secretary, Charles Clarke, was one of several MPs who told him he should stand aside. Another former minister, Gerald Howarth, had already told the *Daily Telegraph* that Brown was the most unpopular prime minister since Neville Chamberlain and could not be allowed to continue.

Yet Brown's allies, including key ministers, were equally vocal, telling Lobby correspondents he was the right man to take the country through the economic crisis and warning that a leadership contest would further damage the party's reputation. There was no concerted move to oust him and the prime minister battled on.

He suffered a further setback on the night of his big speech to Labour's conference in Brighton, when he'd sought to rally morale, urging delegates to 'never give up' and to 'fight to win'. Hours later the *Sun* withdrew its support for the party, with the front-page headline 'Labour's Lost It'. The tabloid's verdict was a story in itself – reported as another significant blow to the Labour leader's authority. Brown sought to downplay the importance of the *Sun*'s move, saying it was the British people who decide elections, not newspapers, and ruling out the idea that he would stand down before the country went to the polls. Privately he was furious at what he saw as further proof that the Murdoch press, and others in the media, were out to damage his prospects for their own political reasons.

Labour went into the 2010 election behind in the polls and with most of the papers supporting the Conservatives under David Cameron. Even the *Guardian* had turned against Brown, with its influential columnist Polly Toynbee writing an article with the headline 'Gordon Must Go'.[20] She said the Labour leader had 'been tested and found in want of almost every attribute a leader needs' and highlighted his failure to deal with what she called 'squalid dealings by his poisonous inner circle'.

Brown's campaign failed to turn around his standing with the voters. It was dominated by the televised leaders' debates in which the Liberal Democrat leader, Nick Clegg, outshone his opponents from the two bigger parties. Any hopes within the Labour Party of a late recovery were flattened by Brown's infamous confrontation with Gillian Duffy, a Rochdale voter who challenged him over immigration and crime. As Brown was driven away, he described her as a 'bigoted woman', not realising that the microphone he was wearing was still switched on. It sparked a huge row and Brown delivered a humiliating apology, saying he'd misunderstood what she'd said and was mortified by what had happened. Lobby colleagues on the Brown battle bus told me the mood among the prime minister's team was grim as the drama dominated the final week of the drive for votes.

Despite the epic fallout, I learned that there was a similar incident just days later when Brown was wearing a microphone for broadcasters to record his chats with a group of voters. After the event, he walked off and went to the lavatory, before realising that every sound of his personal visit was still being transmitted back to the television crews. On this occasion the recording was not made public. Yet it was another extraordinary oversight from a leader obsessed with his media coverage.

Brown's campaign never really recovered, despite a passionate and highly personal speech just days before the country went to the polls. As Lobby correspondents who'd been out on the road returned to Westminster on election night, few were prepared to predict who would form the next government.

8 TORY TRAVAILS

'I loved being prime minister. I thought I was doing a
reasonable job.'
David Cameron, 26 April 2017

O ut on the road for the 2010 election campaign, I was once
again squashed alongside my cameraman in a tightly
packed media pen as the man tipped to be our next prime minister strode down the steps of his battle bus. It was uncannily
reminiscent of the moment, thirteen years earlier, when I had
witnessed Tony Blair kick off his drive for power. We were back
in the Midlands, but this time I was assigned to cover David
Cameron's efforts to convince the country to vote for change.
It was another carefully choreographed tour with a series of
whistle-stop events in marginal seats, where the Conservative
leader would deliver his stump speech to small groups of voters,
many of whom were already party supporters.

The month-long tour involved many hours' travelling by
plane and train, as well as the battle bus, and although we
were not always with Cameron, he made a point of frequent,

informal chats with the accompanying press pack. He would wander down the bus, in his socks, to share a beer and a laugh at the end of a long day, a leader comfortable unwinding in the company of journalists. It was all off-camera, of course, but when we asked him if we could quote one of his remarks on how he felt the campaign was going, Cameron said he always assumed that anything he said to any correspondent would be reported, whatever the supposed ground rules. From conversations with colleagues, I realised that our experience was rather different from that of our counterparts who were travelling with a reserved and defensive Gordon Brown.

Cameron's team certainly tried to look after the Lobby journalists and camera crews on board, providing sandwiches, fruit and plenty of coffee on the long journeys. There was a tiny oven inside the bus and one Sunday, Joey Jones of Sky News managed to cram in a leg of lamb, complete with plenty of garlic and rosemary, which provided wafts of a traditional lunch as we travelled across the country and was almost cooked by the time we had completed the day's campaigning. Those who enjoy their lamb gently pink on the inside certainly had a treat as we headed back down the motorway that evening.

Cameron's final push for votes was a US-style, non-stop, thirty-six-hour tour of key constituencies in an attempt to demonstrate his energy and drive. It was an exhausting exercise, at the end of many long, relentless days travelling and meeting broadcasting deadlines. At each stop I did a quick live update for the BBC News Channel, before jumping back on the bus to provide radio commentary and an hour-by-hour diary for the website. I have vivid memories of Grimsby fish market at dawn, where I realised it was a mistake to be wearing such long trousers, which trailed into the fishy water underfoot and carried an unmistakable smell on to the bus as we moved on for an endless series of visits to warehouses, schools, supermarkets and, for some reason, a zoo. It was at least another twelve hours before I finally had a chance to shower and change at a hotel at the other end of the country. Long before anyone had heard of coronavirus, the receptionist made a point of remaining at a very safe distance.

It is impossible to judge whether this last frenetic charge around the country made any difference. When the votes were counted, the Conservatives emerged with the most seats but no overall majority, and David Cameron went straight into four days of hectic and highly charged negotiations, ending with the historic coalition deal with the Liberal Democrats.

The Tory leader had worked to change the image of the Conservative Party; there was the scenic trip with huskies across the Arctic to highlight his concern over climate change, the 'hug a hoodie' speech, suggesting some young offenders needed more love, and his support for gay marriage. He wanted to be a radical social reformer, to stop his party 'banging on about Europe', though of course that did not quite go according to plan.

In Opposition, the Conservative leader had focused on the broadcast media, getting on to the main television bulletins, and on expanding direct communication via webcasts and social media. Initially, he'd thought the idea of politicians wining and dining newspaper proprietors and editors was outdated, declaring: 'I hadn't relied on newspapers' backing to win the leadership (in fact much of the Tory press had been hostile). Why would I rely on them to win the election?'[1] Yet, after two years as Opposition leader, he had realised that he did need to do more to get the papers on his side. 'The press was a force to be reckoned with, and I needed someone to grip it, a heavy-weight media operator who knew how our tabloids worked.'[2]

Eyebrows had been raised when Cameron hired Andy Coulson as his director of communications in July 2007, just six months after he had resigned as editor of the *News of the World* on the day the paper's former royal editor was jailed for four months for phone-hacking. Coulson had said he took 'ultimate responsibility' for the behaviour of his paper's journalists, though he insisted he was not aware any of them had been involved in phone-hacking. He reiterated those assurances when he was interviewed by senior Tory figures and by Cameron himself, who decided to give him a second chance. The Tory leader said the 'Essex boy-done-good' became a popular member of his team and 'put the wind back in our sails'.[3]

Coulson became an influential adviser, and I found him invaluable in giving a real steer on Cameron's thinking and his approach to the issues of the day. He did not address the regular Lobby briefings when Cameron took office. That job went to Steve Field, who had been director of communications at the Treasury. He became the PMOS, continuing the practice of leaving this task to a civil servant who has to remain politically impartial. By this time these gatherings had become routine, useful for obtaining advance notice of announcements and speeches, and for getting the official government line on stories. They were very rarely a source of news and it is clear that Field had a limited, defined role: he doesn't even get a mention in Cameron's memoirs.

The divide between the official government briefings from a civil servant and the political spin from special advisers was well established by now, even if the line was sometimes blurred. In coalition, there was another dimension: the Liberal Democrats had to find a way of getting their message across too. Sean Kemp headed the party's media team in Downing Street when its leader Nick Clegg was deputy prime minister. He said the regular Lobby briefings were about 'what the Tory prime minister would want to say, rather than what the Lib Dem deputy prime minister would want to say'. So Kemp and his colleagues would tour the offices of Lobby journalists in the Commons every day to try to convince them to reflect their ministers' angle on the stories they were running.

Kemp acknowledges that it was not easy to make it clear where the Liberal Democrats disagreed with their Tory colleagues without undermining their overarching goal of making sure the coalition functioned effectively. The two media teams shared an office at No. 10, an arrangement that did work most of the time, according to Kemp: 'I think if we had been in different offices we would have briefed against each other, been at each other's throats a lot more,' he told me. They usually tried to avoid public disagreements, but on occasions such as the huddle after Prime Minister's Questions in the Commons, Kemp and his colleagues would loiter at the back while their Conservative colleagues were speaking, before trying to catch journalists to make their own separate points. 'It was extremely important always to be out there,' he told me, 'because we had to try to find some way of having a voice in what was going on, because when the prime minister is Conservative, and you're the smaller party in coalition, you have to be there, to say . . . this is our take, this is what we stopped, and this is what we have delivered.'

Kemp had a good relationship with most of the correspondents, but the one theme that the Westminster hacks were keen to pursue was the extent of the difficulties between the two parties. There were plenty of issues on which the two parties diverged; the biggest fallout was over welfare reforms, and in 2014 Liberal Democrat ministers defied the Tories to back changes to the controversial 'bedroom tax', which reduced benefits to claimants who had a spare room. Kemp says that, with hindsight, his team worried too much about reports of 'government splits', and should have disagreed more, to get greater credit for their own influence on government policies.

Within months of the 2010 election, the relationship between politicians and the media was engulfed by further revelations that some tabloid journalists had worked with private investigators to access messages on thousands of mobile phones. The prime minister had stood by his close adviser Andy Coulson, even when fresh claims emerged over his role in phone-hacking when he was at the *News of the World*. Cameron later admitted that his trust in Coulson was misplaced: 'It wasn't only that I believed his assurances, it was that I very much wanted to believe them. And that always affects your judgement,' he wrote.[4] In January 2011 Coulson resigned, saying the wave of allegations made it impossible for him to continue in his job. 'When the spokes-man needs a spokesman, it is time to move on,' he said. Three years later, Coulson was jailed for eighteen months for plotting to hack phones when he was in charge at the *News of the World*. Cameron could only apologise, saying 'I am extremely sorry I employed him. It was the wrong decision.'

The hacking scandal then took a further grave twist when it emerged that the police were investigating claims that the *News of the World* had hacked the phone of the murdered schoolgirl Milly Dowler. Both the Liberal Democrats and the Labour Party called for an independent public inquiry, led by a judge. On 13 July 2011, the prime minister announced that Lord Justice Leveson would conduct an inquiry into the 'culture, practices and ethics' of the press. In six months of hearings, it took evidence from celebrities, civilians, the police, journalists, newspaper pro-prietors and politicians, including the prime minister himself.

Though no Lobby journalists were directly involved in the scandal, it was an uncomfortable time for anyone in the media, as the 'Hacked Off' campaign highlighted the trauma of victims and pressed for tighter controls on the press. It is worth noting that at the end of the police inquiry, in which well over sixty journalists were arrested or charged and dozens more were questioned, just nine were convicted.

The Leveson inquiry concluded that politicians of all parties had developed 'too close a relationship with the press in a way which has not been in the public interest', though it found no evidence of any impropriety or wrongdoing by the prime minister. Leveson proposed a new system of self-regulation, with what he called 'statutory underpinning', meaning it would be backed by legislation. On this Cameron strongly disagreed, opposing any arrangement that would give Parliament or government control over what the press could report, and warning against 'any legislation that has the potential to infringe free speech and a free press'. Many of the newspapers were outraged at Leveson's suggestion, with the *Sun* declaring that it was 'deeply alarmed by his main proposal for new legislation that could bring in state control of newspapers'.

A compromise was eventually agreed for a new press watchdog, backed by Royal Charter, with the power to impose big fines or force prominent apologies from UK publishers. Many newspapers refused to accept the new body and signed up to an alternative, independent press regulator. Lobby members working for newspapers were subject to the new arrangements and all its journalists were acutely aware of the damage to public trust in their profession and the pressure for tougher sanctions on those who behaved improperly. The BBC, like other broadcasters, is regulated separately by Ofcom, so the new press watchdog did not directly affect my work or that of close colleagues. It was, though, a time when it was clear the behaviour of a small number of journalists had undermined the wider reputation of the media.

The whole issue of press regulation also became a political story for Lobby journalists as this was a topic on which the Liberal Democrats completely disagreed with their coalition partners, arguing that much stricter controls on the press were needed. When the prime minister delivered a speech in Downing Street setting out his response to the Leveson proposals, Sean Kemp lurked at the back of the State Dining Room until the speech was over, before gathering the assembled journalists to tell them why his party believed Cameron's plans were wrong.

After many months of headlines and soul-searching, it is hard to argue that the changes introduced as a result of Leveson were as far-reaching as some had expected. Campaigners for greater curbs on the press were clearly disappointed. In 2018, the government confirmed that it would not go ahead with the second part of the Leveson process, which would have looked at the relationship between journalists and the police. Cameron himself later reflected that 'the press and politicians are as close as ever'.[5]

Some of Leveson's other suggestions on the behaviour of reporters, 'requiring transparency on the sources of quotes, requiring transparency on the method by which any story has been obtained', received rather less attention and were quietly buried. This is hardly surprising, given that protecting your sources has always been a fundamental principle for journalists. Many of the most significant stories of recent years would never have seen the light of day if everyone involved had known they would be named publicly. Whistleblowers take risks when they reveal wrongdoing, as do government insiders when they tell reporters what is happening behind the scenes. The exchange of information secretly, privately or off the record is an essential part of the correspondents' work and, without it, not only would we all know less about what is really going on, but some serious misdemeanours might never be exposed.

For Lobby journalists, the politicians or aides who are happy to pass on a vital snippet of information or gossip during those quiet words in the corridors, lobbies and bars of Parliament often have good reason for not wishing their identities to be revealed as the source of a story, yet the information they provide undoubtedly enriches the coverage of political life.

It is worth noting that until the Lobby rules were updated in 2018, Rule 3 stated:

'The cardinal rule of the Lobby is never to identify its informant without specific permission. In any case, members of the Lobby must always take personal responsibility for their stories and their facts.'

And the principle is preserved in the latest edition, even if the language is less draconian. Rule 10 declares: 'Lobby journalists should never name the sources of any off-the-record briefings they may receive from MPs, peers or their advisers and civil servants. They should also do all they can to ensure their sources are not identified inadvertently by themselves or others. This preserves the convention known as "Lobby terms".' While that doctrine of 'Lobby terms' is as important as ever, other rules have been dropped, lifting some of the secrecy that was once an intrinsic part of the Lobby. The latest version has scrapped the old rule 7, which until 2018 declared: 'The Lobby frequently invites Ministers and others to meet it collectively, to give information and to answer questions. Members are under an obligation to keep secret the fact that such meetings are held and to avoid revealing the sources of their information.'

Instead, the current edition sets out the arrangements for briefings from the PMOS twice a day from Monday to Thursday when the House is sitting, and says members should 'bear in mind that the purpose of the meeting is to elicit information, not to score political or debating points'. The PMOS is not usually named by reporters, though his or her identity can be found easily through public sources, such as the government's own website. These sessions are on the record – everything can be quoted – but the words are usually attributed to the PMOS.

David Cameron wanted to modernise the arrangements for communicating the government's message after Andy Coulson's departure and sought a replacement who understood the rapidly changing media world. When Craig Oliver was appointed as his director of communications in 2011, he was the first person from outside the newspaper industry to take on the role. I had known him when he was a senior editor at BBC News, and he went on to become head of English Services at BBC Global News. Oliver told me that although the Lobby was still important in speaking to 'the bubble' of a few thousand people closely involved in Westminster politics, and could set the narrative for how a government was perceived, he believed its journalists often failed to see the bigger picture. His attitude was to 'make sure that they're fed, have plenty to write about and are getting a positive view of the government', but he stressed that could only be one part of the strategy. 'If you only do that . . . you are failing to reach beyond the bubble to most people who push politics to the corners of their lives.' Oliver pointed to recent elections and the EU referendum as examples where the 'received wisdom had often been very wrong', and believes this is partly because the Lobby tends to be 'inward-focused and navel-gazing', lacking a real sense of what is going on across the country.

Oliver, who was knighted in Cameron's resignation honours list, now works for a communications agency, and believes the increasing power of digital media means that Lobby journalists working for the mainstream newspapers have to realise that 'almost no one reads their stuff'. Oliver told me that David Cameron questioned whether it was time to change the arrangements completely. Oliver was sympathetic, believing the regular briefings had become a 'shadowboxing game'. He still queries the entire structure: 'Do we have to have this system whereby somebody who is nominally a civil servant is a spokesperson for the government, isn't allowed to say anything political, but goes out there every day and gives the government message, while the people who are in charge of shaping and focusing that message aren't even allowed in the room?' He told me the result was a pantomime, with those who conduct the briefings 'playing defence' all the time, trying to avoid creating a story, while special advisers, who can address the political issues, work around the formal system.

Oliver sees the Lobby as one of the last closed shops in Britain and acknowledges that any move to get rid of it would provoke a backlash from its journalists, but he did become exasperated at what he calls their 'stupid games'. He recalls an occasion when fuel bills were rising, and the Liberal Democrat energy secretary, Ed Davey, had suggested that people should wear warm jumpers to save on heating bills. Amid controversy over whether the government was sufficiently sympathetic to those struggling to pay their energy bills, a junior spokesman took one of the regular Lobby briefings. Oliver said the transcript showed he was asked more than twenty questions by journalists demanding to know whether the prime minister believed people should wear a woolly sweater. Under pressure, he eventually said it was 'something that people may wish to consider'. The result was newspaper stories suggesting the prime minister had told people to put on a jumper if they were cold, an assertion which was then flatly contradicted by a No. 10 spokesperson who declared: 'It is entirely false to suggest the prime minister would advise people they should wear jumpers to stay warm. Any suggestion to the contrary is mischief-making.' Yes, this really is the sort of thing that sometimes becomes part of a day's work at Westminster.

Oliver told me they did seriously consider putting the briefings on camera, but thought the idea through and decided at that stage that it probably would not work. They were forced to acknowledge that the reason the system had continued for so long was that it suits both the journalists and the government. Oliver said that when there were complex, unfolding stories, there was always another opportunity to sort out confusion or give information that might not have been available when an issue was first raised. 'The pressure is not on and you can wind things back and there's not something on tape,' he said. He still believes televised appearances would be 'a high-stakes, high-wire act', with pressure on the spokesperson not to misstep and to deliver the right line all the time. He points out that everyone makes a slip occasionally. 'If it's on camera, then the ability for that to be played dozens and dozens of times and the government be held to account for it is incredibly difficult.' Similar concerns led Boris Johnson's government to drop its plans to televise briefings a decade later.

Oliver is clear that no one can do the job of speaking publicly for the prime minister without having direct access to whomever is in power, and that raises questions about the structure of the Downing Street press team. If the spokesperson is answerable to the director of communications, he or she would also want access to the leader and there is a limit to how many press people can be around the prime minister during important meetings. Add to that the concerns that high-profile appearances from a spokesperson could lead to some bruised egos among ministers who found themselves upstaged, and it is no surprise that David Cameron shied away from any fundamental changes to the arrangements.

At the Westminster correspondents' dinner in January 2014, Cameron acknowledged that the relationship between politicians and journalists was often a confrontational one. 'You slag us off, we rage about you, repeat ad infinitum,' he said, yet he defended the work of political correspondents. 'Yes, rowdy, tenacious, sceptical, uncontrollable, often uncomfortable for our politicians. But British political reporting is deservedly respected around the world for the way it probes, it inquires, it scrutinises, and these things are linchpins of our democracy.'[6]

Graeme Wilson had himself made life uncomfortable for the prime minister when he was deputy political editor of the *Sun*, telling his readers how Tory MPs believed their leader was 'out of touch', but in 2013 he was brought into Downing Street to become the prime minister's press secretary. Wilson was a widely respected political journalist with many friends in the Lobby, but he found it a nerve-wracking experience when he faced his former colleagues for mass briefings after Prime Minister's Questions in the Commons. Having worked for many years on the other side, he told me he was well aware of the risk of saying something unhelpful when 'surrounded by a mob of very skilful journalists who are all trying to find a way to trip you up'. Wilson is mild-mannered and polite, defying the caricature of a shouty spin doctor, yet his understated approach of trying to persuade rather than confront reporters was effective. He would wander the press area of the Commons to brief his former colleagues on forthcoming announcements and, at the same time, ascertain the mood among the hacks, often getting an early indication of trouble. It was, he said, 'a two-way process'. Some senior journalists were also invited to Downing Street for 'fireside chats' over an early evening drink with the prime minister.

Wilson also recognised the importance of talking to people beyond 'the Westminster bubble' and frequently travelled with the prime minister on regional tours around the country. In the run-up to the 2015 election, they would head out of town almost every week for visits that would include speaking to local broadcasters and press, an opportunity to reach a different audience, although local media, armed with evidence of how policies are affecting people in their patch, can often conduct some of the most challenging interviews.

In 2013, when the prime minister announced his intention to call a referendum on Britain's membership of the European Union, it certainly helped to rally the Eurosceptics in his party and to blunt the appeal of the UK Independence Party, which was campaigning to leave the EU. It would have immense consequences for the nation, yet it was by no means the biggest issue in the election campaign two years later.

In 2015 I was out on the road with the Tory leader as part of a pack of other Lobby journalists, news reporters and camera crews as he spoke to small groups of voters in factories and high streets across the country. At the end of five weeks on tour, those of us who had been with Cameron throughout the relentless drive for votes enjoyed supper in a pub with him and his team. Cameron did not make any predictions, but he made it plain he was not expecting a clear victory and his demeanour was not that of a politician on the brink of triumph. Another hung Parliament appeared to be the most likely outcome. Yet the final result was a slim Tory majority of eleven MPs and Cameron returned to Downing Street, promising he would 'bring our country together', a pledge which was to be trampled in the Brexit battles.

Much has been written about the referendum and its consequences. It is, however, worth reminding ourselves how David Cameron sought to continue the regular Lobby briefings, even though members of his government took up opposing sides on

Brexit. Cameron decided to suspend collective cabinet responsibility, whereby all ministers are expected to stick to the agreed
line, but only on issues relating to the referendum. His objective
was to prevent the Tory Party tearing itself apart, to avoid 'blue-
on-blue' attacks, a military phrase for friendly-fire incidents. It
patently did not work, and Cameron's dismay and anger at the
way close colleagues including Boris Johnson, Michael Gove
and Priti Patel took such prominent roles in the Leave campaign
is well documented. The prime minister's policy was to stay in
the EU, but the so-called 'purdah' period in the run-up to the
poll meant the government was not supposed to play any part
in the campaign. When David Cameron stood outside Downing
Street to make a speech on the dangers of leaving the EU, he
was accused of breaching the rules.

Civil servants, who are not allowed to get involved in political issues, were left in a curious position. Helen Bower, the first
woman to take on the role of PMOS, had the unenviable task of
handling the regular Lobby briefings on behalf of the government
throughout this intense phase. Those attending did so to make
sure they did not miss government announcements, though the
real story was clearly elsewhere. Craig Oliver saw it as a stark
example of how outdated the Lobby system had become.

Cameron clearly believes that the attitude of the newspapers
towards the EU was a significant factor in the outcome. 'The
referendum sent the Eurosceptic press into overdrive,' he wrote,
adding that while some of this was predictable, 'the scale of the
onslaught was ferocious.'[7] Cameron was particularly unhappy at
the way the BBC reported the campaign, believing that it 'lost its
way in terms of understanding the difference between balance
and impartiality', so that the voices of thousands of businesses
arguing for Remain were given equal treatment to just two prominent company bosses coming out for Leave.[8] At the same time,

Leave campaigners also accused the BBC of bias and dishonesty. This is another issue that has been debated in great depth. While no organisation can claim to have a perfect record, I know from my own experience at the time that at the BBC's political unit we went to huge efforts to try to cover every twist and turn of the campaign accurately, fairly and impartially, despite enormous pressure from both sides.

The result undoubtedly shocked not just the political establishment, but even some of those who had campaigned to leave the EU. Within hours, David Cameron resigned as prime minister, believing that, as the man who had led the drive to remain in the EU, he would have no credibility in seeing through the process of leaving it. When the leadership contest was cut short by a series of unexpected twists, the task of delivering Brexit fell to the home secretary, Theresa May, who'd maintained a subterranean profile throughout the campaign. Her entire premiership would be overwhelmed by the immense political clashes over the issue.

The new prime minister struggled from the outset to convey a clear message of her vision and strategy. Her initial slogan, 'Brexit means Brexit', was quickly mocked and her decision to bring a balance of Leave and Remain supporters into the cabinet meant she faced endless threats of resignation from one side or another. Her early talk of tackling the 'burning injustices' in society was sidelined by the complex and highly contentious Brexit process, and tensions among her own advisers added to the difficulties.

Her first director of communications, Katie Perrior, was well known and popular with political journalists. She believed that the Lobby was 'massively important' and had to be treated seriously, but she too wanted to reach out beyond the Westminster bubble. She struggled on both counts. 'The prime minister didn't really want to do any form of media,' Perrior told me, 'it just wasn't her thing.' She said that because of May's shy, reserved nature, the idea of sitting down with a political editor for an in-depth, one-to-one interview would 'fill her with horrors'. It meant that Perrior was unable to offer such opportunities to try to get the papers on board and May's message across. Perrior then found that some Lobby journalists, particularly those from Sunday newspapers, had got used to being fed several stories every week by David Cameron's team and were annoyed when this handout dried up. She said her 'grid' of key announcements and speeches was frequently half empty because ideas were blocked by objections either from ministers or advisers.

When Theresa May was persuaded to pose for photographs, for a feature about her home life in the *Sunday Times*, it was a disaster. One of her closest advisers, Fiona Hill, had arranged for top designer Amanda Wakeley to send some clothes for the occasion and the prime minister was photographed apparently relaxing at home, wearing a pair of designer chocolate-brown leather trousers that cost £995 and spotless Mulberry trainers, as you do on your day off. I am still amazed that May herself did not realise how it would look to voters. There was quite a row – Perrior had not been involved in the arrangements and was furious. She realised immediately that for a government which had declared it was on the side of the so-called 'JAMs', those Just About Managing, the photo shoot was a fiasco.

Perrior had wanted May to go on a Brexit tour around the country, to engage with voters about their priorities for life outside the EU, but she was overruled. She wanted the prime minister to appear on non-political programmes such as the BBC's *One Show*, or on Mumsnet, the popular online parenting website. Instead, she believes the No. 10 press machine became hamstrung by the demands of the twice-daily Lobby briefings, with decisions made in haste or announcements slipped out before they had been properly thought through. Perrior said that rather than being a genuine opportunity to deliver information, often the spokesperson would resort to 'survival techniques so they could get though the next forty-five minutes without being killed'. Although she has friends in the Lobby and respects its journalists, Perrior would have liked to reduce the briefings to perhaps one a day, despite the outcry it would have caused. 'I hate to think how much policy has been made, just because we needed an answer for the Lobby over the years, which is quite crazy if you think about it.'

Perrior also had to contend with the rising tensions within May's cabinet. There were huge differences over the approach to Brexit – even between its supporters – which spilled into personal rivalries. The discord was laid bare when Boris Johnson, then foreign secretary, was deemed to have stepped out of line. At a conference in Rome in December 2016, Johnson said that Saudi Arabia, an important UK ally, was engaging in 'proxy wars' in the Middle East. The prime minister had just returned from a tour of the Gulf, where she had dined with the Saudi king and thanked him for co-operating on security over the years. At the morning Lobby briefing her spokesperson delivered a clear rebuke, saying the foreign secretary had expressed his own views, which were 'not the government's position'. Johnson was furious and phoned Perrior, who had worked closely with him in the past, demanding an explanation. Perrior said it was Fiona Hill who had issued instructions for Johnson to be 'slapped down' and had told Helen Bower, the PMOS, to deliver the line at the Lobby briefing, even though Bower is a civil servant and had resisted getting involved in the row. Such are the complexities and arguments played out before potentially far-reaching words are uttered to Westminster's journalists.

Perrior believes many of the prime minister's problems were exacerbated by her powerful chiefs of staff, Fiona Hill and Nick Timothy, and she was staggered at their arrogance and lack of respect for others, including senior ministers. Yet, she said, it was rare for the prime minister to challenge them, adding, 'Normally we would all sit there while Fiona would raise some batshit crazy idea and not say a word.'[9] Perrior spoke out about the 'rude, abusive and childish' attitudes of the two advisers after she left No. 10. She was one of many who criticised the mistakes they made in the snap 2017 election, when they ran a presidential-style campaign totally unsuited to May's personality.

Timothy was blamed for controversial social care proposals that were abandoned rapidly in the midst of the campaign, in a humiliating U-turn. Hill was at the centre of clashes with the media which added to the problems facing the struggling prime minister. Sky News was excluded from some briefings and, for a while, blocked from joining the prime minister's battle bus because Hill objected to some of its reporting. In an earlier incident, its top frontman Adam Boulton (nicknamed Bunter), an experienced Lobby hand, had speculated that May might be calling a news conference because of ill health and then read out a text message from Hill live on-air which said: 'You might want to tell Bunter that he should watch what he is saying about my boss's health, utterly unfounded and untrue.' Sky and other broadcasters found their bids for interviews with cabinet ministers were rejected, a move that further reduced the Tories' chances of getting their message across to voters.

Though the overall strategy was supposedly to keep the focus on the prime minister and her promise of 'strong and stable' leadership, she also ducked out of doing TV debates with her opponents. The rancorous and misjudged campaign ended with a disastrous result for the Conservatives, who lost their parliamentary majority.

In the inevitable fallout, a series of senior figures called on the prime minister to sack the duo described by one minister as 'the monsters who propped her up and sunk our party'. When both Hill and Timothy resigned from their posts, one northern MP welcomed the departure of the two advisers, who he said had been 'instrumental in delivering the worst Conservative election campaign in living memory'.[10]

There was open speculation as to whether Theresa May could survive as leader, with the former chancellor George Osborne describing her as a 'dead woman walking'. May did apologise to party workers and MPs who had lost their seats, but vowed to get back to work. Yet she struggled to maintain discipline, as senior ministers began positioning for a future leadership contest.

Gavin Barwell, who became May's chief of staff and now has a seat in the Lords, said her biggest problem was that so many of the government's deliberations leaked to well-connected Lobby correspondents before a line had even been agreed. Barwell told me that after the 2017 election May had to contend with 'the most leaky cabinet we have ever had'. The chancellor, Philip Hammond, who had backed Remain during the EU referendum, was a frequent target, with staunch Brexiteers presumed to have discreetly passed on various unfavourable stories about him. Two months after the election, Tom Newton Dunn, then political editor of the *Sun*, reported that Hammond had sparked a row over sexism, saying that driving a train was so easy 'even a woman can do it'. The comment was said to have been made in front of the entire cabinet and to have prompted a rebuke from the prime minister. Hammond himself publicly denied he'd made the remarks and told the BBC's Andrew Marr that the claims were generated by people who were not happy with his agenda. An unnamed ally of Hammond's then accused Michael

Gove, who'd been a leading figure in the Leave campaign, of leaking the story, prompting Gove's allies to deny the charge, telling *The Sunday Times* that he had nothing to do with it. The prime minister ordered her colleagues to stop revealing details of cabinet discussions to the papers, only to find her own words reported within hours.

Barwell said the behaviour of some ministers was 'hugely frustrating' and affected decision-making, as the prime minister became wary of discussing sensitive issues with the entire cabinet. Barwell said he often had a very good idea who was responsible for what he regarded as unhelpful stories, but it was impossible to find proof.

Paul Harrison joined May's political staff as press secretary in that summer of 2017 and one of his first tasks was to brief the media after her big speech to the party conference in Manchester. Harrison admitted he was a bit nervous in advance: 'The stakes are high and you want to do justice to the prime minister and the speech writers,' he told me. The post-speech huddle is always an important opportunity for the leader's team to try to shape the coverage and Harrison had memorised six key points. They became totally irrelevant after what will go down as one of the most disastrous conference speeches of all time. A comedian interrupted May to hand her a mock P45. She then suffered a prolonged bout of coughing, almost completely lost her voice and struggled to continue. I was in the audience at the time and it was agonising to watch, as everyone wondered whether she would even make it through to the end. As she finally croaked to her conclusion, letters began falling off the conference slogan displayed on the screen behind her. For May's many detractors, it was symbolic of her whole performance as prime minister.

May left the stage to sympathetic applause from party members and Harrison went to the press room to brief the assembled members of the Lobby. He had not had an opportunity to speak to May, but it would not have helped. No amount of positive spin would have made any difference. The only thing Harrison could tell them was that Manchester police had arrested a man for a breach of the peace. He told me some of the assembled hacks were kind enough to ask about policy: 'It was one of those times when your trousers are on fire and you are trying to pretend very gallantly that your trousers aren't on fire.' The speech went down as 'calamitous', 'a car crash' and a 'disaster', at a time when her leadership was already fragile.

It was by no means the last difficult briefing that Harrison faced, as the prime minister battled to get her Brexit deal through the Commons and went down to a series of heavy defeats. After big parliamentary occasions, Harrison would address the huddle of Lobby correspondents in the Press Gallery, just outside the section of seats reserved for the media looking down on the Commons Chamber. He would be armed with a folder containing all the information he might need on policies, facts, figures and lines to take. On his first such outing he discovered that he could not possibly open the vital folder because he was literally surrounded by reporters who would be delighted to get a glimpse of the confidential notes, including those headed 'DO NOT SAY . . .'. Harrison admitted he found the first of these gatherings 'really daunting' and had to develop techniques for dealing with the barrage of questions as the prime minister suffered setback after setback.

It was not an easy task. Harrison recalls an occasion when there was rising speculation of a leadership challenge if thirty-five Tory MPs submitted letters calling for a contest and he was asked in one of these Lobby huddles whether May would stand and fight if this happened. The usual response would be to decline to comment on a hypothetical scenario, an escape route

I have heard on numerous occasions. On this occasion, Harrison feared that any attempt to duck the question would signal she was prepared to throw in the towel and decided he had to confirm that she would indeed take on any challenge. His answer then led to stories saying 'May – I'll fight confidence vote'. It was not incorrect, but it was not the message he had wanted to put across at that moment, and meant the focus was on the threat to May's position rather than on the case she was making to MPs, with another key Brexit vote looming. A few weeks later May did face a confidence vote, which she won comfortably. Nevertheless, with a third of her MPs failing to support her, her days in power were numbered.

While Harrison spoke to the media on political issues, the daily Lobby briefings were taken by James Slack, the PMOS, a former journalist on the *Daily Mail* and the only member of her press team who went on to work for Boris Johnson. In November 2020 he was promoted to director of communications in recognition of his calm professionalism through some extraordinary upheavals. Harrison says Slack handled the regular meetings with enormous skill through some 'pretty sticky moments'. Finding a convincing message, when it was apparent the government was heading for defeat, was clearly an almost impossible task. May's team tried to crystallise the case they were making to MPs, to set out the positive reasons why Parliament should vote for May's withdrawal agreement, but Harrison acknowledges that 'we weren't really able to do that successfully enough'.

Most Lobby journalists have a huge amount of respect for Slack and recognise how hard it was for him to give them the information they were seeking, especially when his guidance would sometimes prove to be incorrect within hours, when May changed her position. Slack would be pressed by Lobby correspondents to say whether a particular Commons vote was going to be delayed and would insist that the government was still planning to press ahead with it, which was almost certainly true at the time. Yet that would be overturned at a moment's notice, when ministers decided to pull the vote in order to buy more time to try to win over more MPs. Despite this, Rob Hutton of Bloomberg told me he believed that 'James did a fantastic job for Theresa May, and did a fantastic job for us, in trying to help us understand what her position was.'

In addition to the formal briefings, the separate, discreet chats between journalists and advisers continued as ever. As Theresa May battled to get her Brexit deal through Parliament, these conversations with her senior media team developed into what became known as the 'dark Lobby'. While this sounds dramatic and rather sinister, it was an apparently genuine attempt by May's senior team to explain some of the intricacies and underlying factors behind its approach to the negotiations with the EU, which it did not want to put on the record for fear of jeopardising a possible breakthrough. One No. 10 insider told me: 'There are certain things that you can say privately, which you could not explain if there were loads of people barking at you, some of whom you don't know, with their little tape recorders on.' He downplayed the significance of these discreet huddles: 'You just need to have private conversations with people you trust and give them a bit more background to help them explain the policy.' All those involved said these conversations were not so different from the many other off-the-radar chats between correspondents and senior aides, yet most were reluctant to talk openly about the so-called dark Lobby. One senior journalist said it was not a spin operation. 'There's a whole load of stuff that the British government can't say on the record,' they told me. 'It's the kind of conversation that we have all the time with all sorts of people, it's just a way for us to develop our understanding, and governments generally benefit from more accurate reporting of what they're doing.' Another said, 'Don't believe everything you're told about the dark Lobby,' pointing out that it was open to any of those who attended the regular briefings and the small group was not restricted to privileged senior correspondents. John Pienaar, a highly respected figure at Westminster who was the BBC's deputy political editor at the time, told me the so-called 'dark Lobby' wasn't actually all that dark, just a 'more subterranean level of briefing'. He said it was 'pretty factual, with a certain amount of insight into what the government's actually doing and thinking which, for understandable reasons, it would not want officially attributed to No. 10'. Others saw this as a throwback to the early days of the Lobby, when the very existence of the briefings was a closely guarded secret.

At the same time, Theresa May was setting out her plans for Brexit and beyond through a series of big speeches – in Downing Street, in Lancaster House, in Florence and on the floor of the House of Commons. It was part of the strategy to ensure that the public would hear the prime minister explain her case in person, rather than learning about it through the prism of political journalists.

Robbie Gibb, who replaced Katie Perrior as May's director of communications in July 2017, had been in charge of political programmes at the BBC and had a clear understanding of the difficulties of conveying the prime minister's message given the hostility of much of the press. Gibb, who received a knighthood in May's outgoing honours list, said that despite the expertise of his colleagues who delivered the regular Lobby briefings, 'we often had our message distorted or interpreted in a way that we didn't necessarily agree with'. He told me it was not that the journalists were misrepresenting the government's arguments: 'Their objective is to find a new angle and a new top line to make their newspapers or bulletins as exciting as possible; the objective of government can be to repeat some of the underlying messages that the public may not have heard when they were originally said, but are crucial for the understanding of a particular policy.' While Gibb admits to frustration at the difficulties of cutting through what he calls 'the noise of Westminster', his team did not consider televised briefings. Theresa May needed to confront the questions about her leadership in person, he explained, 'therefore she needed to be out there herself, appealing for support and explaining what she was trying to do to get Brexit over the line,' and the key audience in all this was her own MPs.

While the briefings behind the scenes were important, this was a time when much of the drama was played out live in the Commons and broadcast across the globe, as the fate of the prime minister and Britain's place in the world hung in the balance. For Lobby journalists seeking to tell the inside story and to find out the next moves, the place to be was often Portcullis House, where they would catch passing MPs for a quiet word, find out about the latest motions to be debated and develop their intelligence on the likelihood, or not, of a forthcoming vote getting approval.

Rob Hutton told me how day after day he would be poised on the cushioned benches, ready to grab every passing MP for a quick chat: 'What do you think? How are you going to vote tonight? Where do you think it's going?' Some of those he accosted would be more forthcoming than others, but he would also spot key rebels chatting to one another, or one of the prime minister's allies talking to a wavering MP, all helping to build up a picture of the next likely moves.

Broadcasters were allowed to book a specific spot near the entrance to Portcullis House, where they could seize those who were prepared to speak publicly about their intentions, to feed their comments into the rolling coverage of the constantly shifting story. On-air they may have been slightly more cautious than when speaking off the record, but the scale of the opposition to May's plans was evident. Outside Parliament, rival groups of demonstrators with their banners, chants and musical accompaniment added to the atmosphere.

The problem for Theresa May was not communications but the arithmetic in Parliament, with opposition to her deal both from those who wanted a cleaner break with the EU and from those who wanted a closer future relationship, and without an overall majority in the House. This meant she was fighting on two flanks simultaneously. May's position was further undermined by senior ministers continuing to leak their own version of events, so that her media team lost control of the flow of information. Robbie Gibb said that while they worked as a 'unified, disciplined team' and did everything they could to convey a compelling message, with hindsight they were pursuing a 'fool's errand'. With Labour opposing the deal, a divided party, a leaky cabinet and no overall majority it became impossible for them to succeed.

Even Theresa May's offer to stand down did not prevent a third, shattering defeat in the Commons on her Brexit proposals. On 24 May 2019, after almost three difficult years in power, she delivered an emotional speech in Downing Street, confirming that she was quitting as party leader, paving the way for a contest to decide the next prime minister. Her voice broke as she declared she would 'leave the job that it has been the honour of my life to hold'. After months of political turmoil, parliamentary drama and deadlock over Brexit, the coverage of her departure was hardly sympathetic. 'Teario Theresa, Hello Bojo' was the *Sun*'s front page, correctly predicting victory for Boris Johnson in the race to succeed her.

Despite a dedicated and hard-working communications team, the cautious and reserved Theresa May had struggled from the outset to win over the media and failed to unite her divided party. Boris Johnson arrived at No. 10 with the Brexit-supporting press willing him to succeed. He was a journalist himself with friends in the Lobby and relished performing for the cameras. Yet many of his former colleagues were wary from the outset, and his arrival in Downing Street would mark the start of a new round of ferocious battles with journalists at Westminster and beyond.

9　LOBBY ON TOUR

'A journey is like marriage. The certain way to be wrong is to think you control it.'

John Steinbeck

Setting off on tour with the prime minister is one of the great traditions of the Lobby. While its journalists are based at Westminster, when the prime minister travels overseas, a select group of its reporters and camera crews goes too, seizing the chance for different experiences and good stories. Successive leaders have realised that this is the only way to ensure that they can continue to make the headlines wherever they are. The risk, of course, is that the stories that emerge may be very different from those that No. 10 were hoping for. For the lucky few correspondents on board it is like being on a particularly intensive package tour, with scarcely any time to take in your surroundings, let alone investigate what is happening locally, but with the sort of access to the prime minister and his or her senior advisers that rarely occurs back at home.

Colleagues with longer memories than mine recall trips when there was ample time to mull over stories before filing them to their news desks, long lunches and even days off when excursions were laid on for the press. Alas, those days were over by the time I became a political correspondent for the BBC. The demands of rolling news and the complex logistics of filing television and radio reports meant that such trips were frequently frantic and exhausting, though nonetheless unforgettable.

I remember tightly gripping the seat in front of me as we raced through the outskirts of Islamabad at terrifying speed, our battered minibus crammed with journalists, cameras and broadcast equipment, struggling to keep pace at the back of the column of gleaming limousines. Motorcycle outriders with sirens wailing swarmed around us and armed guards, their backs to the road, lined the route through busy, dusty markets, where local people barely glanced at the passing commotion. It was 2009 and I was covering Gordon Brown's trip to Pakistan, the final stop on a tour that had already included visits to Delhi, Kabul and the British military base in Afghanistan, all in the space of one weekend. Though the pace of this trip was particularly intense, I was well aware of the challenges and the extraordinary opportunities that arise when travelling with the prime minister.

It is no wonder that a place on these trips is one of the most sought-after perks of Lobby life. 'You get to go in a motorcade into Manhattan, with cop cars in front of you and cop cars behind you, swerving across the interstate highway. Ever done that? It could become a habit.' That's one recollection, from the *Guardian*'s former political editor Michael White, of a trip with Tony Blair. Andrew Marr of the BBC has a rather different view, however: 'These are long journeys, often in coaches, rattling across deserts or up badly made roads. Everybody's tired, it's late at night, you're in close proximity to the prime minister's team.

That's when really quite indiscreet things can be said that will then become hugely important days or months later.' Another former BBC political editor, Nick Robinson, described the tours as 'absolute heaven'. He told me 'You're going to exciting places, staying in the swankiest hotels in the world, because you have to stay in the same hotel as the prime minister for security reasons, and then you get to ask the prime minister questions, usually daily, if not more, whereas you might wait months to do that in normal times . . . Then you go out for dinner with your mates in the evening, have a few drinks, put it on expenses, I mean what's not to like?'

My own experiences of the Lobby tour included plenty of rattling across deserts and the occasional night, or at least a few hours, in a swanky hotel. I loved every minute, despite the constant stress of trying to ensure stories and pictures got back across the world to meet deadlines in London. Yet these tours are loathed by some leaders and their close aides, who find themselves torn between the international diplomacy that is the purpose of their journey and the demands of the accompanying media, who are usually determined to pursue a completely different agenda.

One notable exception was Sir Bernard Ingham, who visited fifty-five countries with Margaret Thatcher when she was in power, flying 500,000 miles, and clearly enjoyed escaping the Westminster bubble. Thatcher's image as the 'Iron Lady', unbending in her opposition to communism yet prepared to forge new relationships across the world, meant she was often greeted with far more enthusiasm on her foreign visits than in the UK. These tours helped to bolster her standing at home, as well as overseas, and rarely failed to deliver good stories and pictures. It is hardly surprising that Lobby journalists never missed an opportunity to join what became known as 'Maggie's Flying Circus'.

Sue Cameron, a political journalist who worked for the *Daily Telegraph*, the BBC's *Newsnight* and Channel 4, recalls the excitement of her debut trip with Thatcher in 1986. It was the first visit to Israel by a British prime minister and people lined the streets to welcome and applaud her. The prime minister liked to travel by RAF VC10, part of the Queen's Royal Flight, a plane described by one of the more experienced hacks as 'the Queen Mother of the Skies'. When she asked why, Cameron was told: 'Well she's very graceful, rather elderly and full of gin.'

Ingham told me they were always superbly looked after by the crew on these flights, as the prime minister and her close advisers worked in the VIP area at the front of the plane before being served with cocktails and dinner. The travelling press had their own area at the rear, with their own bar, and Ingham would provide them with briefings on the official business ahead. Thatcher herself usually came to chat to the journalists, the real privilege of these journeys, as she talked off the record about her personal views on the issues of the day. On the way back from successful trips there were even occasions when she joined reporters as they unwound over drinks, which were always in plentiful supply. The hacks often rounded off their journey singing their own comic lyrics to some popular tunes. Trevor Kavanagh of the *Sun* said that on one memorable flight back from Washington, 'Margaret Thatcher kicked off her heels, ordered a large glass of scotch and joined the press for what became a traditional end-of-trip sing-song.'[1] She then astonished the US ambassador, who was on board, by opening President Reagan's Christmas present in front of the press pack. It was a sparkling emerald brooch, and a moment of sheer gold dust for those journalists.

The prime minister's trip to Moscow in 1987 was groundbreaking – she had famously described the Soviet leader Mikhail

Gorbachev as a man she could 'do business with' and the visit was bound to be a big story. It also coincided with the boycott of the Lobby by the *Independent*, *Guardian* and *Scotsman*, and Ingham refused to allow those journalists who would not attend his regular briefings to join the official media party. The *Independent*'s political editor, Anthony Bevins, tried to persuade Ingham to take him along by offering to make himself scarce when Ingham was addressing the press pack, but the approach was rebuffed. During a brief and tetchy meeting, Ingham questioned whether Bevins was planning to lock himself in the on-board lavatory at the appropriate moment and await a knock on the door to tell him it was safe to come out, a scenario the press secretary was not prepared to entertain.

Joe Haines had stopped journalists from travelling with the prime minister when he was press secretary to Harold Wilson, but when he returned to his previous role as a journalist, working for the *Daily Mirror*, he was all too keen to cover Thatcher's Moscow trip. His request was also turned down – hardly surprising given that Haines described his relationship with Ingham as one of 'mutual contempt'. Haines, though, was not prepared to be thwarted. He and a handful of others decided to make their own arrangements, despite the difficulties of getting visas, flights and details of the planned tour.

Somehow, they managed to arrive in Moscow at about the same time as the prime minister. Haines had been in touch with a friend, Nicholas Luis, who happened to be the son of a colonel in the KGB, with a senior role in Soviet press relations. Luis turned up to meet Haines in his Bentley, believed to be the only one of its kind in the city. He'd agreed to loan the car and his driver to Haines for the duration of the prime minister's visit. In a city of beaten-up Ladas, the Soviet delegation assumed this impressive British vehicle was part of the prime minister's entourage and waived it into place in the official convoy, which swept along the priority lanes with accompanying outriders.

Bernard Ingham was surprised and far from pleased to see the uninvited hacks when they arrived with the official party for a visit to a monastery. Ingham ensured that his Lobby pack had unrivalled access to Thatcher's unexpected walkabouts and historic meetings with President Gorbachev. Julia Langdon, then political editor of the *Daily Mirror*, was even greeted enthusiastically by a military band when she got separated from the rest of the group and stepped out on to a parade ground during a visit to the Ministry of Defence. The welcoming party had mistaken her for the prime minister.

Haines, Bevins and the other journalists outside the accredited Lobby group received very different treatment, facing endless struggles with Soviet bureaucracy. They had been unable to book into the same hotel as the official posse, so missed out on the briefings and ended up in bleak hotel rooms in the wrong part of town with no direct-dial phones, which made it immensely difficult for them to file their stories. They eventually struggled to the airport, having booked a return journey with Aeroflot, an airline which was not known for its luxury service.

The flight home for the official Lobby party was quite an occasion, as all those on board celebrated a hugely successful trip. For the team from No. 10, it had exceeded their expectations in resetting international relations and prompted almost entirely positive coverage. For the journalists, it had been three days of front-page headlines, dramatic news conferences and great pictures. On board the VC10, Mrs Thatcher wandered down the aisle of the plane to chat to the reporters, asking them if they were enjoying the champagne, served from a silver tray. The journey was a classic example of how Ingham treated those he described as his 'friends in the Lobby'. It also demonstrated why political journalists covet an accredited place on the prime minister's tour party – it is almost impossible to cover these trips properly without it.

When Robin Oakley was political editor of *The Times* he went on a trip to the Gulf with Thatcher, shortly after he'd written an article that had been critical of her leadership. Thatcher went out to address the crew of a Royal Navy vessel deployed in the region and most of the journalists were taken by launch to cover the event. Oakley and two others were told that, due to a shortage of space, they would be taken separately by helicopter. Their initial enthusiasm for the plan evaporated swiftly when they had to be lowered by winch from the helicopter on to the heaving deck of the ship. They managed to complete their nervous and rather awkward descent, to find Ingham grinning broadly at their discomfort. It was, Oakley told me, 'our penance for the nerve we'd had in writing something critical of the "Great leader"'.

Some journeys are more exotic than others, and gatherings of international leaders can often result in the media being corralled in their own zone, well away from the real action, with long hours waiting for something to happen. Ingham recalls the lengthy negotiations at the European summit in Dublin in 1980, where Thatcher famously asked for a rebate, telling other leaders: 'I want my money back.' At two o'clock in the morning, Ingham tried to brief the press pack, many of whom had spent rather too long at the bar as the talks dragged on. 'There were people who were very merry,' he told me; 'there were people who were asleep, and there were people who were too drunk to ask a question.' Those who had indulged rather too much certainly risked missing a big story. Ingham, though, is remarkably forgiving, and told me that he once fell asleep himself while he was supposed to be addressing a group of journalists. He'd been on an overnight flight across the Atlantic after a demanding trip and had agreed to speak to some German reporters. 'They were incredibly nice,' he told me, 'and waited until a press officer nudged me and gently reminded me that I was giving a briefing.'

Given the gruelling nature of these tours, I am full of admiration for Julia Langdon, who was pregnant when she went on another Moscow trip with Thatcher. Langdon was amazed when the prime minister offered her own bed on board the plane to the expectant journalist. Langdon felt she could not accept and insisted she would be fine on the floor of the press cabin, a decision which is now her 'greatest regret in journalism'. Langdon said it showed the extraordinary intimacy of the tours, particularly with a leader like Thatcher who had the confidence to chat openly to the press and a down-to-earth touch when it came to the practicalities of life. Langdon recalls talking to her about the problems of arrangements for laundry on a lengthy trip to Australia and the Far East.

There is a real camaraderie that develops between the travelling media and the team around the prime minister on these journeys, frequently reinforced by late-night chats over a glass or two of wine. The personal rapport is often a good thing, though Robin Oakley warns of the need to be wary of letting objectivity slip and allowing 'boys-on-the-bus' syndrome to take hold. I have seen little evidence that Lobby journalists ever let the mood on tour outweigh their instinctive nose for a story, but there are occasions when they demonstrate their appreciation for all the information and guidance they receive. During a break in proceedings at the G7 summit in Toronto in 1988, the travelling hacks marked Bernard Ingham's birthday by presenting him with a cake, a teddy bear and a chorus of 'Happy Birthday'. Ingham was clearly touched, reflecting that it was 'the first recorded time

that a No. 10 press secretary has not had to put up with aggrava-
tion from the media'.

In the days before journalists were under constant pressure
to meet the demands of the twenty-four-hour media, the pace of
these tours was very different. At times when the prime minister
was in private meetings, Downing Street would lay on entertain-
ment and excursions to keep the press pack out of trouble. John
Major's former press secretary Gus O'Donnell recalls taking a
group of them on a perilous white-water rafting trip during a
break in a Commonwealth summit in Zimbabwe. It was only
when they were in the midst of the rapids that he discovered that
several of those on board the makeshift craft could not swim.
His boss's joke – 'Just make sure you don't come back with all
of them' – was rather too close for comfort. The BBC's Robin
Oakley also had a worrying moment. He'd gone to a safari park
instead and found himself stranded with a burst tyre on a remote
track as dusk approached, with several hungry lions nearby.
Such tales, of course, were not reflected in the coverage. I regret
to say that by the time I started travelling with prime ministers,
such diversions were no longer on offer.

The rules of engagement on these trips are complex. The
conversations between prime minister and press are usually considered to be off the record, unless some on-the-record quotes
are agreed. However, when the supposedly informal chat discloses a good line or revelation, journalists will huddle together
and work out how and when they can get the story out. They
may go back to the press team and ask if they can use the quote,
and if that doesn't work they may attribute the words to a 'friend
of the prime minister' or report that they 'understand the prime
minister believes . . .'. Sometimes they reach an agreement on
when to reveal a particular story. It does not always work, and
their competitive spirit means they will always strive to get their

own genuine exclusives; but those who break an agreement with their colleagues over the coverage of a collective briefing will face a backlash and find that they cannot expect any help if they miss a quote or have technical problems.

John Major frequently made his problems worse by making careless comments to reporters on his overseas trips. He was battling the Eurosceptic rebels in his party, whom he'd famously described as 'bastards' in an earlier unguarded moment, when he went to Japan in the autumn of 1993. Rumours were swirling of a leadership challenge, with suggestions that a maverick Conservative, Sir Richard Body, might stand as a 'stalking horse'. When the press pack on the plane asked the prime minister what he thought of the idea, Major remarked that he could 'hear the flapping of white coats' when some of his 'barmy' critics complained about his leadership. His words were recorded by one of the reporters and the story inevitably got out, fuelling the animosity of the Tory rebels.

It was on this same trip that the usually polite and unflappable Gus O'Donnell lost his patience with John Sergeant of the BBC. A brief doorstep interview had been arranged as John Major emerged from the British embassy in Tokyo and O'Donnell had made it clear to the media that they should ask about his meeting with the Japanese prime minister before questioning him on other matters. Sergeant, frustrated that Major's comments on the plane about the rebels in his party had been off-camera, went straight to the story of the moment and asked the prime minister what he thought of a possible leadership challenge. Major was furious and walked off without answering, telling his press secretary to make his annoyance clear to the BBC. 'You jerk,' was how O'Donnell put it to Sergeant, in front of several other journalists. The confrontation became newsworthy in itself, much to Sergeant's pride, and O'Donnell later apologised.

He told me he was annoyed because Sergeant's approach had spoiled the opportunity for everyone else to ask questions, but realised he'd overstepped the mark.

On the flight back from Tokyo the chancellor Kenneth Clarke boarded the prime minister's plane at the last minute, after technical problems grounded the aircraft on which he was due to return. After take-off, the prime minister came for a brief and uneventful conversation with the accompanying journalists, before declaring that he was going to catch some sleep. The media were unwinding with glasses of champagne when the chancellor came to join them. Rather than briefing them on the trade deficit or unemployment figures, he regaled them with tales of jazz and football. Everyone was enjoying the anecdotes, laughing at his jokes, when Philip Webster of *The Times* felt a tap on his shoulder. It was the prime minister. 'What's he talking about?' asked an anxious John Major, preoccupied by the questions over his leadership. Webster reassured him that Clarke was talking about Nottingham Forest rather than European policy. Major then joined the assembled media to listen in, though it is unclear whether he was enjoying the jokes or keeping a close watch on his cabinet colleague.

Despite his frequent clashes with the media, Major always wanted to chat to the journalists accompanying him on these trips. O'Donnell had hoped this would help reporters understand that Major was a decent and genuine man, but after several occasions when these informal conversations led to unhelpful headlines he began to wonder whether they were a good idea. By the time he handed the role of press secretary to Christopher Meyer, O'Donnell had reached the conclusion that the pitfalls of these occasions outweighed any potential advantages and suggested to his successor that he should 'get a grip' on the arrangements for foreign travel.

Meyer swiftly realised he was right. There were too many dangerous moments when Major would wander down the aircraft to speak to the Lobby members, certain that 'he'd be able to convince them that he was taking the right course'. 'He lost all sense of discipline,' Meyer said. 'We would have constructed for the trip a very tight line, and who was the prime violator of that tight line? The prime minister himself, who would say something to journalists which would be the headline the next day, completely wrecking everything.' Meyer decided to take a robust approach and told the prime minister to stop these informal chats with the press pack.

The ruling lasted for two trips, which were seen as a success by the No. 10 press team but not by the journalists, who were deprived of a prime source of stories. Meyer was taken out for lunch by a group of senior Lobby hacks, including Trevor Kavanagh of the *Sun*, who pressed him to lift his moratorium. At the same time, Major himself said that on the next trip he would make use of the flight to speak to the reporters on board, convinced that his personal approach could result in more sympathetic coverage. Meyer lost the battle, to the delight of the media.

Jonathan Haslam, who worked alongside Meyer before becoming director of communications at No. 10, was well aware of the risks. He told me he always tried to make sure he knew in advance what the journalists were after and gave the prime minister a note intended to guide him through the supposedly informal chat. It had a limited effect, however, at a time when every trip was dogged by new twists in the rows over Europe and sleaze.

For reporters, the biggest stories are always those which are not planned by the Downing Street team. Jonathan Haslam told me that Charles Reiss, who was political editor of the *London*

Evening Standard for many years, constantly badgered him to be as close as possible to the prime minister throughout their journeys. When Haslam asked him why this mattered so much, Reiss told him it was just in case the prime minister died unexpectedly. He wanted to be on the spot as he breathed his last words.

Not only do the media and No. 10 have very different agendas on these trips, but often the press pack can catch out an unprepared prime minister with questions on political developments back at home. Nick Robinson, who travelled with several different prime ministers for both the BBC and ITN, said this meant the tours were 'enormous fun if you're a travelling journalist, but the politicians loathe them and they go wrong again and again'. Indeed, Alastair Campbell has said that while it made sense, logistically, to take along a group from the Lobby when Tony Blair was travelling overseas, it reached the point where Blair felt that taking journalists on his plane was 'like a football team taking the away fans with them'.

Sometimes huge stories break while the prime minister is abroad. In 2003, Tony Blair was en route to the Far East when news of scientist David Kelly's death was received. Nick Robinson was one of the Lobby journalists on board. 'I realised this might be the biggest story I had ever covered,' he told me.

Godric Smith was with the prime minister in the first-class cabin at the time and recalls the sense of shock at the news as Blair struggled to talk to colleagues in London, via an intermittent satellite phone. 'It was pretty clear the government needed to say something by the time we landed,' he said.

Ten minutes from touchdown in Tokyo, Smith gave the journalists a handwritten note, saying the prime minister was profoundly saddened by the death of Dr Kelly and there would be a 'proper independent inquiry' to establish the facts. The announcement of what became the Hutton inquiry, hastily formulated mid flight, was conveyed around the world within minutes.

Blair himself made a brief statement to camera, confirming the announcement, as he arrived at his hotel, but his ordeal was far from over. It was at his news conference, standing alongside the Japanese Prime Minister, that Jonathan Oliver of the *Mail on Sunday* shouted 'Have you got blood on your hands, Prime Minister? Are you going to resign?' It was a phrase that would haunt Tony Blair for years to come.

From 2001, I travelled with successive prime ministers to visit British troops in Afghanistan and Iraq, amid a grim backdrop of mounting casualties. If you were lucky, the first stage of the journey would be on a chartered civilian plane from Heathrow airport. After lengthy security screening at the VIP suite, you would be deemed to be part of the Downing Street party and whisked through many of the usual formalities for the rest of the trip. On several occasions we flew direct to Afghanistan from either RAF Northolt or RAF Brize Norton on military cargo planes, a journey of at least eight hours. It was not the most restful way to start a demanding trip, but I found that a sleeping bag on the floor was certainly preferable to the cramped seating on your average cut-price airline.

Travelling to a war zone inevitably requires stringent security measures. This means not just flak jackets and helmets, some nervous moments and the need to comply with the barked instructions of military commanders, but also complicated arrangements on what you are allowed to report and when it can be broadcast. Frequently you will be told you cannot reveal news of the trip in advance. News organisations understand the need for such restrictions where there are real security concerns, but problems do arise if a member of the press pack breaches the agreed plan. I recall one correspondent from a rival broadcaster getting a full foghorn of abuse from a senior army officer when he got on-air via his mobile phone as soon as we had landed at the British base in Afghanistan. Keen to be first to break the news of the visit, the correspondent had ignored an agreement that it would be kept secret until the prime minister's potentially risky trip to troops on the front line had been completed. My rival narrowly avoided being left behind in the desert camp as punishment.

Tony Blair's visits to Iraq, after the fall of Saddam Hussein in 2003, were dominated by the continuing controversy over the decision to go to war and growing questions over whether British troops were being put at risk by a lack of equipment and protective vehicles. I joined the Lobby party on several of these trips, often just before Christmas when Blair went to thank the British military for their dedication and professionalism. These journeys were run to a tightly controlled timetable, with the prime minister on the ground for a few hours. We would get the chance to ask a few questions for a brief broadcast interview before the prime minister was whisked away for private briefings. There were scant opportunities to speak to any of the British soldiers on their tour of duty. It was always a scramble to try to set up satellite equipment, transmit our pictures and interviews and fulfil a list of demands from different BBC programmes before we were hastened back on to the plane. Under such circumstances, it was not easy to get a proper grasp of the situation in the country. Having reported for the BBC from other war zones over the years, with the freedom to roam more widely, I was struck by the constraints of travelling with the prime minister. You have access to whomever is in power and their close advisers and you may get to places that would otherwise be difficult to reach, but, once there, it is very difficult to assess what is really happening locally. Lobby journalists taken on tour may spot the political significance of a chance word or phrase from the prime minister of the day, but they are not best placed to judge the effectiveness of British missions in complex and dangerous places such as Afghanistan or Iraq.

In 2006, the controversy over Blair's relationship with US President George Bush was ongoing when the two leaders met at a G8 summit in St Petersburg. The microphones picked up what they had thought was a private conversation. 'Yo, Blair. How are you doing?' was the president's greeting. The prime minister's spokesman Tom Kelly, who was travelling with him, only learned about this when he started taking calls from the Lobby journalists on the trip. He realised he would have to speak to Blair before responding. 'I have rarely seen the prime minister completely flummoxed,' Kelly told me, 'but he stood there with his mouth open for several seconds while I conveyed this to him.' Blair had not noticed anything significant in the president's choice of words and thought it was just a friendly greeting. Kelly knew the press saw it very differently, an indication of how the US president treated his British ally. Kelly admitted it became 'a horror show', dominating the coverage of the summit and fuelling the accusations that Blair was the puppet of the American president. With hindsight, Kelly said he could see the amusing side of the episode, but he understood why this was not shared by the prime minister.

News organisations pay for places on these prime ministerial tours and expect their journalists to demonstrate that this is money well spent by providing plenty of good copy and pictures. Downing Street aides are well aware that the additional pressure on reporters to keep their news desks happy, even when there are no significant developments, can lead to all sorts of unhelpful coverage. Godric Smith, who replaced Alastair Campbell as Blair's spokesman, told me they would bring along domestic stories to feed to the media on days when the visits and meetings were not 'news-rich', though not all of them made the newspapers and bulletins.

Smith has much experience of the way that trivial issues can become a preoccupation when journalists are cooped up together in the press pack. At a Commonwealth heads of government meeting in Australia in 2002, reporters spotted that the pale-pink shirt worn by Tony Blair was from the top British designer Paul Smith and had pictures of a naked, kneeling woman on each cuff. The prime minister had tried to ensure that no photographers got any shots of the racy design, but that did not prevent a flurry of stories, with the *Daily Mirror* even providing a mock-up of the shirt, with cuffs exposed, for its readers. Blair then chose a long-sleeved blue casual top by another designer, Nicole Farhi, for an evening barbecue. He was snapped with beer in hand, chatting to other world leaders whose outfits were noticeably more formal. The prime minister's fashion sense became the subject of numerous articles, including in the broadsheet newspapers. Smith told me he faced days of increasingly bizarre questions about the prime minister's wardrobe, culminating in a classic quote from the exasperated spokesman: 'Mr Blair got his shirt from a shop that sells clothes.'

There can also be tensions among the journalists, as Robin Oakley found on his last foreign trip as political editor of the BBC. On a flight back from a G8 summit in 2000, he was keen to have the usual chat with Blair before recording a radio interview with him. Oakley was surprised and concerned to learn that the prime minister had suggested coming to speak to the press pack, but that his offer had been rejected by John Sergeant, political editor of ITV News, who was chairman of the Lobby at the time. The two journalists had a history of rivalry, dating back to the time when Sergeant was Oakley's deputy at the BBC. Oakley was informed that Sergeant had settled in to watch the in-flight movie after enjoying a good dinner and had told Blair's staff that if the prime minister wanted to speak to the journalists he should wait until the film had finished, a response which, understandably, did not go down well with the team from No. 10. Oakley was furious and went to talk to Blair's officials to stress that Sergeant did not speak for all of the reporters on board, who were keen to see the prime minister as soon as he was available. Oakley then had what he describes as a 'forceful exchange' with Sergeant, delighting the rest of the Lobby who duly described the scene in their diary columns the next day. Fortunately for Oakley, the prime minister saw the amusing side of the incident and came back for a friendly chat with the journalists, though Sergeant was unusually quiet during the discussion.

On another trip to Australia in 2006, Tony Blair was under huge pressure to spell out a timetable for his departure from office when he came down the plane to speak to the assembled Lobby journalists. His press secretary at the time, David Hill, had told them this was a private chat and his words were not to be reported. Philip Webster of *The Times* asked him if he had a date in mind for when he might stand down. 'Yes, I have actually, Phil,' was Blair's reply. It was quite a revelation, even though Blair would not tell him when that might be, saying, 'No, I've already said enough, haven't I?' Some of the assembled journalists realised the significance of his comments. Nick Robinson of the BBC, who was on the trip, told me he had been struck by Blair's demeanour. 'He looked crushed, like he hadn't got the fight in him any more, and knew the game was up.' When Blair wandered back to his separate compartment at the front of the plane, they all started discussing how they should handle his comments. A worried-looking David Hill told them emphatically that the conversation was not to be used.

An argument ensued which was still not resolved when they reached Australia.

The British media was determined to find a way to get the story out and primed a local Australian reporter, who had a long-arranged interview with Blair when he arrived, to ask about his plans for leaving Downing Street. Blair's answer was far more cautious, but it was sufficient for the press who had been on the plane to declare that they 'understood' he had a date in mind to stand down. It was far more difficult for the broadcast journalists, who included his bland answer to the Australian reporter in their stories but did not have any footage of the more telling quotes he'd given them on the flight. Nick Robinson recalls how excited he was to despatch what he considered to be a groundbreaking report, only to discover that it was relegated to a lowly position near the end of the bulletins back home. Without Blair's words on camera, revealing that he'd decided when to end his premiership, BBC editors had decided it was not much of a story. It was a classic example of the difficulties of turning an off-the-record chat into a meaningful television despatch, particularly when those producing the news bulletin are in another time zone on the other side of the world. It was more than a year later that Blair finally set the date of 27 June 2007 for his departure, ending many months of speculation.

While Blair's conversations with correspondents became increasingly strained as the rows over the Iraq War intensified, his successor Gordon Brown never seemed at ease in the company of a bunch of journalists. Nick Robinson remembers a trip to the USA, when Brown was under pressure from many in his own party over the government's decision to scrap the 10p starting rate of income tax. The prime minister's tension was all too apparent as he went to chat to the media on his plane. Forced into close proximity with journalists who were all asking hostile

225

questions about the policy, Brown started gripping the headrest of one of the seats with such ferocity that Robinson feared he was about to rip it off and throw it at his fellow travellers.

The trip did not get much better. Brown's meeting with President Bush was a difficult one, as the new prime minister tried to signal that his approach to the American president would be different from that of his predecessor while striving to bolster the close ties between the two countries. The personal chemistry between the two leaders was awkward, and at their joint news conference all the questions from the British side were about the 10p rate of tax. The bemused president later asked why they were all so interested in Tempe, a city in Arizona.

It was a prime example of a Lobby corps that was far more preoccupied with the domestic political agenda than their journey around the world. While Blair's team had begun taking stories with them to fulfil these demands, Brown's spin doctor Damian McBride took the idea further, drawing up a schedule for each foreign trip: 'I needed a good story for the morning we flew out so all the hacks were in a buoyant mood by the time we got on the plane; I needed one strong story for each day of the trip and two belters in my "back pocket" in case something went wrong; and finally, I needed one decent domestic story – often a bit of grid-busting skulduggery – that I could dispense on the final day or on the flight back as a parting gift to the travelling hacks, just so they felt as looked after and catered for as possible.'[2]

McBride recalls some serious partying on the flights home at the end of these trips, which would begin with Brown joining the media for a chat before returning to his cabin to work. This would then be followed by a quiz or other games, with a hard core of hacks drinking until arrival, when, as McBride put it, 'a hardy few of us used to come off those flights – often in the cold light of dawn at Heathrow – absolutely plastered'.[3] At the risk of sounding a complete wimp, that is not something I experienced on my travels with prime ministers, though I certainly unwound over a few drinks on occasion. Usually I found I still had work to do on the return flight, with more broadcasts looming on arrival, and then there was always the need to try to catch some sleep.

Gordon Brown was a notoriously driven, hard-working leader and this was reflected in the relentless pace of the trips on which I accompanied him. That death-defying charge through the streets of Islamabad was on a whirlwind weekend tour taking in Afghanistan, India and Pakistan. The schedule was frenetic, without sufficient time built in to establish satellite links and despatch our reports to London. We argued in vain that there was little point in filming meetings and news conferences if we were hassled back on to the plane before we could send the material back to be broadcast. Our protestations were met with warnings that if we failed to stick to the timetable, we would be left behind and miss the rest of the trip.

The only time we paused for breath was when Brown's talks with Pakistan's President Asif Ali Zardari on tackling extremism in the region went on longer than expected. We waited in searing heat in the beautiful and well-tended gardens of the presidential palace, along with a large group of local media and dignitaries. Podium, flags and microphones were ready for the joint news conference to be given by the two leaders. The lines of chairs on the lawn stood empty as we all sheltered under the shade of nearby trees. Vast numbers of immaculate, uniformed staff bustled around, ensuring the seats were correctly aligned, testing the microphones. As we continued to wait, there were complaints from some of the Pakistani television crews. Trays with glasses of water arrived. Then cables were unfurled, large fans were brought out and, to our bemusement, hosepipes.

Eventually it became clear that the plan was to spray a fine, cooling mist of water over the entire area of the garden, which was laid out for the news conference.

At last we were summoned to our places, with government ministers and officials invited to take their seats first. They sat down for only a few moments before swiftly getting to their feet, realising that they had acquired large and embarrassing damp patches on the rear of their otherwise immaculate clothing. The cooling mist had soaked the cushioned seats of the chairs. A furious row broke out. Hoses were swiftly rolled away, and there was further confusion until we were told that the news conference would be held inside the presidential complex and the media scrambled to relocate to the cool of an air-conditioned meeting room.

The delay resulted in even less time to put together our reports and convey them to London before we had to leave on the prime minister's plane. We ended up recording my reports for the evening news and handing all the material, including our pictures, to a local 'fixer', who took it to the BBC's bureau in the city. Such are the arrangements we frequently have to make to get these stories on-air. I am well aware that, all too often, the logistical challenges of these trips can make it difficult to focus sufficiently on the journalism, but in my view the privileged access to the prime minister and his closest advisers still outweighs all the difficulties.

There was plenty of media interest in Gordon Brown's trip to a G20 summit in Pittsburgh in September 2009, though once again the journalists' focus was very different from that of No. 10. Simon Lewis, who had recently been appointed as the prime minister's director of communications and was on the trip, believes Brown's role in co-ordinating the global response to the financial crash was one of his finest achievements. Yet the coverage of the summit was completely dominated by reports that Brown was 'snubbed' by President Barack Obama. Despite repeated efforts by No. 10 to arrange a one-to-one meeting with the president, the two leaders ended up with a 'walk and talk' for fifteen minutes in the kitchens of the UN. Even the *Guardian* described how Brown had 'lurched from being hailed as a global statesman to intense embarrassment'. Lewis said it was clear from the moment they set off that this was the story the Lobby wanted to run, and his efforts to persuade them that this was a 'side issue' did not wash. He told me how surprised he was at the lack of coverage of the G20 agreement to reform global banking. 'What struck me, to be frank, was how little interest the Lobby had in what I thought were very important matters.'

Sometimes the priorities are determined by news desks back in the UK, particularly when they want reaction to events closer to home. I went on a fascinating trip to Rwanda with David Cameron when he was Opposition leader in 2007. He was there to launch new policies on tackling global poverty, signalling a shift in his party's priorities, and he joined other Conservative MPs working on voluntary projects. The only story my editors back in London were interested in, however, was why he was not in his constituency, which had been hit by flooding. Cameron was even asked about this by a Rwandan television reporter, to the amazement of everyone on the trip. I eventually convinced one of the BBC Radio 4 programmes that there was an important story to tell about the new Conservative approach to international development, but it was quite a struggle. For once, I found myself sharing the frustration of the leader's media aides.

The trip was part of David Cameron's drive to change the focus of the UK's foreign policy and build links with countries that had been overlooked in the past. His wider agenda was given scant coverage and when he became prime minister

Cameron asked his press secretary, Craig Oliver: 'Why the hell do we take a plane full of journalists with us when we go abroad? They are never interested in what's actually happening on the trip.'

That was certainly the case in 2013, when Cameron travelled to North Africa, including Libya, two years after the overthrow of Colonel Muammar Gaddafi, with a party of Lobby hacks on board as usual. They were preoccupied with rumours of cuts in defence spending rather than their travels across the continent. From the outset, the prime minister was fuming at a story in the *Daily Telegraph* suggesting he was planning cuts to the SAS and other Special Forces. He walked down the plane, spotted one of the paper's reporters and said: 'Oh great story today. By the way, you forgot to mention that I'm also going to scrap Trooping the Colour and get rid of the Red Arrows.' The prime minister then turned on his heels and strode back to his cabin. Craig Oliver, realising the potential risks, went to speak to the journalists to tell them that, for the avoidance of doubt, the prime minister was using irony to make the point that the *Telegraph*'s story was not true. Oliver was not entirely convinced he had prevented any of the journalists taking Cameron's words seriously, and as they landed back at Heathrow his Blackberry lit up with queries about the front page of the *Daily Mirror*, which declared 'Red Arrows Face Axe Threat', quoting 'sources with the PM' who had 'suggested that the Red Arrows could be next in line for the chop'.[4] Oliver was furious and confronted the *Mirror* reporter, asking how he could have written a story which he knew to be untrue. He rang the editor to demand a correction. The following day, hidden on page 27, the *Mirror* claimed victory in its 'Save the Red Arrows campaign', saying it had succeeded in getting a guarantee from David Cameron that the RAF display squadron would not be axed. Oliver's team decided that in future the supposedly informal off-camera chats with reporters would be on the record, so that both sides would be more careful with their choice of words.

Later that year the prime minister went to Sri Lanka and made a controversial visit to the north, where he raised concerns over alleged human rights abuses against Tamils. The country was emerging from a long civil war but there were still tensions and the Sri Lankan government had said it could not provide security in the Jaffna region. As he and the whole entourage waited for the internal flight to the troubled zone, Cameron briefed the Lobby on his decision to defy the national government's advice not to go there. Yet Oliver told me the first question the prime minister was asked was whether he had ever eaten horse meat (a scandal had emerged back in the UK over the discovery that horse meat had been mislabelled and used in some beef products). The second question was about his reaction to a suggestion from the comedian Russell Brand about the obscene habits of some Conservative MPs. At that point, it is perhaps not surprising that Oliver called a halt to proceedings and they all boarded the potentially risky flight. 'We literally went into a newspaper office where there were bullet holes and bloodstains on the floor and pictures of the journalists who'd been murdered were pinned on the walls,' he told me. 'And I think at that point a lot of people realised this was evidence of real journalism, people who had died for what they did.'

Oliver reluctantly reached the conclusion that he would have to follow the example of some of his predecessors and take a grid of stories on overseas trips to 'keep the media at bay'. He told me he'd been pressed by James Chapman, then a Lobby correspondent for the *Daily Mail*, who had urged him to provide stories on a forthcoming visit to China. Cameron led the largest-ever trade delegation to the country and announced a series of deals and partnerships. The travelling hacks were also briefed on several domestic initiatives. As they returned from what was perceived as a successful trip, an editorial in the *Daily Mail* questioned why No. 10 had been feeding journalists a diet of stories that had nothing to do with their journey to China. Oliver realised this newspaper would be almost impossible to satisfy.

Despite all the meticulous planning that goes into these journeys, they frequently do not go according to plan. I went with David Cameron to Afghanistan in 2011, when he was due to visit British troops at their base in the south of the country and see the work of the bomb disposal teams. A ferocious dust storm meant that we spent several hours circling in mid-air before being forced to land at Kandahar, the main NATO base. It was minus five degrees and almost impossible to film anything in the gloom of the swirling dust. Cameron's team had their work cut out to prevent the journey being a complete waste of time, but RAF Tornado crews from Lossiemouth got a hastily arranged visit from the prime minister, who stressed his commitment to ending the UK's combat role in the country by the end of 2014.

The USA had made a similar commitment to handing command of security to local Afghan forces by 2014. When Cameron visited the USA in 2012, his team were delighted when President Obama endorsed the 'rock-solid' special relationship between their two countries and laid on a lavish state dinner, in marked contrast to his treatment of Gordon Brown. The visit was not entirely without hitches, though, and the entire press pack almost missed the all-important joint news conference with the two leaders. The press bus is a ubiquitous feature of these trips, but on this occasion they had a driver who inexplicably did not know where the White House was. When it became clear that he was lost in heavy traffic on the wrong side of town, Cameron's spokesman Jean-Christophe Gray had to get out to ask directions from a passer-by. As the time ticked by and the Lobby journalists grew increasingly frantic at the prospect of missing the highlight of the trip, the driver went through a red light and was stopped by the police, adding a further delay. They eventually made it to one of the world's most famous addresses, 1600 Pennsylvania Avenue, just in time to get through security and hear the president welcome his 'friend and partner' David Cameron. Their relief was certainly matched by that of the prime minister's press team.

Afterwards Craig Oliver got separated from the official party and was struggling to cross the gridlocked streets of Washington in a rickshaw, but was in an upbeat mood at the warm words from the American president. He was brought down to earth abruptly by a call from the *Guardian*, asking about the government's plans to cut the top rate of income tax. It later emerged that the Liberal Democrats had leaked part of the forthcoming Budget and the fallout dominated the rest of what would otherwise have been a hugely successful trip.

Even worse for No. 10 was Cameron's trip to Africa in July 2011 at the height of the phone-hacking scandal. They were only an hour into the flight to Johannesburg when news broke that the Metropolitan Police Commissioner Sir Paul Stephenson had resigned after criticism of his decision to hire as his media adviser the former *News of the World* executive Neil Wallis, who had been questioned by detectives on the hacking investigation. The prime minister's team considered turning back and tried to consult senior ministers in London. The secure satellite phones didn't work, so they had to use the Virgin credit card phones available on board. They decided to press ahead with at least part of the itinerary, though it was cut short so he could get back for a parliamentary debate. It was a particularly difficult issue for Cameron, just six months after the former *News of the World* editor Andy Coulson had stood down as his communications chief and questions on the scandal dominated every step of the journey. At Pretoria's Union Buildings, South Africa's President Zuma stood and listened with bemusement as the prime minister faced numerous questions on his handling of the matter, their own discussions hardly getting a mention. Cameron insisted the government was pressing ahead with establishing a judicial inquiry into the allegations, adding: 'Just because you're travelling to Africa does not mean you suddenly lose contact with your office.'

Yet this was one of numerous occasions when Cameron's trips resulted in unplanned controversies. Jason Groves of the *Daily Mail* said Cameron was always a 'good source of stories' abroad because of his tendency to speak more freely away from home. Perhaps his biggest slip-up was on a trip to New York in 2014. The prime minister was filmed chatting to the city's former mayor Michael Bloomberg as they entered the headquarters of his business empire. They were unaware that their conversation was being picked up by the microphones. Scotland had just voted in a referendum to reject independence and Cameron told Bloomberg that when he had phoned the Queen to tell her the result, she had 'purred down the line'. It was a huge breach of protocol which prompted uproar.

Groves and the UK media were working from a nearby hotel bar when they learned what had happened. He said Jean-Christophe Gray, who was with them, put his head in his hands, despairingly saying: 'I don't believe it, every day they send me out, they tell me to say nothing and now he's said this.' The next day the press pack was summoned to a hotel room, where Cameron declared he was 'very embarrassed' and 'extremely sorry' for revealing what should have been a private conversation and said he would be making a personal apology to Her Majesty.

His successor Theresa May was certainly a very different politician, renowned for her careful choice of words. She embarked on several tours of European capitals during the endless negotiations over the terms of Britain's departure from the EU, which dominated her entire premiership. On some of these shorter trips the media had to make their own arrangements, but there was a battle for places when she did embark on longer journeys, as Lobby hacks hoped for an opportunity to get a little closer to the famously reserved leader. She reluctantly accepted that talking to the travelling hacks was part of the deal when their organisations had paid for places on the plane, but there was rarely any spontaneous chat. 'She would never do that, that's too scary, too dangerous,' her former director of communications Katie Perrior told me. 'Theresa May just could not do small talk.' Instead, the prime minister and her advisers would prepare carefully for a question-and-answer session, working out the message she wanted to deliver and rehearsing responses to some of the points that were likely to be raised. Perrior would organise what amounted to a mini news conference in the aisle of the plane, ensuring a fair spread of questions from the journalists on board. There were no cameras rolling, but May's answers were on the record, thus providing the Lobby with fresh lines to report on arrival. Jason Groves, who went on several trips with May, said the chats were 'pretty painful', and although everyone would get to ask a question, it was very difficult to get any newsworthy comments from her. 'She couldn't stand us,' Groves said. 'It's nothing personal, she just didn't like us and didn't trust us.'

On her first major foreign trip, to a G20 summit in China, May seemed somewhat taken aback as she pulled back the grey curtain on the RAF Voyager to find twenty or so journalists poised with tape recorders. 'This is the first time I have done this,' were her opening words. May had to lean on one side of an on-board bar while the reporters jostled for space on the other side, to set out her plans for the international gathering. The governor of the Bank of England, Mark Carney, was travelling with her and was on hand to observe the proceedings. Afterwards he noted the 'collegiate' approach of the correspondents as they tried, with difficulty, to work out what was the best line to report from the stilted and surreal gathering.

Theresa May was the first world leader to visit President Trump in the White House in January 2017, a meeting that her team considered a big success, despite controversy over pictures of the two leaders holding hands. They seemed to have a good personal rapport and the president stressed the importance of the special relationship between their two countries. The prime minister flew on from Washington to Turkey and was in mid-air when Trump announced a ban on people from seven Muslim-majority countries entering the USA. Perrior told me May was reluctant to criticise Trump so soon after their successful summit, particularly when it was difficult to consult colleagues while travelling across time zones with poor communications. The Lobby journalists on board immediately asked for the prime minister's response but were given a bland statement intended to hold for a few hours.

By the time May faced the media for a news conference in Turkey the travel ban had provoked an outcry, and May faced a barrage of questions. Still she refused to give her own view on the announcement, saying: 'The United States is responsible for the United States' policy on refugees.'[5] Perrior herself said this was a 'rubbish answer' that left May 'on the ropes' in a humiliating session in which Lobby reporters pressed in vain for a more explicit British response to the ban. It was not until the following day, when the prime minister had flown back to London, that she finally issued a late-night statement saying, 'We do not agree with this kind of approach.'[6] Her remarks indicated that she was prepared to stand up to the US president, but by then the delay had already prompted stories accusing her of dithering.

It was a lesson in the need to respond swiftly when you have a group of journalists on the prime minister's plane in an era of twenty-four-hour news. May's press secretary, Paul Harrison, recalls a trip to the Middle East the following year, when Donald Trump sparked another row by retweeting three inflammatory videos posted online by a far-right group called Britain First. The prime minister and accompanying Lobby journalists were about to leave Baghdad on board an RAF C-130. They were strapped in for take-off, wearing flak jackets because of the risk of small-arms fire, when news of the president's tweets came through. Harrison managed to show the offending footage to May on his mobile phone and, on this occasion, she made a quick decision. They hastily agreed a statement saying Trump was wrong to share the videos with his followers. Harrison went down the plane, shouting above the noise of its engines, to read the response to the travelling Lobby journalists, while at the same time holding his mobile phone so his colleagues in London could hear the agreed words. When he had to take his seat for take-off, Harrison was unsure whether anyone had heard him. 'You age a few years in those moments,' he told me.

In the autumn of 2017, May was in New York for a meeting of the UN General Assembly, but Brexit was once again the only story of interest to the accompanying media. Boris Johnson, who was also in town, had threatened to resign as her foreign secretary over concerns that the prime minister was preparing to pursue a deal with the EU that would leave the UK tied to many of the rules and regulations of the European Single Market. As senior political journalists, including Sky's Beth Rigby and the BBC's John Pienaar, gathered in the lobby of a hotel where they were due to interview the prime minister, Boris Johnson came in through the swing door, sweating after a four-mile run around Central Park. He headed for the lift and the reporters seized their chance, with Beth Rigby holding the doors so they could all pile in with him.

Characteristically unbothered by the unorthodox surroundings and his less than pristine red running shirt, the foreign secretary happily told them he had resolved his differences with No. 10. 'We are a government working together,' he said. 'We are a nest of singing birds.'[7] It was a great sound bite for the evening bulletins, ensuring that Johnson stole the limelight from his boss once again – an unexpected encounter that underlined why many Lobby journalists love these foreign trips.

Theresa May's last big trip as prime minister was to the G20 summit in Japan in 2019 after she had announced she was standing down. During the formal proceedings May was as businesslike as ever, urging world leaders to do more to tackle climate change and delivering an uncompromising message to Russia's President Putin. On the plane home she finally relaxed a little, knowing she was about to shed the burdens of high office. The outgoing prime minister even made an unprecedented foray down the plane to chat to the accompanying Lobby hacks, after enjoying a glass of wine with her husband Philip. There were no big revelations, of course, from the famously cautious politician, but the journalists did at last get a glimpse of her human side, just as she was preparing to make way for a very different leader.

Boris Johnson, as a former journalist, had always seemed comfortable in the press's company in the years before he got to No. 10. Many Lobby correspondents who knew him had high hopes of trips with a prime minister who seemed to relish a high-risk photo opportunity and was rarely reluctant to express his views in colourful prose. Nonetheless, he appeared determined to adopt a more statesmanlike approach as he set out to establish his credentials as a world leader. At his first G7 summit in Biarritz Johnson pulled off a delicate balancing act, maintaining positive relationships with EU leaders and the US president, but further travel plans were shelved by the Covid-19 crisis. Conversations via Zoom not only deprive the participants of opportunities for those private chats that can help forge important bilateral relationships, they also leave journalists reliant on the official read-outs, which rarely tell the full story.

These trips have certainly become tougher over the years, as journalists race to meet the demands of twenty-four-hour rolling news channels and newspaper reporters compete to be first to update their online editions. Yet while the brief breaks from Westminster were certainly no holiday, I will never forget the unique experience of such tours, whisked through the VIP channels at airports, tagging on to the high-speed convoys with outriders clearing the route and huddling around the most powerful person in the land, hoping he or she will let their guard down sufficiently to let slip a newsworthy phrase. The shared experiences and camaraderie endure long after touch-down. When international diplomacy does return to something resembling normality, Lobby journalists will be battling for the coveted experience of accompanying the prime minister on their next overseas trip.

10 SEXISM AND SCANDALS

'Just pat her on the bottom and send her on her way . . .'

Boris Johnson's advice in 2005 to his successor as editor of the *Spectator* on how to deal with the magazine's publisher.

In autumn 2017, the #MeToo movement swept through the lofty corridors of Parliament, causing soul-searching and nervousness among some of its members and forcing significant changes to its rules. The tales of the shenanigans at what became known as 'Pestminster' eventually ended several ministerial careers and revealed the hidden hazards facing women in the Lobby.

Anyone reading such stories of harassment and sexist comments would be forgiven for thinking that Westminster is a dreadful place for a woman to work. I must stress that this has not been my experience, nor that of most of the female journalists I know. In more than twenty years as a political correspondent, I never once felt intimidated or threatened and indeed was treated with consideration and respect by most of those I encountered, especially more senior members of the Lobby.

Certainly, I did not have to confront the open hostility faced by the pioneer women journalists who first beat a path into the political jungle many decades earlier. In 1890, a certain Miss E. Blain (no one seems to know her first name) applied to report from the Press Gallery of the Commons for the *Women's Penny Paper*, an early suffrage publication. The Serjeant at Arms turned down the request on the grounds that 'the consequences were too difficult to conceive'. At the time, women could only observe proceedings in Parliament from a separate Ladies' Gallery, with grilles over the windows so the women could see out but the men could not see in. It was nicknamed 'The Cage'. It was not until Nancy Astor became the first woman MP in December 1919 that two female journalists were allowed into the Press Gallery. Marguerite Cody of the *Daily News* and Miss E. Cohn of the Central News Agency were admitted just long enough to witness the historic moment when Lady Astor took her seat before they were ejected.

Five years later a redoubtable reporter called Stella Wolfe Murray became the first woman to work in the Lobby. She worked for the *Daily Sketch*, wrote a column in the *Leeds Mercury* and was also an accomplished pilot, co-writing a book entitled *Women and Flying* with the record-breaking aviator Lady Heath. Murray broke new ground, writing about women's issues and the campaign for equal pay, ensuring there was coverage of the contributions from the nine women who had been elected to Parliament. Of course, there is no record of Murray's early conversations with MPs in the Lobby outside the Commons Chamber – such encounters would have been strictly off the record – so we can only imagine the reactions as she became the first woman journalist to accost politicians as they went about their business.

In 1946, Patricia O'Brien became the first female reporter for the Press Association in the Press Gallery, though she believed she only got the job because she'd called herself 'Pat' on her application and her editor assumed this was short for Patrick. In an article for the *Norwood Press* she wrote: 'I am called in when descriptions are needed of clothes worn by women ministers and members and my opinion is sometimes sought when a reporter is writing a newsletter on things which affect women.'[1] She was sacked when she became pregnant and was only reinstated after pressure from MPs including Labour's Barbara Castle. She was fired again when she was expecting her second child.

Attitudes were slow to change, and almost forty years later there were still only seven women Lobby journalists, an imbalance that was reflected in Parliament itself, where 97 per cent of MPs were male. Harriet Harman, who became Labour's deputy leader, has been a lifelong campaigner for equality for women. When she was first elected in 1983 she was struck by the 'self-serving cosiness' between all the men in the Commons and all the men reporting on their work. She was mocked for trying to put issues such as childcare, domestic violence and maternity rights on to the political agenda and has described how delighted she was whenever she spotted a female journalist. 'I would think, "Thank God a woman has arrived." I would give every possible story to her, to try to help her find her feet and be a voice for women.'[2]

Julia Langdon began working as a Lobby journalist at Westminster in 1971 and told me that although there were often no other women around, she was always surprised when others remarked on the fact. She went to cover a lunch in the city where Denis Healey, then chancellor, addressed his audience as 'Gentlemen and Julia . . .'. She had not noticed till then that she was the only woman at the event. Langdon became the first female political editor of a national newspaper, the *Daily*

Mirror, in 1984, and Elinor Goodman became political editor of Channel 4 in 1988. They became friends at a time when women were still quite a rare sight in Parliament, apart from those serving in the cafés and bars. On one occasion, when the two journalists were chatting together in a corridor of the Commons, they overheard a Tory MP observe to his colleague: 'This place gets more like the Reeperbahn every night.' He was referring to Hamburg's red-light district.

They were also frequently mistaken for one another, to their mutual annoyance, something which continued to happen for years. It seems this was a common problem for women at Westminster. When Theresa May was one of just thirteen female Tory MPs elected in 1997 she was frequently mistaken for Teresa Gorman, a leading Eurosceptic. They were very different characters and did not even look alike, but it happened so often that May said she considered wearing a badge reading 'No, I'm the other one.'[3]

When I first arrived at the Lobby in 1996 the formal briefings still had the atmosphere of a gentlemen's club, especially when the morning sessions were held in a sitting room at 10 Downing Street, and it was not unusual to be the only woman attending. At the time, I genuinely did not feel at all concerned by this. I had spent many years working as a news correspondent, frequently travelling overseas, and was often the sole female member of a BBC team. When you have had to deal with an inebriated gunman pointing a Kalashnikov at your head, facing a rather florid MP invading your personal space does not seem so serious. Of course, I do understand that other women at Westminster have found themselves in situations where they have felt uncomfortable and even frightened.

As a new arrival in the Lobby, it never occurred to me to question the unspoken rules that ensured the political editors of the major national papers, all male, sat on the big sofa at the front, while more junior reporters squeezed in at the back of the room, or in my case, sat literally at their feet. There was a clear hierarchy, with opening questions always coming from the blokes in the front row. One of my former colleagues, Carolyn Quinn of the BBC, said that although she found it unnerving at first, she later realised how much of it was an act. 'It was all a bit showy,' she said. 'The pecking order was a bit more formal, so you waited your turn to ask your question.'

Beth Rigby, now Sky's political editor, says that even in 2010, when she began working in the Lobby, she found it completely intimidating. Rigby was appointed senior political correspondent for the *Financial Times* and had fifteen years' experience as a journalist but said she hated her first few months at Westminster, trying to make her way in a new world with its own rules and cliques, where she did not feel she belonged. 'It's like going to a party,' she told me, 'where everyone knows each other and they're all in a social group and you're the newbie standing in the corner, just desperate for someone to say hello.' She said she was often the only woman in the room at the daily briefings. 'It was very male, there was a lot of testosterone around and the blokes all sat and gossiped with each other and no one talked to you.'

The culture can have significant consequences. Rigby recalls an episode soon after she ventured on to the political beat, when Prime Minister David Cameron was under pressure to say whether Prince Andrew should keep his job as a trade envoy. It was the spring of 2011 and stories had emerged of the Prince's association with the convicted sex offender Jeffrey Epstein. Rigby was with a group of other Lobby journalists at a Conservative spring conference where there was a briefing from one of Cameron's senior aides. He told them the prime minister still had 'full confidence' in the Prince, but then qualified this by adding that Cameron 'would not shed many tears' if the Duke of York were to relinquish his voluntary role. Afterwards, Rigby noticed a group of political editors, all men, huddled together and discussing the story. She was not included in their discussions. Rigby told her news desk what she saw as the substance of the briefing. It was only much later that she realised she had failed to flag up sufficiently the question mark over the Prince's future. Those who were part of the huddle of senior hacks had collectively unpicked all the answers and decided the real message was that Cameron wanted Prince Andrew to stand down. Their stories for the next day's newspapers all made much of the revelation that the prime minister 'would not shed many tears' if the Prince were to quit. Rigby's bosses at the *FT* questioned why she had failed to get the story. Months later the Duke of York did indeed stand down from his role as trade envoy, though he continued with his royal duties for several more years.

Rigby was miserable and now realises that she missed the significance of certain phrases, partly because she was new and did not understand the Westminster code, but partly because she was left out when the boys got together to decide the top line. 'I just wasn't in the gang and that was a real rite of passage for me.' Today, Rigby is hugely respected for her judgement and ability to cut through the complexities of political debate. She says that many of the Lobby's male grandees have been helpful and generous, but it took time to understand its structure and to build contacts among senior politicians.

Traditionally, the best way to get to know MPs and pick up gossip was to frequent the bars and cafés within the Palace of Westminster. In her early days at Westminster, with a minority Labour government clinging to power, Elinor Goodman realised that the place to talk to many of the party's traditional trade-union MPs was Annie's Bar. She admits, however, to feeling out of place in this legendary drinking den: 'It was a very different environment to the kind of thing I was used to, but you had to go there to find out what was going on.'

Sue Cameron who worked for the BBC and Channel 4, though, enjoyed the atmosphere in Annie's Bar, often euphemistically described as 'convivial'. It was also known as the Kremlin, because of the largely left-wing, northern clientele who enjoyed the cheap pints of what was known as 'Fed', Federation Ale, specially supplied from a Newcastle brewery. With many journalists among the regulars, someone would often rush in to spread word of what would be breaking news on our mobile phones today. Cameron said there was certainly plenty of drinking and smoking, but it was 'good and gossipy, a great source of stories and it was fun'.

For Andrew Marr, Annie's was at the heart of the drinking culture that prevailed at Westminster in the 1980s. Marr worked for the *Guardian* in that era and told me how its legendary political editor, Ian Aitken, would stand at the bar, drinking with a couple of cabinet ministers: 'Many pints and many whiskies would be poured down their throats,' he told me. 'Then towards the end of the evening, Ian would reach across and beckon to the barman, who would pass him the telephone from underneath the bar. Aitken would call the *Guardian* news desk, and, without any notes at all, dictate a word-perfect splash for the next day's paper. He didn't hesitate, he didn't stop, and the prose flowed as freely and fluently as the beer had done.' Marr describes this as a 'very male story' from a time when if you wanted to be considered a 'proper journalist' you would go to the Press Bar and stay until it closed – not ideal if you had a family to consider.

Annie's Bar closed in 2006, but it was still a good place to gauge the political mood when I started working at Westminster in the 1990s. The clientele had become more mixed, but it was nevertheless a favourite haunt of Labour MPs sceptical of Tony

Blair's modernising agenda and was still a smoke-filled room, largely the domain of men with pints. Like Goodman, I too felt that I was intruding on unfamiliar territory, with some of the older regulars eyeing me with surprise initially, though the offer to pay for a round quickly broke down their reserve.

Most politicians and advisers were perfectly well behaved and treated me with respect, but, as a 'new girl' in the Lobby, there were certainly occasions when I felt I was being patronised or when discussions with contacts strayed towards flirtation. When I first ventured into the Members' Lobby outside the parliamentary Chamber to speak to MPs about a forthcoming vote I was asked, 'What's a nice girl like you doing in a place like this?' by a senior Tory who is still in the Commons, as he leaned in slightly too close for comfort. I was rather irritated by the condescending tone, although not remotely surprised – such an approach was not unusual in those days.

There was also a real battle to avoid being pigeonholed into covering what editors considered to be women's issues. Jane Merrick said that when she was the only woman on the *Mail*'s political team in 2003 she was always asked to write about MPs' wives during elections. The idea of an article on MPs' husbands never seems to have been considered. Childcare and equal-pay stories were assigned to Merrick too, while her male colleagues covered defence and economic issues.

Merrick had joined the Lobby as a political reporter for the Press Association two years earlier. Arriving from Liverpool at the age of twenty-six, she told me she felt like a 'wide-eyed girl from the provinces' as she was taken along to the afternoon Lobby briefing from the PMOS to be formally introduced. Colleagues had told her to 'bob' when her name was announced, which she duly did, and everyone clapped. It was, she said, like being inducted into a secret society.

The clubby atmosphere is something that has struck men as well as women. The BBC's Nick Robinson said that when he first joined, he found it 'utterly male-dominated . . . smug and self-satisfied and obsessed with its own codes and ways of doing things'. The *Sun*'s Tom Newton Dunn, who ensured those rules were updated, said it still felt like an 'old boys' club' when he arrived in 2009, although there were significant changes over the next decade. Simon Lewis, who came from a business background to become Gordon Brown's spokesman, said he too was surprised to face an almost exclusively white, male audience when he addressed the Lobby.

This was despite the changes introduced by Alastair Campbell a decade earlier, which were intended to open up the Lobby and make it accessible to a wider circle of journalists and publications. His own briefings felt more like a clash between rival groups of football fans than a gentleman's club. He has admitted the daily confrontations became counterproductive and told me, 'I probably did swear too much.' Jane Merrick said she found the adversarial tone of these meetings daunting, and initially hesitated before wading in with her questions, although she found Campbell himself generally helpful when she dealt with him on a one-to-one basis. I did not feel cowed by Campbell, perhaps because I had got to know him during Tony Blair's first election campaign. Most of the time I got the courteous, charming approach, apart from a few occasions when he took exception to my stories and the blast down the phone was somewhat unnerving. In my experience, he was more likely to have a go at male journalists, though this may have been because so many of the senior hacks in the room were men.

Indeed, there were occasions when it was an advantage to be one of the few women in the Lobby. That is certainly the view of Elinor Goodman. 'There were MPs who were attracted to you and told you things they would not tell a male journal-ist,' she said. 'They weren't actually chatting you up, but they wanted you to think they were worth talking to.' Goodman told me she was wary when more female journalists started work-ing at Westminster, fearing they would get the stories instead of her. She admits this may have been part of a wider insecurity at the time, when she was convinced that male journalists were all 'getting terrific stories in the gents'.

Julia Langdon became friends with many of her contacts at Westminster and frequently got to know their partners too. In an overwhelmingly male Parliament, this meant establishing a rapport with MPs' wives – invaluable when trying to speak to politicians when stories broke late at night or over the weekends. She found that, as a woman, many senior figures would not only share the latest gossip but would confide in her with personal issues too. She remembers one cabinet minister sobbing on her shoulder but prided herself on being trustworthy and never revealing her sources. It is hard to believe they would have behaved in the same way with a male Lobby correspondent.

Sue Cameron also believes her gender was an advantage. She thinks MPs were more friendly and less suspicious towards her than they were with men, though some could be patronising. 'I think they thought, "There, there dear, I tell you what, I'll just give you a little snippet." Well, I didn't mind. If they gave you a story, that was great.' Cameron says she benefited from their efforts to be helpful and found that although characters like Bernard Ingham could be 'a bit of a bully', he was more likely to get tough with men than with women.

I was certainly aware that I needed to make the most of any possible advantages in a world where the rivalry and ambition among correspondents matched that of the politicians. In the BBC's political team there were more men called John than there were women. These included John Sergeant, Jon Sopel and John Pienaar, who worked alongside Huw Edwards, Mark Mardell, Steve Richards and Jeremy Vine – all now in high-profile roles in broadcasting and journalism. To say the atmosphere in the office was competitive is something of an understatement. One of my few female colleagues was Carolyn Quinn, now a BBC presenter, who remembers the 'big characters, big egos, all jostling for stories'. In the days before twenty-four-hour news we were all vying to get on to the BBC's television and radio bulletins. 'The ladies had to fight to get on,' Quinn said; 'there was almost an assumption that the men did so, and we had what was left over.'

It was taken for granted that nothing would get in the way of finding stories and broadcasting to the nation. That meant not only staying late when there were unexpected developments to be covered but spending time 'networking' in the bar to pick up tip-offs and establish better contacts. When I first joined the BBC's political team in the 1990s, I had two children under the age of two and certainly found that juggling journalism and childcare was quite a challenge. My female boss warned me she 'did not want to hear any crap excuses about getting home for my baby'. At the time I thought this was a perfectly reasonable attitude, and was careful to make sure senior colleagues did not overhear my frequent, frantic scrambles to rearrange pick-up times and beg favours from other mums on the many occasions when stories broke late in the day. I did not want or expect any favourable treatment and felt I needed to prove my commitment and ability if I was to have any chance in the battle with the boys to get on-air.

There were few other mothers around to confide in, to bolster morale, and there were moments when I struggled with sheer exhaustion. It was only when I left the BBC a few years ago that several younger female colleagues told me that I had been a role model for them, proof that you can pursue a high-profile career and raise children at the same time. I was surprised and proud to hear their comments, especially as, with hindsight, I could have done more to challenge working arrangements and attitudes that did little to encourage other women to pursue the career path I found so rewarding. I was so busy just trying to stay on top of the competing demands that I rarely stepped back to consider the wider picture.

Attitudes have undoubtedly changed since then, with greater recognition of family commitments in most workplaces and parenting duties shared far more equally. Most fathers in the Lobby are also trying to balance the demands of work and home. It is not easy in the fast-moving and unpredictable political world. In the five years from 2014 there were two referendums, three general elections and numerous other crises, including government defeats, high-profile resignations and leadership contests. Beth Rigby, who has two school-age children, says she believes the relentless pressure and twenty-four-hour news cycle does deter some women from pursuing a career in political journalism. 'It's not just a job, it's a vocation, it's your life,' she told me. 'You never stop and it's very difficult to balance family life while doing this.'

Changing attitudes to work patterns are making a difference. The *Guardian*'s decision to appoint Anushka Asthana from Sky News and Heather Stewart from the *Observer* to share the role of political editor in 2015 was groundbreaking at the time and demonstrated that such flexible arrangements can work successfully. It was equally encouraging to see one of my former colleagues at the BBC, Chris Mason, take six months off to care for his young daughter.

While strides have been taken towards greater equality of the sexes, the lack of ethnic diversity in the Lobby is still striking. When Anne Alexander got her first job at Westminster in 2002 it was a real culture shock for her. She was deputy political editor for one of the biggest regional papers, the *Daily Express & Star* in the Midlands, and the first black woman in the Lobby. Soon after she arrived, she joined colleagues at a reception on the terrace overlooking the Thames, a good opportunity to talk to some of the MPs from her patch. As she stood chatting with a small group, an MP casually handed her his empty glass before turning to continue his own conversation. He had assumed she was a waitress, at an event where the only other people of colour were the serving staff. It is an incident typical of the attitudes that Alexander has since confronted on numerous occasions.

She shared an office in Parliament with five other reporters from agencies and regional papers, all of them white and male. Media staff from various parties would frequently drop in with press releases and advance copies of speeches. One of them arrived with a new young colleague whom she introduced to each of Alexander's colleagues before adding: 'And this is Anne, their PA.' When Alexander corrected her and explained that she was in fact a deputy political editor, there was huge embarrassment and red faces as the press officer tried to explain why she had made the mistake.

Alexander, who grew up on a working-class estate in the Midlands, believes the attitudes she has faced as one of the very few black, female political journalists are shaped by a combination of unconscious sexism, racism and classism. She told me that when she began appearing on BBC programmes as a political pundit, some colleagues reacted with surprise. '"Oh gosh you're really quite articulate, you know, you're really quite good," they said, as if they were surprised that I could actually string a sentence together.' She still finds it can be a struggle to be taken seriously. If she is talking to certain politicians with a couple of white male colleagues, they will often address their remarks to the others rather than to her.

Alexander, who is now senior political producer at ITV's *Good Morning Britain,* believes the lack of diversity in the Lobby is an overlooked issue. While the number of black and other minority-ethnic MPs has increased in recent years, there are still only a handful of non-white Westminster journalists. Certainly, when she attended her first Downing Street briefing she found it a daunting experience. There was a fraught confrontation between Alastair Campbell and some of the more senior political correspondents, not unusual at the time. Alexander was sitting at the back of the room, noting the exchanges, when Michael White, political editor of the *Guardian* and a Lobby stalwart, leaned back, introduced himself and declared in a loud stage whisper: 'These people take themselves far too seriously.' It was a welcome moment of light relief and warmth.

While I too benefited from friendly advice from some senior characters in the Lobby, it was a somewhat blokeish club then, with football as much a part of the conversation as politics. On a Monday morning, the Lobby boys would all be joshing with the Downing Street aides about the performance of their respective teams and Campbell would join in with the latest on the performance of his beloved Burnley FC. Some of the reporters and government advisers played football together; there was always a Lobby v MPs match at the Labour Party conference and these shared experiences were undoubtedly part of a bonding process from which I felt excluded. I was not alone in this. Many female correspondents have since admitted they too got fed up with the endless talk about football.

Of course, football is not just a male sport, and perhaps I should have tried harder to get involved. I can only applaud Jo Tanner, the communications strategist who set up the Parliamentary Women's Football Club in 2018, bringing together journalists and MPs from all parties. They train regularly and have begun holding their own party conference match, before the men take to the field.

A sense of camaraderie among the Lobby women developed during the Blair years and led to the creation of our own lunch club. The idea was to invite senior ministers or Opposition figures to come and talk to us, a smaller, female version of the long-standing Press Gallery lunches. It caused quite a stir, partly because it was all too successful. In 2003, Peter Mandelson, a key Labour figure who was then outside government but still hugely influential, joined us for a fascinating and entertaining discussion over white wine and delicate plates of food in a private room at a Westminster restaurant. Mandelson told us that Gordon Brown, then chancellor, had outmanoeuvred the prime minister over policy on the euro. It was a good line on a highly contentious issue and gave us quite a story. There was a big discussion over the status of the remarks, whether or not they could be attributed to Mandelson himself, but once he had been named as the source by the Press Association the story was out.

The men who had missed out on the scoop were, unsurprisingly, miffed. There were complaints about sexism because men had been excluded from the gathering, and the club was referred to as the 'lezzy Lobby'. The columnist Paul Routledge used the term in his write-up of the row in the *New Statesman*, prompting quite a backlash. He insisted he was merely reporting the facts. 'Lezzy Lobby is what the male hacks call it. I didn't make it up,' he wrote. The following week Routledge kept the story bubbling with some advice to Brendan Barber, the new TUC general secretary, who had been invited to address the next women's lunch. He warned him that 'the lezzy Lobby, as it is disgracefully called among jealous male hacks, is never happy unless the guest's scalp is on the menu'. Routledge added that Barber 'would be well advised to hurry back to Great Russell Street to put out his own spin before the harpies (I'm sorry: ladies of the media) get back to their screens'.[4]

I do not believe Routledge's remarks reflected the views of the majority of men whom I knew at Westminster, but there was undoubtedly huge resentment at the way the women had worked together to get their stories. I have never been particularly keen on women-only organisations, believing we are quite capable of making contacts and proving our abilities without trying to emulate outdated exclusively male institutions. Yet I have come to realise their value and to enjoy the atmosphere, without any self-important men around. Of course, it was also great to have the opportunity to get stories that could not be nabbed by my male colleagues. It is not always easy for a junior reporter to go out on a limb, to convince their editors that they have a decent scoop. The women's Lobby lunches undoubtedly gave a collective helping hand to some of the less-experienced female correspondents trying to establish themselves at Westminster. Yet the controversy deterred some politicians from accepting invitations to join us and the Westminster Women's Lobby Club did not last long.

A decade later a group of senior female politicians, including ministers such as Amber Rudd and Margot James, began hosting drinks receptions for women in the Lobby. These were some of the most interesting and convivial occasions in my time at Westminster, a chance to enjoy relaxed conversations and establish contacts with some female high-fliers. These gatherings do help female reporters when there are many other informal cliques and groups of men who get together to wine and dine senior MPs and ministers. For women MPs, who are still a minority in Parliament, they are also an opportunity to get to know journalists who may be interested in covering their pursuit of particular causes.

The support of other women has clearly been important in lifting the lid on incidences of improper behaviour that have been hidden for too long. Despite the headlines, cases of harassment at Westminster are still rare, though the attitudes of a few male MPs do appear to be stuck in a very different era.

In the 1970s, Julia Langdon spent many long evenings hanging around Parliament as the minority Labour government battled to get its legislation through and the Commons regularly sat until well after midnight. Drinks and dinners with MPs were very much a part of the job, then as now. Langdon, whose first marriage had recently ended, said her social life became political and there were inevitable 'misunderstandings' when she asked male politicians out for dinner. 'People would think, well this young woman, what's she offering. Answer – a paragraph in the newspaper.' There was a very senior civil servant who took his shoes off in an upmarket French restaurant and started playing footsie with her under the table. A minister insisted on driving to her house, after she mentioned they might get together for a chat, and had to be told he was certainly not being invited in. There were plenty of 'hands on knees' that had to be firmly removed, but Langdon said she did not feel intimidated or scared. 'I can look after myself, I'm enough of my own woman to tell people to get lost,' she told me, though she is glad such behaviour is now considered unacceptable.

Even in the 1990s, the scene could become quite raucous. Late-night votes meant the bars were often packed, lively and a good source of stories and tip-offs. In those days, what we used to call 'wandering hands' were a routine hazard, not only at Westminster but at the office bash and in the pub. I generally found that a decisive thwack of the offending hand and a loud expletive worked pretty well, forcing the man in question to back off, even if he happened to be an MP. At the time, I did not even consider making any complaints about such incidents. After all, in one of my first jobs in journalism, more than a decade earlier, the editor of the main evening programme would invite me to come and sit on his lap to discuss the running order. I told him, in no uncertain terms, to keep such ideas and his hands to himself, but other young female colleagues who felt under pressure to comply with his requests were 'rewarded' with plum assignments.

All too often, the inappropriate behaviour towards women at Westminster and beyond is due to an imbalance of power. Pippa Crerar is now political editor of the *Daily Mirror*, but was in her twenties when she joined the Lobby in 2001 and has written of her experiences. Towards the end of a late night in a bar with a group of fellow journalists and MPs, a politician twice her age began stroking her collarbone with his finger and propositioned her. She said she giggled and beat a hasty retreat. There was an MP who tried to kiss her and a peer who sent inappropriate text messages. Crerar told me: 'There was the odd hand where it shouldn't have been, on the knee or the bum, and I gave those men short shrift to be honest.'

At the time, she feared any form of complaint would lead to being blacklisted by MPs or considered a troublemaker by her bosses. Crerar felt that if she wanted to get on as a Westminster journalist she could not make a fuss about the behaviour of older male politicians, particularly if they were established figures. Looking back, she admits to feeling guilty and wonders if she was 'doing the sisters a disservice, by not making more of it'. Instead, she shared stories with female friends and colleagues about whom to avoid in the bars late at night. My approach was similar: I would warn my female mates about certain MPs but often made light of flirtatious approaches and it never crossed my mind to make a formal complaint.

One of my former colleagues, Carolyn Quinn of the BBC, also recalls joking about particular MPs who should be avoided after a few drinks. 'There were those rather heavy-handed older men who would pin you against the wall, breathing meaty, beery breath all over you,' she told me. 'It was awful, and my personal space was being infringed, but I never felt physically intimidated.' Quinn says she would not put up with such behaviour today, but at the time she did not give it a second thought. 'I didn't feel that I was at the heart of some sort of misogynistic empire, because I had nothing to compare it to. It was just the way it was.'

Jane Merrick, who is now policy editor at the *i* newspaper, was also prepared to overlook incidents such as the MP who remarked to a passing colleague: 'Jane Merrick's legs make me proud to be British.' On another occasion a well-known peer texted to invite her to lunch and asked her to wear the cowboy boots he'd spotted her wearing that day. But in 2003 there was a more serious incident. She had recently begun working as a political reporter for the *Daily Mail* when she went for lunch with Michael Fallon, a chatty, media-savvy Conservative MP who was then chairman of the Treasury Select Committee and an influential MP. They had enjoyed a few glasses of wine, as was usual in those days, and were walking back to their respective offices through a dark corridor just off Westminster Hall when he 'lunged' at her and tried to kiss her on the lips. It was 'completely out of the blue', Merrick told me, 'and I was so horrified and taken aback that I didn't challenge him and say, "What the hell are you doing?" I just basically ran away because it was so unexpected.' Merrick told her colleagues, who all happened to be male, but she did not say anything to her bosses at the paper or report the incident to the Conservative Party whips. Merrick said that at the time she feared such action would backfire.

'I remember thinking the whips would be more interested in defending Michael Fallon than helping me, and then I'd be blacklisted and would not be able to lunch Tory MPs, which I needed to do.' Merrick said nothing publicly about the episode until fourteen years later, when new allegations surfaced about Fallon's behaviour.

In the autumn of 2017, Julia Hartley-Brewer, the Talk Radio presenter and former political editor of the *Sunday Express*, described an incident when a senior Conservative had put his hand on her knee while they were having dinner during a Conservative Party conference in 2002. 'I calmly and politely explained to him that, if he did it again, I would punch him in the face,' she said. 'He withdrew his hand and that was the end of the matter.'[5] Hartley-Brewer said she did not consider herself a victim and did not name the politician in question, but shortly afterwards the *Sun* revealed that it was Michael Fallon, who was by this time defence secretary and had received a knighthood in 2016. His spokesman said Fallon had apologised and both he and Julia Hartley-Brewer considered the matter closed.

Merrick was still reluctant to speak about her own experience, but then she learned of other, more recent allegations of Fallon's unwelcome approaches to younger journalists. She was 'horrified' to think that her silence many years earlier had left other women vulnerable to similar incidents. Merrick consulted a senior minister whom she knew well, then phoned Theresa May's chief of staff, Gavin Barwell, to tell him she wished to report the defence secretary for sexual harassment. She made it clear she did not want her name to become public because of her young daughter. Within hours Fallon had resigned from the government.

In an interview with the BBC, Fallon said: 'What might have been acceptable fifteen, ten years ago is clearly not acceptable now.' Merrick was furious that he still appeared to believe that his past behaviour had been 'acceptable' at the time, and decided to tell her own story in full, with an article in the *Observer*. Merrick told me she realised she had lived with a 'power imbalance' for years whenever she had to deal with Fallon: 'I always felt like he had something on me because he had sexually harassed me.' It was the only serious occurrence Merrick experienced in her twenty years as a Lobby correspondent, but after she spoke out publicly other female journalists told her of occasions when certain MPs had made them feel uncomfortable or intimidated too.

It was a time when Westminster was awash with lurid rumours. The *Sun* published a 'dossier' of allegations by staff working for Conservative MPs, including a minister described as 'handsy with women at parties'; a backbencher said to be 'perpetually intoxicated and very inappropriate with women'; and crude propositions made to secretaries. A WhatsApp group among female researchers and aides revealed how they shared warnings about MPs who were 'very handsy', 'not safe in taxis' or 'groped my arse at a drinks party'.

In the fallout, International Trade Minister Mark Garnier was sacked after he admitted calling his secretary 'sugar tits' and asking her to buy him sex toys. Former Welsh secretary Stephen Crabb apologised for inappropriate behaviour, after sending explicit texts to a nineteen-year-old woman who'd applied for a job in his office. Another Conservative MP, Chris Pincher, stood down from the whips' office after claims that he had made inappropriate advances towards a party activist.

Charlie Elphicke, then Conservative MP for Dover, had the party whip withdrawn after serious allegations were passed to the police. He was eventually jailed for two years for sexually assaulting two women. One of his victims, a parliamentary worker in her twenties, said the assaults in 2016 had left her with a feeling of 'fear and helplessness'.

Political journalism thrives on personal contacts, the gossip over a drink, the tip-off over coffee about the next potential rebellion. When do light-hearted remarks stray into flirtation? Is it OK to accept some mildly sexist comments from a somewhat unreconstructed old hand whom you have known for many years? Is it worth staying for an extra drink when you suspect you are about to hear a juicy tale? My own approach was always to put the potential story first, particularly as I never felt physically threatened, and let's not forget that some of these get-togethers at party conferences or in the bars were often really good fun. I do, however, acknowledge that in my early years covering politics I put up with behaviour that I would certainly challenge today. It is only recently that I have wondered whether my failure to take a stand in the past contributed to the very real difficulties that others have faced. I have struggled to think of an occasion when I could realistically have lodged a formal complaint.

Yet perhaps I should learn from the admirable stance adopted by Isabel Hardman, assistant editor of the *Spectator*, who took to Twitter to reveal an exchange with an MP whose behaviour she considered unacceptable. In April 2016 she described how the MP, whom she had only met a couple of times, said to her, as his opening gambit: 'I want to talk to the totty.' Hardman, a respected Lobby journalist, passed the name of the MP to the whips, who deal with party discipline, and received a contrite apology. She did not reveal his name, tweeting: 'I don't betray sources. But I will betray sexists.' She said she had chosen to speak openly about what had happened because she wanted the small number of MPs who behave in that way 'to know it's not on'.

Attitudes at Westminster towards women and on wider issues of diversity have been slow to move with the times, and there is plenty of scope to go further. When Andrea Leadsom, then Leader of the House, announced a new independent scheme to deal with allegations of abuse and sexual misconduct in July 2018, with tougher penalties for those who breach it, she said it was 'the beginning, not the end of our efforts to change the culture of Parliament'.[6] Under the new complaints and grievance procedure, allegations are assessed by an independent panel, with harsher punishments for those who fail to comply with an updated Code of Conduct. If a serious complaint against an MP or peer is upheld by the Committee of Standards, it could ultimately lead to the culprit being sacked and a by-election called. Hundreds of callers have contacted a hotline established for staff to seek advice and report their experiences.

There has been criticism of the decision to grant anonymity to those under investigation, and some victims of alleged assault have said more needs to be done to ensure really significant change. Those who feel they have been improperly treated can, nevertheless, now raise their concerns anonymously through an independent panel rather than consulting their own bosses, who may be the source of the problem in the first place. Some of the new mechanisms are targeted at parliamentary staff and would not necessarily apply to journalists. Still, I believe the fallout from the #MeToo campaign has led to a wider recognition that inappropriate conduct must not be swept under the carpet and has forced many of the less enlightened men at Westminster to think hard about their behaviour.

Yet there is another worrying hazard for female journalists and politicians – the growing tide of online abuse. It is telling that Andrea Leadsom herself was targeted on social media as she was overseeing the overhaul of the rules at Westminster. A story emerged claiming that the former defence secretary Michael Fallon had made a suggestive remark to her about where she could put her cold hands to warm them up. Leadsom denied she had ever spoken about the claim, but she faced a wave of hostile comments, including being called a 'lying b******' on Twitter. Leadsom said the reactions she faced demonstrated how difficult it was for victims of inappropriate behaviour to raise their concerns. She has since warned that women are being turned off politics by the levels of online abuse, which have led to several female MPs quitting Parliament.

The former shadow home secretary, Diane Abbott, has spoken of the 'frightening' abuse she frequently receives on social media. Abbott, who was the first ever black woman to be elected as an MP, regularly has to report violent threats to the police. Abbott could not say how much of this was because of the colour of her skin, but it is surely notable that she receives more abuse than anyone else in British politics. Many of her colleagues have spoken of the everyday sexism and racism they face. In February 2020, the shadow culture secretary Tracy Brabin prompted huge controversy when she wore an off-the-shoulder dress in the Commons. She posted her own tweet, mocking the reactions. 'Sorry I don't have time to reply to all of you,' she wrote, 'but I can confirm I'm not a slag, hungover, a tart, about to breastfeed, a slapper, drunk or just been banged over a wheelie bin.' Her experience, and her response, were quite a story, but many other incidences of online abuse go unreported.

A survey by the International Federation of Journalists recently found that more than 40 per cent of female respondents had been trolled online and only half of the victims reported the attacks to their managers. Like most of my former Lobby colleagues, I have had plenty of sexist or misogynistic comments on social media. I try to ignore the unpleasant posts and, thankfully, have not had to deal with any serious incidents. Those with higher profiles, such as the BBC's Laura Kuenssberg, have faced frequent and sometimes serious threats. She has said she's stopped reading the comments posted about her television appearances and at one stage considered leaving social media because of the levels of vitriol. She was given extra security at a recent Labour Party conference because of concerns for her safety.

There are more female correspondents than ever in the Lobby, providing the public with their political news. Yet women in public life say they still face a constant battle to counter sexism in the coverage of their work. Even those who reach the top of the political ladder find they are not immune. In March 2017, then prime minister Theresa May met Scotland's First Minister Nicola Sturgeon for talks on Brexit and a possible second Scottish referendum. The front page of the *Daily Mail* featured a large picture of the two leaders, with their legs highly visible in the shot, and the headline 'Never Mind Brexit, Who Won Legs-it?'. The paper's article described how Sturgeon's legs were 'tantalisingly crossed' in what it said was a 'direct attempt at seduction', with the message 'come, succumb to my revolutionary allure'. It sparked a huge row, with former minister Nicky Morgan saying it was 'deliberately demeaning'. Yet the story was written by the columnist Sarah Vine, who said it was intended to be light-hearted and accused her critics of 'a slight sense of humour failure'.

When the famously reserved and resilient Theresa May announced on the steps of Downing Street that she would stand down as prime minister and spoke of her 'enormous and enduring gratitude to have had the opportunity to serve the country I love', she broke down in tears. Her chief of staff, Gavin Barwell, said he believed there was an 'element of sexism' in the way this was reported, given that any human being would have been upset in that situation. He told me May was cross with herself for getting emotional, realising the papers would be 'full of photos of a woman crying', and she was right. May herself later said that if a male prime minister's voice had broken with emotion, it would have been reported as 'what great patriotism, they really love their country', but when a female prime minister did so it was 'why is she crying?'.

Yet the emotion of her statement was clearly an important element of that story, after the weeks and months of stalemate as May failed to get approval for her Brexit plans, conveying the personal strain of her political struggle. Her tears were reported by female as well as male correspondents, with Pippa Crerar's account in the *Daily Mirror* headlined 'First the Iron Lady, now the Crying Lady'. On this occasion, the coverage would seem to be less about sexism than a ruthlessly accurate description of the poignant moment when our second female prime minister was forced out of Downing Street.

The coverage of a later drama, however, involving Boris Johnson's partner Carrie Symonds, revealed the extent of the laddish culture in some parts of Westminster. Symonds is a former ministerial adviser who was briefly head of media for the Conservative Party and clearly had an influential role in the huge upheavals in Downing Street at the end of 2020, which culminated in the departure of two of the prime minister's most powerful advisers, Dominic Cummings and Lee Cain.

The *Daily Mail* reported that allies of Cummings and Cain had been referring to Symonds as 'Princess Nut Nut' for months. This insulting phrase went viral after the paper described how the nickname had been used so frequently in text messages during the 2019 election that it was conveyed using emojis of a princess and two peanuts. Downing Street denied that the prime minister had decided to get rid of the two colleagues with whom he'd worked closely during the referendum campaign because they'd been briefing against his partner. Yet supporters of Symonds believe she was subjected to rank sexism as part of the vicious internal battles. The former sports minister Tracey Crouch told the *Observer*: 'People are playing the girl not the ball, knowing she can't defend herself,'[7] and said the insults were patronising. Others pointed out that there was no such criticism of Philip May for his role in supporting his wife Theresa during her difficult premiership.

At the end of the shake-up at No. 10, the views of Carrie Symonds and her allies had clearly prevailed – or, as the *Daily Telegraph* put it, 'How "Carrie's Crew" saw off the "Brexit Boys"'. *Grazia* magazine was appalled at the way the entire episode had been reported, exposing what it said was 'rampant misogyny running wild in the tabloid press'. The publication's senior features writer, Georgia Aspinall, said women such as Symonds 'should be allowed to express their expert opinions without being made out as calculated "hen-pecking" power grabbers forming a "girl gang" to take down men in power'.[8]

Such episodes are a reminder that the attitudes of some at Westminster have not kept pace with the significant changes taking place around them. Almost one-third of MPs are now female, as are the first ministers of Scotland and Northern Ireland, although, as I write, there are just six women around the cabinet table. The political editors of the BBC, Sky News, the *Guardian* and *Daily Mirror* are all female. This very visible shattering of the glass ceiling undoubtedly sends a powerful message to younger colleagues as to what women can achieve in a highly competitive profession.

In 2018, the year that Parliament celebrated the centenary of votes for women, both the Lobby and the Press Gallery were chaired by women. Emily Ashton, then senior political correspondent of BuzzFeed, who took on the Lobby role, said she hoped that such a line-up would soon become unremarkable.

'We need to be able to show as an organisation that the Lobby isn't an all-boys club, because it isn't.'[9] She hoped her appointment would encourage more young female students to consider pursuing a career in journalism. Ashton has a young daughter and believes the long hours and late nights, which are an inevitable feature of political journalism, can still make it a difficult career for women to pursue. Kate McCann, now a political correspondent for Sky News, who chaired the Press Gallery for a year said she hoped the increase in the number of senior political journalists who are also mothers would lead to a shift in attitudes.

The *Guardian* recently wrote that women are enjoying a 'golden age for telling the nation's political stories'. It is no longer remarkable that the first questions at news conferences are often put by the BBC's Laura Kuenssberg or Sky's Beth Rigby, and rightly so. The current generation of female correspondents are shaping the political agenda as well as the way it is reported and demonstrating a ruthless professionalism in holding our politicians to account.

Some female journalists and politicians still feel they face greater hurdles than their male counterparts, still have to confront outdated conventions. Often they are the ones taking responsibility for the juggling of childcare, and Covid-19 brought the additional challenge of trying to supervise home-schooling. Nevertheless, the Lobby these days is a very different place from the club I joined more than twenty years ago, and that is to be welcomed. The public needs to be informed about the decisions that affect our lives by journalists with a broad range of perspectives and backgrounds. Sexism still exists, more scandal will be uncovered, but the revelations and rule changes of recent years have swept away many of the old attitudes that have been lurking in the historic corridors of Westminster for far too long.

11 SURVIVAL

'Freedom of the Press, if it means anything at all, means
the freedom to criticise and oppose.'

George Orwell

'Let the healing begin,' Boris Johnson declared as he stood
outside the door of 10 Downing Street on Friday,
13 December 2019. Five months after winning the Conservative
leadership contest to succeed Theresa May, he had won his
own mandate at the general election with a thumping majority
of eighty seats. He wanted to move on from the battles over
Brexit that had dominated the UK's politics for more than three
and a half years. He was, of course, unaware that the scars
of those clashes would seem almost trivial in comparison
with the terrible pain the Covid-19 pandemic would inflict on
the nation.

The prime minister announced that his government would
unite and level up the country. Yet it was clear from the outset
that his administration would not flinch from confronting anyone deemed to be obstructive, that it was ready to challenge

established ways of working and that several in his team saw the Lobby as a troublesome and outdated institution.

Relations with some broadcasters and newspapers had been severely strained during the election campaign. There was the high-profile row with the BBC's tough interrogator Andrew Neil after Johnson failed to appear on his show. Ministers refused to give interviews to BBC Radio's flagship *Today* programme. Channel 4 decided to 'empty-chair' the Tory leader and put an ice sculpture in his place when he declined to take part in a debate on climate change. Then came the clash with ITV's *Good Morning Britain* after one of its reporters tried to grab a live interview with the prime minister, prompting him to hide in a fridge. There were other incidents, including the moment during an interview when Johnson refused to look at a photograph of a four-year-old boy who was sleeping on the floor while waiting for treatment at a Leeds hospital. As an ITV reporter tried to show him the picture on his mobile the Tory leader put the phone in his pocket, though he did later look at the image and apologise to the boy's family. Such episodes are not unusual in the heat of a hard-fought campaign and are generally forgotten when normal politics resumes. Yet when Johnson returned to No. 10, bolstered by his solid Commons majority, his media team made it plain that, as far as they were concerned, the hostilities were far from over.

Many of those in the prime minister's inner circle then were key players from the Vote Leave campaign in the 2016 EU referendum, when they successfully adopted the tactics of insurgents taking on the Establishment. Their chief strategist was Dominic Cummings, who became the prime minister's chief political adviser. Frequently snapped in his beanie hat, with his shirt half undone and low-riding trousers, Cummings's sartorial style reflected his contempt for traditional thinking and his determination to shake up Whitehall. At Vote Leave he had masterminded a plan which broke new ground, using analysis of data to target specific groups of voters directly through social media, sidestepping the mainstream newspapers and broadcasters.

His chief lieutenant was Lee Cain, the Lancashire-born former tabloid reporter who had been head of broadcasting strategy at Vote Leave. Cain was relatively inexperienced; his role in the 2010 election campaign had been to dress in a chicken suit for the *Daily Mirror* and chase David Cameron and other senior Tories around the country. Yet during the referendum battle he created powerful messages that resonated across social media and cut through to the public, building strong loyalties among the Vote Leave gang. He was subsequently appointed as special adviser to Boris Johnson when he became foreign secretary, then headed the media team for Johnson's successful bid for the Conservative leadership in the summer of 2019, before accompanying the new prime minister into Downing Street as his director of communications.

When politics resumed at Westminster after the New Year break, Cummings made headlines with his blog calling for 'weirdos and misfits with odd skills' to come and work at the heart of government. In the same piece, he criticised the way communication in SW1 was 'generally treated as almost synonymous with talking to the Lobby' and declared: 'With no election for years and huge changes in the digital world, there is a chance and a need to do things very differently.'[1] Cummings said he wanted to recruit deep experts on TV and digital platforms to explore the possibilities of 'the intersection of technology and story-telling'. It was clear the strategy was not just to bypass Westminster journalists, but also to undermine the main broadcasters, considered by some in Downing Street to have become too big for their boots.

For months, ministers continued their boycott of the *Today* programme, which a No. 10 source had described as speaking only to a 'pro-Remain metropolitan bubble in Islington, not the real world represented by Wakefield and Workington'.[2] The show's editor at the time, Sarah Sands, accused the government of trying to 'put its foot on the windpipe of an independent broadcaster' and resorting to 'Trumpian' tactics,[3] emulating the former American president's feuds with the media. At the same time, aides in Downing Street were ramping up suggestions that the BBC licence fee could be scrapped, with one source quoted as saying: 'We are having a consultation and we will whack it.'[4] The government's increasingly hard-line approach caused concern among some of its own MPs and ministers, worried it could alienate some of the party's core supporters. Huw Merriman, who chaired an all-party parliamentary group on the BBC, warned against 'ramping up an unedifying vendetta'[5] against the corporation. The former home secretary Amber Rudd said the threats to the BBC and the continuing boycott of the *Today* programme were a disgrace and warned that Westminster was becoming 'the wild west of politicians making it up as they go along'[6] while refusing to accept proper scrutiny.

There were arguments over the prime minister's address to the nation on the night the UK finally left the EU. On occasions like this there is usually a 'pool' arrangement, in which one broadcaster records the event and shares it with all the others, but Downing Street declared that its own in-house digital team would film Boris Johnson's three-minute video, to be aired at 11 p.m. on 31 January 2020. The BBC and other broadcasters saw this as an attempt to undermine their independence and feared it would set a dangerous precedent whereby No. 10 would choose who covered the prime minister's appearances. They refused to use the footage provided for their live programmes on the historic night, although shorter clips were shown in news reports and the speech was available in full on Downing Street's social media feeds.

As all this was going on, No. 10 also had the Lobby in its sights. Dominic Cummings made his intentions clear when he was asked about his plans for the Westminster press pack at a Christmas drinks party, drawing a finger menacingly across his throat. At the beginning of January the regular briefings were moved, without consultation, from the Commons to No. 9 Downing Street. You will be forgiven for thinking this is a minor practicality, and some senior journalists do not think it made a huge difference, but the change did have wider repercussions. Those attending the briefings had to enter through the gates at the entrance to Downing Street, thus allowing the government to control who had access. Although the new location was only a five-minute walk from Parliament, there were security controls to pass through, and many regional papers with fewer reporters ended up missing important debates or committee hearings. Initially, mobile phones were confiscated, underlining the government's control of proceedings. Senior Lobby journalists raised their concerns, and the Society of Editors sent an open letter, signed by every national newspaper editor, calling on the government to reconsider the move, which it said would 'create barriers to covering democracy and impede the vital work of a free press'.[7] No. 10 refused to budge.

'Cummings Declares War on the Lobby' was the headline on the right-wing website Guido Fawkes, which had close links with many at the heart of the No. 10 operation and itself has a record of scathing attacks on the whole Lobby system. Its reporters began tweeting lines from the No. 10 briefings as soon as they were delivered, breaching the long-standing rule that nothing should be published or broadcast until the meetings are finished. This may also seem like a small matter, perhaps inevitable in a world where there is intense competition to be first with the latest developments and social media is an increasingly important source of news. Yet there are reasons for this agreement. Some of the information may be market-sensitive; there may be operational guidance which is restricted for security reasons; and some comments are given in advance to help journalists, but are embargoed until such time as statements are made to Parliament.

Senior Lobby correspondents objected to the behaviour of Guido's reporters and asked them to stop live tweeting. News agencies were particularly annoyed that they were being beaten by a website which was breaching the rules. There were some forthright exchanges and the issue was raised with the prime minister's spokesman, James Slack. He said it was a matter for Lobby journalists, rather than for No. 10. Paul Staines, the Irish-born former political bag carrier who created the Guido Fawkes blog of 'plots, rumours and conspiracy', was unrepentant. He told me: 'Everyone outside the Westminster bubble thinks it's bonkers, people can't understand what all the hoo-ha is about.' For Staines it was all part of his campaign to, as he put it, 'crack the cartel' of the established media organisations. The top echelons of the Lobby decided it would be counterproductive to make a huge fuss over the issue and give further prominence to Guido's efforts to break up the entire structure. The result was that if one of Guido's reporters attended a briefing, all those present were allowed to tweet throughout the proceedings. If they didn't turn up, the old rules were observed. It was an unhappy compromise and a direct result of the disruptive tactics of someone who, like many of his friends in No. 10 at the time, wanted to shake up the Westminster establishment.

Relations between the government and the Lobby deteriorated further when the government began holding briefings by senior officials to which it invited only a handful of political editors, leaving out those who had fallen foul of No. 10. Jason

Groves, the political editor of the *Daily Mail* who had recently taken over as Lobby chairman, raised concerns with Downing Street and tried to resolve the issue behind the scenes. Senior journalists met to discuss what to do but failed to agree on a course of action.

Matters came to a head when seven political editors were offered a background briefing on the EU trade talks from David Frost, who was then the prime minister's chief negotiator. Word spread through the Lobby and other journalists turned up at the appointed time. As they waited in the entrance hall of No. 10, a security guard read out a list of names. Those who had been invited were told to stand on one side of a rug on the black-and-white chequered floor, while everyone else was ordered to the other side and told they would not be granted access. Those who were barred included the political editors of the *Daily Mirror*, the Press Association, the *Independent*, PoliticsHome and HuffPost UK. The prime minister's director of communications Lee Cain then arrived and bluntly told them that only those on the list would be allowed in. When challenged, he said: 'We're welcome to brief whoever we like, whenever we like.'[8] Pippa Crerar, political editor of the *Mirror*, one of those who was turned away, said she had never experienced anything like it in many years as a Westminster journalist. It was, she said, 'literally, physically, divide and rule'. At that point, all of the journalists walked out together, including the BBC's political editor Laura Kuenssberg and Robert Peston of ITV News. They had not planned to do so in advance but had agreed in principle that they should try to stick together. Jason Groves, who was also on the invitation list said: 'The situation in the hallway behind the No. 10 door was so farcical that they made the decision for us . . . we were not going to stand there and watch these people being marched out, we'd go with them, and yes, it did feel like a moment.'

The walkout then became quite a story and was picked up internationally, forcing Downing Street to back down. From that point, technical briefings were offered to all Lobby correspondents. They had demonstrated that, for all the strains to the system, they were still prepared to act collectively to protect the wider interests of political journalism. Yet most of them believed Johnson's media team had performed no more than a tactical retreat in the face of all the adverse publicity. Groves said at the time: 'If No. 10 have plans to give the Lobby a kicking and break us up, well they've been parked for now.'

Selective briefings are not new. For decades, governments have given stories to particular newspapers or called in specialist reporters to give more details of their policies. This, though, was a briefing from officials, who are supposed to be politically neutral. It was on a mainstream issue on which all political journalists would want to be as well informed as possible, to provide accurate coverage for their readers and viewers. Lobby journalists are hugely competitive with one another, but also recognise the importance of standing together when they believe certain principles are being undermined. Andrew Grice of the *Independent*, who's been a Westminster journalist for almost forty years, said he had witnessed 'many bouts of arm-wrestling as politicians of different hues tried to tame the media beast', but believed relations had sunk to their lowest ebb. Grice drew parallels with former President Trump's attacks on what he liked to call the 'fake news media' and warned: 'Team Boris wants to get its message directly to voters, unmediated by what it views as an anachronistic Westminster institution out of touch with the real world.'[9]

The Labour Party waded into the row, with its future leader Sir Keir Starmer writing to the cabinet secretary to complain that banning sections of the media from briefings on important matters of government was 'damaging to democracy'. He added: 'The media's access to the prime minister's chief negotiator should not be determined by political favouritism.'[10] The party put down an Urgent Question, forcing the Cabinet Office minister Chloe Smith to address the issue in the Commons. She said the government was committed to being open in its dealings with the press and no journalists had been barred from official media briefings hosted by the PMOS. She added: 'It is entirely standard practice for the government to host additional technical specialist briefings, as was the case yesterday.'[11] Smith was backed by Conservative MPs including Damian Green, a former journalist himself, who questioned whether the widely reported walkout was all 'fake outrage and a mass outbreak of snowflakery'.[12] Other Tories were quick to point the finger at Labour for its record of selective briefings to favoured reporters. At Prime Minister's Questions the following day, Boris Johnson sought to dismiss suggestions of a wider onslaught against the media, declaring: 'I am a journalist – I love journalism.'[13] While this was an important signal, it was also a classic example of Johnson's ability to deliver an appealing sound bite without addressing the specific concerns of Westminster's press pack.

The prime minister's own career in journalism won him friends as well as enemies and he has maintained good relations with many, though not all, of his former colleagues. His record was undeniably chequered: he was sacked from his first job with *The Times* for making up a quote. Yet he went on to make a name for himself as a foreign correspondent for the *Daily Telegraph* in Brussels in the early 1990s, writing tales of outrage at the meddling and ridiculous rules of the EU, some of which were only loosely based on facts. In 2005, Johnson told the BBC's *Desert Island Discs*: 'Everything I wrote from Brussels I found was sort of chucking these rocks over the garden wall . . .

and I listened to this amazing crash from the greenhouse next door over in England. It really gave me this, I suppose, rather weird sense of power.'[14] Even when he began wielding real power as a politician, he continued to pursue a parallel career in journalism, becoming editor of the *Spectator* while he was MP for Henley. He kept up his regular column for the *Telegraph* until he became foreign secretary in 2016, frequently stoking outrage with his provocative language and views. The publicity he generated for his paper clearly helped to justify his salary of £275,000 a year, and when he resigned from the government the *Telegraph* was quick to rehire its star columnist. He has never belonged to the Lobby, instinctively wary of being part of a pack, and has always prided himself on his readiness to challenge orthodox thinking. Importantly, though, he has frequently declared his support for free speech, and personally remained open and friendly towards the media, even if that could not be said of some of his closest aides.

This freedom-loving commentator could never have imagined that he would have to impose restrictions on the lives of the public that were unprecedented in peacetime. On 23 January 2020 the health secretary, Matt Hancock, made a statement to the Commons on an outbreak of Covid-19 in the Chinese city of Wuhan in which seventeen people had died. He said that 'the whole of the UK is always well prepared'[15] for these types of infections and announced checks on flights from China. Exactly two months later, the prime minister gave a television address to deliver his instruction to the British people: 'You must stay at home.'

Even before the announcement of the first national lockdown, the emergence of the deadly threat of Covid-19 had prompted the government to reconsider its confrontational approach to the press and broadcasters. On 3 March 2020, when fifty-one cases had been confirmed in the UK, Matt Hancock broke the ministerial boycott of the BBC's *Today* programme to warn that the virus could become widespread in the UK within weeks. Later the same morning Boris Johnson called for responsible reporting of the crisis, saying: 'The media has an important role as does social media. I am sure they will want to convey the right messages and the right balance of risk.'[16]

Two weeks later, Lee Cain called for a fresh start, turning up unannounced to a Lobby briefing to declare: 'The slate is wiped clean. It doesn't matter what political spectrum any of us are on or who you write or work for – whatever, we will deal with everybody the same with an entirely transparent position.'[17] He even praised reporters for their responsible and sensible coverage of the pandemic thus far. It was an attempt to build bridges that was welcomed by the assembled correspondents, but few were naive enough to believe the battles were over.

The truce was called on the day the government announced the start of its daily televised Covid-19 briefings, with a senior minister and scientific advisers answering questions, initially from Lobby correspondents, though the cast list was soon expanded to include other journalists and members of the public. Ministers clearly wanted to demonstrate transparency at a time when there was an overriding need to keep as many people as possible on side. The sessions also exposed those asking the questions to an unprecedented degree of scrutiny as millions tuned in to hear the latest on the epidemic.

The reporters putting their queries about the response to the crisis via video-conferencing screens faced waves of criticism, with accusations that they were either ridiculously hostile at a time of national crisis or soft-pedalling and in the pockets of the politicians. Robbie Gibb, Theresa May's former communications chief, led the charge from those on the right of politics who accused journalists of misjudging the public mood, with 'cheap, political business as usual questions', at a time when the public was seeking scientific and practical information about the virus. He was particularly annoyed when Channel 4 News asked the home secretary Priti Patel if she would apologise for problems with the supply of protective equipment to staff in the NHS and care homes, a question he viewed as 'absolutely outrageous'. Gibb, who was head of the BBC's political programmes before he went to No. 10, told me: 'It isn't about avoiding scrutiny, it's the tone and language around it that grates. It's jarring, because it isn't commensurate with culpability.' Others accused the journalists of failing to challenge the government over its shortcomings. Alastair Campbell said: 'I don't like this idea that because the crisis is so big, that somehow we should give ministers an easy ride. I just don't think we should.' Campbell went on: 'With some exceptions, much of the media has not been holding the government's feet to the fire and that is the role of the media, whether it's a crisis or not.'

Pippa Crerar, who chaired the Parliamentary Press Gallery at the time, was given the task of choosing which reporters from print and digital media would get to ask questions, while Downing Street organised the broadcast side. Crerar tried to ensure there was a fair mix of representatives from national and regional newspapers as well as some specialist publications. She defended their approach: 'We're not there to make good television; as print journalists we're there to ask the questions that will give us an answer which will help to develop a story.' She acknowledged it could be frustrating when they asked for specific information and were given the government's pre-prepared stock answer, in a format that made it difficult to press for a proper response. Crerar believes that during the initial weeks of the outbreak, with Parliament on Easter recess and the Opposition waiting for its new leader, it was easy for people to lump all their criticism and frustration on the handful of journalists who appeared on their screens. 'I would not pretend the press is nailing down everything,' she told me at the time, 'but we all obviously feel our job is to inform the public and hold the government to account and we have all been working really hard to do that.'

While the televised news conferences exposed the work of journalists to unusual levels of public scrutiny, the routine Lobby briefings continued away from the cameras. Once the lockdown was imposed, these too had to be conducted remotely. Instead of twenty or thirty hacks gathered in a room to fire questions at the prime minister's spokesman, they had to dial in to join the meeting online. The Lobby chairman, Jason Groves of the *Daily Mail*, faced the novel challenge of posing questions on their behalf from his laptop on a fold-up camping table upstairs at his home in south-east London. Lobby correspondents submitted their queries in advance via WhatsApp and were able to pass on follow-up points for Groves to raise while the proceedings were under way. The WhatsApp group, which had previously been used to share information on timings of briefings, embargoed reports and other useful snippets, became a vital tool for the Lobby.

Attendances rocketed to well over a hundred people, including many journalists who had never been seen at Lobby briefings before but took the opportunity to access them remotely, at a time when the government's message had never been more important and most other political gatherings were cancelled. It wasn't easy to handle, particularly when some forgot to mute their microphones. 'We've had dogs barking, children crying, toilets flushing and people arguing about what temperature to roast a chicken,' Groves told me. There were some who queried whether it was right for a *Daily Mail* journalist to be the conduit for everyone, but Groves made sure that he asked all the questions that others wanted him to raise, whatever his own views on the matter. Every journalist I spoke to was full of praise for his skill and tenacity. Rob Hutton, then UK political correspondent for Bloomberg said: 'Jason has done an amazing job and I haven't heard a whisper of complaint about the way that he's doing it.'

With questions raised on every aspect of the government's handling of the crisis, follow-ups submitted throughout the session and no limits on how many times a particular point could be pursued, the virtual meetings frequently lasted for up to an hour and a half. They also yielded far more information than the televised news conferences, where ministers and advisers were often defensive and determined to stick to agreed lines.

What the Lobby journalists really missed during the lockdown, however, were the opportunities to wander around Parliament, catching MPs for a quick informal chat or a coffee. Even when the Commons resumed, limited numbers of MPs were allowed into the Chamber and many worked from their constituencies. Most of the reporters also began working from home, relying on phone calls rather than the chance encounters that so often yield stories or new developments. Jason Groves said that while he was able to do the basic elements of the job, he regretted the lack of opportunities to pick up gossip: 'You bump into someone in a corridor, you stop and have a chat and they tell you something. They would never have thought to ring you up to tell you and you might not have thought of ringing them up, but you learn things just by being there.' Rob Hutton said he hated being unable to lurk in the atrium of Portcullis House, where he would usually be able to grab passing MPs to hear their views and test the political temperature. It was, he said, 'deeply frustrating', particularly when the sense of everyone pulling together in the face of a national crisis began to fray.

When Boris Johnson himself was admitted to intensive care in early April after being struck down by the virus, there was a profound sense of shock in Downing Street. Several of his key aides were also taken ill, as was the health secretary. Johnson came close to death but emerged after a week in hospital to thank the NHS for saving his life. When he returned to Westminster after recuperating at Chequers, he was greeted with messages of goodwill. His near-death experience had not only shaped his response to the pandemic but also won him considerable sympathy, with early polls suggesting huge support for the prime minister and his government. It did not last long.

MPs adapted to the new arrangements for the Commons with restricted numbers in the Chamber and opportunities to join proceedings via video link. Once Sir Keir Starmer was installed as Labour's new leader, ministers faced tough questions over their decisions on lockdown, the testing programme and the high numbers of cases in care homes. As some restrictions were eased, there was confusion over the government's message to the public and disputes over policies on schools, testing and quarantine.

The politics of the crisis entered a new phase when two left-leaning newspapers, the *Daily Mirror* and the *Guardian*, broke the story that the prime minister's most powerful adviser, Dominic Cummings, appeared to have breached lockdown rules by driving from London to his parents' home in Durham with his wife, who was suffering Covid-19 symptoms, and their four-year-old son. The account was written by Pippa Crerar, a respected figure in the Lobby, and Matthew Weaver of the *Guardian*. It would have huge consequences for the government and for public attitudes to the restrictions they would face for many more months.

Initially, No. 10 tried to dismiss the tale, telling journalists: 'We will not waste our time answering a stream of false allegations about Mr Cummings from campaigning newspapers.'[18] Then what was described as a 'friend', but was clearly Cummings himself, told the *Daily Mirror* he was 'not remotely bothered' about the claims, adding 'there is zero chance of him resigning'.[19] Cummings believed he had done nothing wrong, and told the No. 10 communications team not to give detailed responses to the numerous questions from journalists. This attitude undoubtedly made matters worse for Downing Street, as it faced accusations that one of those responsible for the rules had failed to follow them himself.

As the row gathered pace, the prime minister defended his adviser with a Sunday evening news conference declaring that Cummings had acted 'responsibly, legally and with integrity'.[20] It failed to halt the furore and the following day Lobby correspondents were summoned to the Rose Garden of No. 10, a setting usually reserved for prime ministers and visiting world leaders, where Cummings delivered an extraordinary hour-long explanation of his behaviour. Wearing what was for him a remarkably pristine white shirt, he said he'd decided to undertake the 260-mile drive to Durham because of a 'complicated, tricky situation' when his wife became unwell, he was concerned about childcare and feared that he too would be infected. During their two-week stay in a cottage on his parents' farm Cummings did become extremely ill, though his wife recovered sufficiently to care for their son. Then, when they were preparing to return to London, he said he was worried that his eyesight had deteriorated, so he took a forty-five-minute test drive to Barnard Castle, a local beauty spot, with his wife and son. Cummings did not apologise for his actions and said he did not regret what he'd done, though he did acknowledge that 'reasonable people may well disagree'.[21]

Plenty of people did indeed disagree strongly. MPs were deluged with letters from their constituents, questioning why there appeared to be one rule for a senior adviser and one rule for everyone else. The drive to Barnard Castle, with a child in the back of the car, to test his eyesight was ridiculed. Some leading scientists said he'd undermined efforts to control the virus, more than forty Conservative MPs called for Cummings to be sacked and even church leaders criticised his behaviour. Yet at this stage the prime minister was determined to ride out the storm. Johnson had come to rely on Cummings for his ability to cut through the complexities of governing, to focus on the bigger picture and provide some operational grip. He did not want to lose his unconventional adviser.

Cummings faced an angry mob outside his home and his reputation for understanding the public mood was severely undermined. Usually, when the adviser becomes the story, it's time to stand down, but Cummings always liked to defy conventional rules and he survived, at least for a while.

Cummings did not routinely brief the Lobby, preferring to set out his views in lengthy blogs, but senior political journalists did speak to him individually. Cummings would also occasionally appear unannounced in Portcullis House or the Commons Press Gallery to set out his latest thinking to Westminster correspondents, who would swiftly gather around. His frequently abrasive words to the weekly meeting of other special advisers were unerringly picked up by Lobby journalists, who ensured they reached a wider audience. While Cummings played a significant part in establishing the overall message, he left the day-to-day chats with journalists to his ally Lee Cain and the PMOS James Slack, who took most of the daily Lobby briefings.

Despite the pandemic – and the more constructive approach to the media – it was clear that Boris Johnson's team wanted to deliver their message directly to the public wherever possible and continue their efforts to reduce the power of Lobby journalists to set the agenda. The address to the nation by the prime minister, announcing the start of the lockdown on 23 March 2020, was watched by more than 27 million people, one of the largest-ever television audiences. This was at a moment of unprecedented national crisis and subsequent news conferences saw a return to more modest viewing figures. Yet the success of these regular sessions, with ministers and scientific advisers answering questions on camera, convinced Boris Johnson and his closest aides that this was by far the most effective way of communicating with citizens across the country.

In July, Steven Swinford, then deputy political editor of *The Times*, a Lobby correspondent well known for his scoops, exclusively revealed that No. 10 had decided to introduce daily White House-style televised briefings hosted by an experienced broadcaster. They would replace the off-camera Lobby briefings in the afternoons that had been part of the Westminster routine for almost a century, though the morning sessions would continue as before. The speculation about who would take on the role – and the recruitment process – began immediately. So did the arguments about the merits and risks of the plan.

The story sparked a huge debate across mainstream and social media, with Lobby journalists and those with experience of addressing them divided on whether it was a good idea. Pippa Crerar said it would be 'win-win' for No. 10, with the real business of the day done off-camera at the morning meetings and the on-camera gatherings allowing the prime minister's team to look transparent. Jim Pickard, chief political correspondent of the *Financial Times*, said there was no harm in it as 'most journalists believe in transparency'. But other newspaper journalists were not convinced they would gain much from the change to the long-standing arrangements. Oliver Wright, policy editor of *The Times*, said that Boris Johnson might come to regret the plan, pointing out that 'if his spokesman is on a sticky wicket it will be beamed to the nation'.[22]

Broadcasters, understandably, were delighted at the prospect. Sky's Beth Rigby said she had always thought that 'sunlight is the best disinfectant' and believed that televising the briefings would reveal when the government was failing to answer certain points and show the diligence with which journalists press for answers. The prime minister said the daily Covid-19 news conferences had shown that there was a public appetite for this kind of approach. 'We do think people want direct engagement and stuff from us, so we're going to have a go at that,' he told LBC Radio, and confirmed that he would himself continue to 'pop up from time to time'.[23]

The plan was the brainchild of Lee Cain, who saw this as another opportunity to 'take back control' of the agenda, recalling his experience on the Vote Leave campaign. He believed it was a way of delivering key messages straight to voters, bypassing Westminster journalists who were always ready to confront the government and expose its shortcomings. Robert Peston, political editor of ITV News and an experienced Lobby hand, said there were mixed emotions among its members. The traditionally private briefings 'confirmed a certain sort of power and authority on those people lucky enough to have a pass to go along'[24] and he pointed out that privilege would be lost once some of the proceedings were televised.

The papers, meanwhile, delighted in speculating about who would get the job. Daytime TV hosts Richard Madeley and Anne Diamond were tipped, with senior BBC correspondents Vicki Young and James Landale also in the frame. In fact, the three names on the final shortlist were Angus Walker, a former ITV correspondent, Ellie Price, a BBC political reporter, and Allegra Stratton, who emerged as the choice to become the public face of the prime minister.

Stratton is a former Lobby journalist and presenter who worked at the BBC, where she was political editor of *Newsnight*, and at ITV News, where she was national editor. In April 2020 she left to become director of strategic communications for Chancellor Rishi Sunak and did much to raise his profile. Stratton was responsible for the 'Eat Out to Help Out' slogan for the discount scheme to encourage us all to support restaurants and cafés when restrictions were eased over that summer. Her connections to the chancellor were well established long before she went to work for him. Sunak was best man at her wedding to James Forsyth, political editor of the *Spectator* and an astute member of the Lobby. The couple were also on good terms with the prime minister's fiancée, Carrie Symonds, who invited them to Chequers. Boris Johnson personally helped to persuade Stratton to take on the challenge, ringing her several times to convince her to accept the job. Some saw her appointment as a move by Johnson to poach Sunak's star player, but most recognised it as a shrewd choice given her media and political experience.

Previous press secretaries who had addressed the Lobby, though without the cameras present, had mixed views on the whole idea. Simon Lewis, who had wanted to introduce televised briefings when he worked for Gordon Brown, said it was inevitable that such a change would be introduced, and it was 'a very good step forward'. Lewis told me it was sensible to choose a former TV presenter who was used to answering unpredictable questions with authority. Older hands were more sceptical. Lord O'Donnell, who was John Major's press secretary, said he thought it was 'a dreadful idea' that would result in the spokesperson having a higher profile than many cabinet ministers. Sir Bernard Ingham, who famously handled press relations for Margaret Thatcher, also opposed the change. He told me: 'Parliament, to defend its supremacy, should create such a fuss that they abandon the whole idea.'

Yet, with extraordinary irony, the change intended to ensure that Downing Street could convey a clear message to the public led to a ferocious bout of infighting among those around the prime minister. It would result in the resignation of Lee Cain, the original architect of the plan.

Cain was unhappy with the choice of Allegra Stratton to take on the high-profile task and clashed with her from the outset, when she insisted that she needed regular access to the prime minister. Johnson then offered Cain a different role as his chief of staff, which in turn prompted a backlash from some senior Conservative MPs who objected to his confrontational attitude. Carrie Symonds, herself a former Conservative adviser, also opposed Cain's appointment because of what she saw as the 'macho culture' he embodied. In the vicious briefing war that ensued, stories appeared in newspapers in which Symonds was described as 'Princess Nut Nut', who was not content to be the power behind the throne but wanted to be 'a new Princess Di Character'.[25] The insults went viral and as we know, allies of Symonds, along with many female MPs and commentators, were furious at what they saw as rank misogyny.

For Boris Johnson the briefing against his fiancée had been the final straw. He'd had enough of the toxic behaviour of his two powerful aides and ordered them both out immediately. The pictures of Cummings leaving Downing Street with his belongings in a cardboard box dominated the front pages of all the papers. There was a collective sigh of relief from many special advisers across Whitehall who would no longer be subjected to his regular tirades and unpredictable demands. Some senior Conservative MPs, including those who'd worked with Cummings and Cain on the Vote Leave campaign, also welcomed their departure from No. 10. The former cabinet minister Theresa Villiers said there had been concerns about their 'dismissive attitude' and there was 'a good opportunity for a fresh start'.[26] Sir Bernard Jenkin, a senior Conservative MP who had himself clashed with Cummings, said it was 'an opportunity to reset how the government operates and to emphasise some values about what we want to project as a Conservative Party in government'.[27]

Their departure also removed the two figures who had been intent on curbing the power of the Lobby. Throughout this turbulent phase James Slack had continued to take the regular No. 10 briefings, dealing with the numerous and detailed questions from journalists on the government's handling of the pandemic. Slack was a civil servant who had been recruited for the job when Theresa May was prime minister and, unusually, stayed in the post when Boris Johnson replaced her. Slack, a former political editor of the *Daily Mail* who had been in the Lobby for many years, was highly regarded by his former colleagues for his calm professionalism and considerate manner – a marked contrast to the abrasive approach of Cummings and Cain. In the upheaval after their departure, Slack was promoted to take on Cain's old job as director of communications, with Jamie Davies, a civil servant who'd been Slack's deputy, taking charge of the regular Lobby briefings for a time.

At the end of his final briefing as PMOS, on 17 November 2020, Slack made it clear that he not only respected the Lobby but saw it as an important part of our political system. Though the proceedings were all online, it was an emotional occasion. Jason Groves, chairing the meeting, said Slack was the best spokesperson he'd worked with, despite the difficult circumstances. Slack told his audience it had been an 'enormous privilege' to speak to them on behalf of two prime ministers. 'It's not always easy doing this job,' he said, 'but I never once questioned why I need to do it, even when I was walking into a wall of gunfire some days, because what you do keeps all of us in government honest, it exposes problems that need fixing, and it makes sure that we don't ever relax. And that's a good thing.' He concluded: 'I think you're an absolutely essential part of the democracy that we have in this country. And long may the Lobby continue.'[28] The journalists banged their desks in appreciation. It was a clear signal that the war with the Lobby was over, though both sides were well aware that future skirmishes were inevitable.

In a further sign that the new communications team in Downing Street wanted to move on from the battles initiated by Cummings and Cain, ministers resumed appearances on ITV's *Good Morning Britain*. The boycott of the programme had lasted for many months after its outspoken presenter Piers Morgan had described Cain as a 'snivelling little worm'.

These far-reaching changes at No. 10 came as the pandemic was taking another turn for the worse. After the relaxation of the rules on socialising and travel over the summer, with pubs and restaurants allowed to open in many parts of the country and some holidays possible, the rates of infection and hospital admissions began to rise steeply once more. A new system of tiers was introduced, with different restrictions in various parts of the country. A plan to ease the limits to allow family gatherings over Christmas was hastily abandoned at the last minute and, on 4 January 2021 the prime minister announced another national lockdown. In a televised address to the nation, he warned that a new variant, which began in London and the South East of England, was 50 to 70 per cent more transmissible than the original strain and that hospitals were under greater pressure than at any time since the start of the pandemic.

In late 2020, Allegra Stratton began contributing to some of the off-camera Lobby briefings and on her first appearance went out of her way to dismiss an earlier suggestion from an unnamed Downing Street source that trust in the media had collapsed during the Covid-19 crisis. She told Lobby journalists that Boris Johnson believed they had played a 'very good and powerful role' during this time, adding: 'The prime minister, as a former journalist, has spoken publicly about the positive role the media has played during this pandemic in spreading information about what we need people to do, to observe social distancing and so on.'[29] Her comments, on the record, appeared to confirm the change of attitude at No. 10.

Stratton also agreed that she could be named when her words to the off-camera Lobby meetings were reported, a move that would once have been hugely controversial but was accepted without dissent, given that everyone expected her to be appearing on screen shortly.

As a special adviser, Stratton was free to speak about political matters as well as the government's approach; able to provide more insight into Boris Johnson's thinking. Once in post, she quickly established a close working relationship with the prime minister and began conducting calls with groups of Conservative MPs in an effort to address their concerns about the communications operation at No. 10. Many of them had been infuriated by last-minute policy changes and dithering on issues such as free school meals during the crisis, which had prompted angry reactions from their constituents. Senior MPs were impressed by Stratton's contributions and welcomed the sign that the prime minister's new team was ready to listen to their views, which had so often been dismissed in the Cummings era.

By the New Year, Johnson also had a new chief of staff, a little-known former Treasury official and banker, Dan Rosenfield. He, along with Stratton, was credited with a distinct change of tone from the prime minister, usually known for his love of 'boosterism'. After many months when the government had set optimistic targets for lifting restrictions, only to abandon them when infection rates rose, the new watchword was caution. The famously loquacious Johnson stuck faithfully to the line that he would only ease the rules when it was safe to do so.

When on 26 January 2021 the UK became the first European country to reach the grim milestone of 100,000 deaths from Covid-19, the prime minister said he was 'deeply sorry for every life lost' and that he took full responsibility for his administration's handling of the crisis, adding 'we truly did everything we could'.[30] The government was under immense pressure, with the Opposition accusing ministers of acting too slowly to impose tough restrictions to control the virus, while a vocal group of Conservative MPs pressed for a rapid timetable for lifting the lockdown. Johnson was able to point to one positive development, however: the rollout of the biggest vaccination programme in the nation's history.

The regular news conferences, with the prime minister or another cabinet minister accompanied by leading scientific advisers or NHS administrators, had resumed in the autumn of 2020 and the government had decided these should continue while the crisis remained so grave.

Even when the prime minister announced his highly antici-pated 'one-way road to freedom' on 22 February 2021, with plans for a phased easing of lockdown restrictions, he still struck a note of caution. Boris Johnson said that while he hoped all legal limits on social contact could be lifted by 21 June, each step would depend on an assessment of data, including the risks from new Covid variants. No. 10 judged that while this slow process unfolded it was not the right time to change its media strategy: the virtual news conferences with ministers and advisers would continue.

Allegra Stratton's televised briefings had already been delayed once in 2020, with a revised date set for the beginning of January. Once again they were put on hold, with Stratton telling Lobby journalists that the government was 'looking closely at the best ways of communications for the period we now find our-selves in'.[31]

A hi-tech studio had already been created in a vast wood-panelled room in No. 9 Downing Street, and a Freedom of Information request by the Press Association revealed it had cost £2.6 million to install the technical facilities in a Grade 1 listed building. The Cabinet Office gave a breakdown of the outlay: £1,848,695.12 for the 'main works', £198,023.75 on 'long lead items' and £33,394.63 on broadband equipment.[32]

In mid-March 2021, ITV News revealed pictures of the plush new studio with seating for journalists, official Downing Street lecterns and four prominently displayed Union Jack flags. Commentators immediately spotted a red Henry vacuum cleaner parked by the stage, sparking much amusement on social media. A spoof 'Press Office Henry Hoover' account was even set up on Twitter. The studio was used for the first time on Monday, 29 March 2021, but it was the prime minister, rather than his spokesperson, who addressed the media and the wider public.

A new date of 17 May 2021 was set for Stratton's first appearance in front of the cameras but within weeks it was revealed that Downing Street had scrapped the whole idea. Stratton herself confirmed the move to journalists, ahead of the announcement that she was to become spokesperson for the COP26 climate summit in the autumn of that year.

Culture Secretary Oliver Dowden defended the decision, telling the BBC that the new studio would be used by the prime minister and senior colleagues and by future governments. He said the old state dining room at No. 10 which had been used for news conferences was not fit for purpose and it was 'perfectly normal for governments to have press briefing facilities'.[33]

It seems several key figures in Downing Street, including James Slack and Dan Rosenfield, had grave reservations about the plan from the outset. When Slack left Downing Street in March to become deputy editor-in-chief at the *Sun*, he was replaced by his deputy Jack Doyle, a former Lobby journalist for the *Mail*, who also had concerns about the change. They helped to convince Boris Johnson, who'd initially been enthusiastic about the idea, that it would not be in his interests to go ahead with the proposals. The decision was made as Johnson was embroiled in huge rows over leaks of his personal text messages, his dealings with American businesswoman Jennifer Arcuri and questions over who had paid for the refurbishment of his Downing Street flat.

Jason Groves told me they'd realised the dangers of going 'live without a net', with remarks from the prime minister's spokesperson only getting onto news bulletins when things were going badly for the government. 'You'd be asking for trouble,' Groves said, with remarks on camera providing a licence for broadcasters to investigate awkward stories about Boris Johnson's personal life – which they'd otherwise leave to the papers.

Steven Swinford agreed: 'When you've got an ongoing scandal or difficult issue, the on camera-briefings could become very uncomfortable and give significant momentum to stories if the government is reluctant to answer questions,' he told me. 'Ultimately that's why they dropped them. There was a concern that the risk was too great and that actually these briefings could end up being own goals for the government.' Swinford himself had been looking forward to the televised sessions as an opportunity for political journalists to hold the government to account publicly. 'From a Lobby point of view, the more transparency the better,' he said. He believed that although there would have been some grandstanding, they would also have been a valuable source of stories.

Labour's deputy leader Angela Rayner claimed the prime minister was 'running scared of scrutiny' and had wasted millions of pounds of tax-payers' money on 'a pointless vanity project'.[34] Alastair Campbell, who had put Lobby briefings on the record when he was in charge of media relations for Tony Blair, told the BBC it was a 'stupid idea, should never have been considered and I'm just glad it's not happening'. He said he believed the proposals had been drawn up as part of efforts to undermine Parliament, when that is where the 'action had to be', with ministers speaking on behalf of the government. Sir Christopher Meyer, who was John Major's press secretary, agreed. 'One of the problems is you would have had a public personality on TV who would become a rival as a spokesperson to cabinet ministers,' he said. Sir Christopher, who became ambassador to the US, said it was a 'delusion' to think arrangements here could be modelled on the American approach: 'The notion that we could graft onto our system essentially a White House-style on-the-record press conference I thought was lunatic and would not work and I'm glad it's been cancelled.'[35]

Tom Kelly, who'd considered proposals for televised briefings when he replaced Campbell as Blair's press secretary, said he believed the latest plans were abandoned for the same reasons that similar recommendations were not implemented almost twenty years earlier. 'It's always easier to outline the advantages of total transparency on camera in theory rather than in reality,' he told me. Kelly said that while all administrations started out with the best of intentions, once in power they worried about the questions they'd face and whether these would feed controversies that they'd rather put to rest. 'I think people do underestimate the difficulties of the job,' he said. Kelly believes that while none of this is a big issue for the general public, the problem for successive governments is that it perpetuates a sense of secrecy in their overall approach.

Jason Groves was unconvinced that the White House-style briefings would have led to greater openness, however. 'It was going to become a circus,' he said. 'You would have some reporters showboating and the prime minister's spokesperson playing for time, and I'm not sure what you'd have added to transparency by doing that.' Swinford told me that the real test of the government's commitment to openness would be whether the regular news conferences from ministers and senior advisers continued in a post-Covid era.

As someone who has worked for broadcasters most of my adult life, I would certainly have welcomed the chance to have regular briefings on camera, though I suspect that after the initial excitement they would have become less newsworthy. I agree that they would undoubtedly have been risky for those in power and would almost certainly have benefitted journalists far more than politicians, which is why, so far at least, successive governments have backed away from the idea.

The latest about-turn came as there were further changes

to the communications team at No. 10. Max Blain, who'd been head of news at the department of health and social care, was appointed as the PMOS. Rosie Bate-Williams, who'd been a special adviser to Boris Johnson since he ran for the leadership, was promoted to replace Allegra Stratton as his press secretary, contributing some political insight to the regular Lobby briefings from Blain, which continued away from the cameras.

Even before all this, the digital team at No. 10 had already found other ways of connecting Boris Johnson directly to voters. A recent survey by the media regulator Ofcom suggested that half of all adults turn to social media to keep up with the news. So Johnson has held live chats on Facebook, which his team viewed as a success, and he is said to have written some of the posts on his Twitter feed himself. Other changes have also been introduced, almost unnoticed. WhatsApp has not only been an essential part of the virtual Lobby briefings but is increasingly used by Downing Street to pass on practical information to journalists and to disseminate lines of response on important issues. Several former press secretaries who worked at No. 10 in previous eras have told me how they wished they could have used such methods to put out information and statements instead of conducting time-consuming rounds of phone calls.

Another of the more recent innovations of Westminster life has been the morning email providing a Lobby insider's guide to the day ahead to anyone who cares to sign up. Many of the papers now provide their own daily newsletters, but one of the first and finest is the London Playbook from Politico UK. For three years it was written by Jack Blanchard, now Politico's UK editor, who recently recorded a podcast describing his sleepless life as a 'setter of agendas, framer of stories and the hub of all gossip'. His 7 a.m. missive became an essential primer for fellow journalists and politicians alike and provided the sort of information and insight that Lobby journalists would once have been forbidden from disclosing.

The Lobby itself has also expanded to include a wider membership. In recent years, left-wing websites such as Evolve and Left Foot Forward have been granted Lobby passes, a sign that the institution is adapting to the changing media environment. Evolve's former editor Matt Turner told me that he was surprised their application was accepted, but that the inclusion of organisations which do not consider themselves part of the mainstream media showed the Lobby was being dragged into the twenty-first century.

Tom Newton Dunn had set about overhauling the rules in 2018 when he was political editor of the *Sun* and chairman of the Lobby, believing it was important to set out in black and white the Lobby's transformation in recent years. 'It's no longer a club where you get exclusive rights for membership if you're the right kind of person,' he told me. 'It's almost a trade body and its sole purpose is to facilitate access to government and Opposition.' The first of the updated rules declares: 'The Lobby is an open and transparent association that exists solely to facilitate the communication of Government and Opposition business to media representatives that are assigned to cover it.'[36] Newton Dunn believes it's a system that provides the 'oil of politics', facilitating the rapid flow of information which allows our democracy to thrive.

As a former Lobby correspondent and a journalist, I know how important it is to spend time getting to know and understand those who are making our laws, those who advise them and those who oppose them. The ability to roam around the corridors and atriums of Westminster is the one privilege I have missed most since I moved on from my job as a political correspondent. I know that today's Lobby reporters are longing for the time when Covid-19 restrictions are eased so that they can resume this essential part of their efforts to find out what is happening in the corridors of power.

It is hard to exaggerate how important this aspect of the job is for any political journalist seeking to build up an accurate picture of what is going on, and to assess how the government's message is being perceived. The Covid-19 restrictions have undoubtedly tested the resourcefulness of correspondents, yet they have clearly found ways of keeping up with their contacts and digging out some great stories. This all proves what nonsense it is for anyone to suggest that the media simply laps up spoon-fed lines from No. 10. Similarly, those who have had the task of speaking for various prime ministers over the years dismiss as laughable the notion that they could somehow dollop out their lines unchallenged.

Of course, it is also important for journalists to report the stance of whoever is in power, never more so than during the pandemic, when government policies have such an immense effect on people's lives and livelihoods. And it is hard to think of a better way of getting to grips with the strategy, the details and the mistakes of the government than by regularly questioning the prime minister's spokesperson, and pressing for proper answers, before broadcasting and writing the stories of the day.

Lobby journalists are among the most dedicated, ambitious and tenacious in the land, explaining the manoeuvrings and personal battles behind the policies and laws that affect every one of us. They may not get everything right all the time, but they undoubtedly strive to give their readers and audiences a clear and comprehensive account of what is going on and what is going wrong.

In an era where we are plagued by conspiracy theories and fake news, they are in the best possible position to sift the truth from the chaff of unfounded rumour. They are in the front row when political history is unfolding, working hard behind the scenes to scrutinise those in power and to enable us all to be properly informed about the decisions that shape our lives.

I am privileged to have been a member of the Lobby and pay tribute to those who continue to ensure that it is such a vital part of our democracy.

APPENDIX 1:
LOBBY RULES, 1982

NOTES ON THE PRACTICE OF LOBBY JOURNALISM

Lobby Practice

1. The Lobby journalist's authority to work in Parliament is the inclusion of his name in a list kept by the Serjeant at Arms for the Speaker. He has complete freedom to get his own stories in his own way; there are no restrictions of any kind on personal initiative. But he also owes a duty to the Lobby as a whole, in that he should do nothing to prejudice the communal life of the Lobby or its ties. This is in the Lobby journalist's own interest and that of his office, as well as in the general interest of the Lobby. It is a responsibility which should always be kept in mind.

2. There is no 'association' of Lobby journalists, but in our common interests we act collectively as the Parliamentary Lobby Journalists. It has been found convenient to have an organisation consisting of Chairman, officers and committee for that purpose.

Individual Lobbying

3. The work of a Lobby Journalist brings him into close daily touch with Ministers and Members of Parliament of all parties and imposes on him a very high standard of responsibility and

discretion in making use of the special facilities given him for writing about political affairs. The cardinal rule of the Lobby is never to identify its informant without specific permission. In any case, members of the Lobby must always take personal responsibility for their stories and their facts.

4. Care must be taken not to reveal anything, even indirectly, which could lead to identification of informants. There are, of course, numerous instances when an informant is perfectly willing to be identified. This is in order as long as the journalist has obtained his permission.

5. The Lobby regularly receives Advance Copies of official documents to facilitate its work. All embargoes on such documents, and on all information given orally or operationally in advance for the Lobby's convenience, must be strictly observed.

6. The Lobby decided by ballot held in April 1982 that: 'It is an abuse of Lobby membership and incompatible with that membership if members pass information gained through Lobby facilities, and not available elsewhere, to interests outside journalism. In no circumstances should advance copies of documents, or information in them, be provided to such outside interests. Any breach may be followed by a recommendation to the Serjeant at Arms that Lobby facilities be withdrawn from the member concerned.'

Collective Lobbying

7. The Lobby frequently invites Ministers and others to meet it collectively, to give information and to answer questions. Members are under an obligation to keep secret the fact that such meetings are held and to avoid revealing the sources of their information.

8. It is recognised, however, that a correspondent has a special responsibility to his Editor. The following Resolution was therefore passed by the Lobby in July 1955:

> 'That it is consistent with Lobby practice that members of the Lobby may tell their Editors, or Acting Editors, the sources of their information at Lobby meetings on the rare occasions that this may be vital, but must, on every occasion that such information is passed on, explain to their Editors, or Acting Editors, that the source is strictly confidential.'

9. DON'T TALK ABOUT LOBBY MEETINGS BEFORE OR AFTER THEY ARE HELD, especially in the presence of those not entitled to attend them. If outsiders appear to know something of the arrangements made by the Lobby, do not confirm their conjectures or assume that as they appear to know so much they may safely be told the rest.

10. The Lobby correspondent should bear in mind that the purpose of a meeting is to elicit information not to score political or debating points.

11. It is a point of honour to stay to the end of a meeting. If there is some compelling reason for a correspondent to leave, he is under an obligation to obtain the permission of the Chairman to do so and, if released, is under an equal obligation not to make use of anything that has been said at the meeting before it ends.

12. When meetings are arranged on the Lobby's behalf, every correspondent should endeavour to attend. The Lobby works most effectively when the courtesy and co-operation shown by Ministers and others are reciprocated in this way.

Parliamentary Privilege

13. On questions of Parliamentary privilege, an up-to-date edition of Erskine May's 'Parliamentary Practice' will be found a useful

guide. In case of doubt, officers of the Lobby and of both Houses are available for consultations.

14. As the case law of privilege is constantly being developed and amended, it is essential that members of the Lobby should acquaint themselves with current practice and bear it in mind when writing anything which might conceivably be held to be a breach.

15. Select Committees of the House frequently meet in public and are reported in the normal way. But any reference to the proceedings of a Select Committee held in private will almost certainly be raised on the floor of the House with the Speaker, with a view to obtaining his opinion as to whether or not it constitutes, *prima facie*, a breach of privilege.

16. References to the reports of Select Committees are covered by the following ruling given publicly by Mr Speaker King on 24th March 1969.

> 'Any publication of a draft report before the report has been agreed to by a Committee and presented to the House is treated as a breach of privilege; but when the report has been presented to the House, though not yet available to Hon. Members in printed form, it is not an offence against the House to publish the findings of the Select Committee. It is certainly inconvenient, however, and discourteous to the House when this is done. I cannot go further than that . . . No question of privilege is involved.'

17. In consequence, the Lobby passed the following Resolution at a special meeting on 23rd April 1969.

> 'That the Chairman and Secretary of the Lobby inform the Speaker that, in the absence of any positive and public ruling, members of the Lobby are free to use any information reaching

them concerning reports of Select Committees of the House
of Commons, once they have been technically laid before the
House.'

The Speaker was informed accordingly.

18. Finally, if you are in doubt about ANY point of Lobby etiquette
or practice, consult the Chairman or Secretary of the Lobby. They
will be glad to help and guide all newcomers, especially in identifying those parts of the Palace of Westminster to which Lobby
correspondents have access.

19. EVERY LOBBY CORRESPONDENT IS UNDER AN OBLIGATION
TO ENSURE THAT A DEPUTY ACTING IN HIS ABSENCE
UNDERSTANDS LOBBY PRACTICE.

July 1982

APPENDIX 2: LOBBY RULES, 2018

RULES OF THE PARLIAMENTARY MEDIA LOBBY

1. The Lobby is an open and transparent association that exists solely to facilitate the communication of Government and Opposition business to media representatives that are assigned to cover it.

2. It elects three officers every year; a Chairman, a Secretary and a Treasurer. It also elects a committee of seven members. Chairmen are not encouraged to serve longer than a year.

Membership

3. Membership of the Lobby is automatically open to all holders of media passes for the Parliamentary estate, which affords attendance at all Lobby briefings.

4. No central membership list is held, but those newly arrived should make themselves known to the Lobby Chairman, who will introduce them at the next afternoon Lobby briefing as a courtesy to others.

Lobby briefings

5. The Prime Minister's Official Spokesman gives briefings about government business twice a day between Monday and Thursday

when the House of Commons is sitting, at 11 a.m. and 3.45 p.m. These take place in the Lobby Room of the House of Commons. Wednesday morning's briefing takes place immediately after PMQs in the Lower Press Gallery, and on Friday, there is only one briefing at 11 a.m. All are on the record. During recess, there is one briefing a week on Monday at 11 a.m.

6. Lobby members should bear in mind that the purpose of a briefing is to elicit information not to score political or debating points.

7. No information revealed during the Lobby briefings must be put into the public domain – via social media or a third party – until the briefings have concluded. It is attendees' individual responsibility to ensure this, though they may communicate contents of briefings to others from their media organisations on this strict understanding.

8. As a courtesy to others, no attendees may leave Lobby briefings until they have concluded. If there is some compelling reason for a member to leave early, they must obtain the permission of the Chairman to do so.

Conduct

9. Lobby journalists have complete freedom to get their own stories in their own way; there are no restrictions of any kind on personal initiative. But they should at all times behave respectfully to media colleagues, Parliamentarians, and all other pass holders on the Parliamentary estate, do nothing to prejudice the communal life of the Lobby, and uphold the highest standards of reporting and a free press.

10. Lobby journalists should never name the sources of any off-the-record briefings they may receive from MPs, peers or their

advisers and civil servants. They should also do all they can to ensure their sources are not identified inadvertently by themselves or others. This preserves the convention known as 'Lobby terms'.

Embargoes

11. Lobby members must abide by embargoes requested by the party issuing the media release, or agreed among other members.

12. It is the responsibility of Lobby members themselves to prevent accidental disclosure, or disclosure by a third party – for example for use on social media – of embargoed material. Material may be shared with third parties in advance, but must be held back from public disclosure in any form until the embargo expires.

13. Media releases offered on the condition of 'no approach' for any comment must be agreed with individual journalists first for the condition to apply. The practice of 'no approach' must be consensual.

14. It is an abuse of Lobby membership and incompatible with that membership if members pass information gained through Lobby facilities, and not available elsewhere, to interests outside journalism. In no circumstances should advance copies of documents, or information in them, be provided to such outside interests.

Members' Lobby

15. Some media pass holders will hold a pass (currently, 28A) that allows them to stand in Members' Lobby. Allocation of these passes is a matter for the House Authorities not the Lobby. Members who do have that privilege must abide by the strict rules laid down by the House, including respecting the highest standards of decorum.

16. Lobby journalists allowed into Members' Lobby are only allowed to sit down if it is on the small bench by the doorway to the Ways & Means corridor.

Please consult the Chairman or officers if clarification of any of the above rules is needed. They will be glad to help and guide all newcomers, especially in identifying those parts of the Palace of Westminster to which Lobby correspondents have access.

January 2018

ACKNOWLEDGEMENTS

This book would not have been possible without the insight and anecdotes provided by those who have worked as journalists in the Lobby and those who have briefed them over the years. I would like to thank all those who have given me their valuable time and recollections.

I am particularly grateful to everyone who agreed to be interviewed. They include the late Chris Moncrieff, Lord Hennessy, Joe Haines, Sir Bernard Ingham, Lord O'Donnell, Sir Christopher Meyer, Jonathan Haslam, Alastair Campbell, Lord Mandelson, Godric Smith, Tom Kelly, Michael Ellam, Simon Lewis, Tom Newton Dunn, Sean Kemp, Craig Oliver, Graeme Wilson, Katie Perrior, Lord Barwell, Paul Harrison, Robbie Gibb, John Pienaar, Elinor Goodman, Trevor Kavanagh, Andrew Marr, Robin Oakley, Nick Robinson, Michael White, Philip Webster, Nick Jones, Julia Langdon, Sue Cameron, Carolyn Quinn, Jon Sopel, Michael Cockerell, Steven Swinford, Rob Hutton, Jason Groves, Pippa Crerar, Beth Rigby, Jane Merrick, Anne Alexander and Paul Staines.

I also carried out research at the Parliamentary Archives.

I would like to put on record my thanks to all those with whom I worked over more than twenty years as a BBC political correspondent, the fabulous colleagues at the BBC, the fellow journalists who helped me out and the many special advisers and spokespersons who answered my numerous queries at all hours of the day and night.

I also must thank Martin Redfern, Diane Banks and the team at Northbank Talent Management, without whom I would not have considered embarking on this project.

I am enormously grateful to Sarah Rigby and Pippa Crane at Elliott and Thompson for having faith in me and for doing so much to improve my manuscript.

Finally, I would like to thank my wonderful husband Tony, who has provided invaluable help and support throughout, and my amazing children Sophie and Gus, who gave me so much encouragement and are a source of such pride and joy.

NOTES

Quotes are taken directly from the author's own interviews unless specified otherwise.

Chapter 1

1 Anthony King and Anne Sloman, *Westminster and Beyond: Based on the BBC Radio series 'Talking Politics'* (London: Palgrave Macmillan, 1973)
2 Lobby Journalists' Committee records 1929
3 Ibid.
4 Lobby Journalists' Committee records 1931/2
5 Lobby Journalists' Committee records 1931
6 James Margach, *The Anatomy of Power* (London: W.H. Allen, 1979)
7 John Evelyn Denison, *Notes from my Journal When Speaker of the House of Commons*, (London: Murray, 1900)
8 Andrew Sparrow, *Obscure Scribblers: A History of Parliamentary Reporting* (London: Politico's, 2003)
9 Sparrow, *Obscure Scribblers*
10 Frederick J. Higginbottom, *The Vivid Life: A Journalist's Career* (London: Simpkin Marshall, 1934)
11 Ibid.
12 Ibid.
13 Lobby Journalists' Committee records 1931/2
14 Lobby Journalists' Committee records 1935/6
15 James Margach, *The Abuse of Power: The War Between Downing Street and the media from Lloyd George to James Callaghan* (London: W.H. Allen, 1978)
16 Richard Cockett, *Twilight of Truth: Chamberlain, Appeasement and the Manipulation of the Press* (London: Palgrave Macmillan, 1989)

17 'Brighter Outlook', *The Times*, 10 March 1939
18 Margach, *The Abuse of Power*
19 Ibid.
20 'The Peace', *Guardian*, 1 October 1938
21 Margach, *The Abuse of Power*
22 Cockett, *Twilight of Truth*

Chapter 2
 1 Warren F. Kimball, 'Churchill, Roosevelt and the reporters', *Finest Hour*, 152 (Autumn 2011), www.winstonchurchill.org
 2 Dr Henry Irving, 'Chaos and censorship in the Second World War', History of Government, www.history.blog.gov.uk
 3 Chris Wrigley, *Winston Churchill: A Biographical Companion* (Santa Barbara: ABC-CLIO, 2002)
 4 Paul Addison and Jeremy A. Crang (eds), *Listening to Britain: Home Intelligence Reports on Britain's Finest Hour, May to September 1940* (London: Bodley Head, 2010)
 5 Ian McLaine, *Ministry of Morale: Home Front Morale and the Ministry of Information in World War II* (London: Allen & Unwin, 1979)
 6 Addison and Crang (eds), *Listening to Britain*
 7 Ibid.
 8 Ibid.
 9 Ibid.
10 Charles Edward Lysaght, *Brendan Bracken: A Biography* (London: Allen Lane, 1979)
11 War Cabinet Minutes, September and October 1940, The National Archives, Kew
12 House of Commons, Public Administration – Sixth Report, Appendix 8, 6 August 1988
13 Margach, *The Abuse of Power*
14 Lobby Journalists' Committee records 1945
15 Oral Answers to Questions, Volume 444, *Hansard*, UK Parliament, 13 November 1947
16 John Carvel, 'My grandfather's budget scoop saw off a chancellor – how times have changed', *Guardian*, 20 March 2013
17 Sparrow, *Obscure Scribblers*
18 William Clark, *From Three Worlds: Memoirs* (London: Sidgwick & Jackson, 1986)
19 Clark, *From Three Worlds*
20 Thomas M. Franck and Edward Weisband (eds), *Secrecy and Foreign Policy* (New York: Oxford University Press, 1954)

21 Clark, *From Three Worlds*
22 Ibid.

Chapter 3

1 *Panorama*, BBC One, 19 October 1964
2 Peter Jenkins, 'My life with Harold Wilson', *London Review of Books*, vol. 1 no. 5, 20 December 1979
3 'The invention of General Election broadcasting: 1960—', Elections, 100 Voices That Made the BBC, History of the BBC (https://www.bbc.com/historyofthebbc/100-voices/elections/invention-3/)
4 Sparrow, *Obscure Scribblers*
5 'An extract from the Cabinet minutes, 16 November 1967', The National Archives, Kew
6 Daniel Harari, '"Pound in your pocket" devaluation: 50 years on', House of Commons Library, 17 November 2017
7 Margach, *The Abuse of Power*
8 Ibid.
9 Barbara Castle, *The Castle Diaries 1964–76* (London: Weidenfeld & Nicolson, 1980)
10 Castle, *The Castle Diaries*
11 Margach, *The Abuse of Power*
12 Joe Haines, *Kick 'Em Back: Wilson, Maxwell and Me* (London: Grosvenor House Publishing Ltd, 2019)
13 Jane Fryer, 'Original Prince of Darkness on today's pygmy politicians', *Daily Mail*, 12 August 2016
14 Haines, *Kick 'Em Back*
15 Nicholas Jones, *Soundbites and Spin Doctors: How Politicians Manipulate the Media – and Vice Versa* (London: Cassell Illustrated, 1995)
16 Lobby Journalists' Committee records, 1970
17 Ibid.
18 Margach, *The Abuse of Power*
19 Castle, *The Castle Diaries*
20 Joe Haines, *The Politics of Power: The Inside Story of Life at No. 10* (London: Jonathan Cape, 1977)
21 Haines, *Kick 'Em Back*
22 Lobby Journalists' Committee records, 1975
23 Lobby Journalists' Committee records, 1974/5
24 Haines, *Kick 'Em Back*
25 Sir Peter Ramsbotham interview with Malcolm McBain, British Oral History Diplomatic Programme, Churchill College, Cambridge University, 9 January 2001

26 Lobby Journalists' Committee records, 1977
27 '"No chaos here" declares Callaghan', On This Day 1950–2005, BBC News, 10 January 1979
28 Margaret Thatcher letter to *Sun* editor Larry Lamb, 24 May 1979, Margaret Thatcher Foundation Archive
29 Margaret Thatcher letter to *Daily Mail* editor David English, 17 May 1979, Margaret Thatcher Foundation Archive

Chapter 4
 1 Robert Harris, *Good and Faithful Servant: The Unauthorized Biography of Bernard Ingham* (London: Faber & Faber, 1990)
 2 Andrew Thomson, *Margaret Thatcher: The Woman Within* (London: Virgin Books, 1989)
 3 Harris, *Good and Faithful Servant*
 4 Iain Dale, *Memories of Maggie: A Portrait of Margaret Thatcher* (London: Politico's, 2000)
 5 Franks enquiry evidence transcript (Margaret Thatcher testifies), 25 October 1982, Margaret Thatcher Foundation Archive
 6 Bernard Ingham, *Kill the Messenger* (London: HarperCollins, 1991)
 7 Margaret Thatcher's Falklands Memoir, 1983, Margaret Thatcher Foundation Archive
 8 John Cole, *As it Seemed to Me: Political Memoirs* (London: Weidenfeld & Nicolson, 1995)
 9 Margaret Thatcher's Falklands Memoir
10 Lobby briefing, Margaret Thatcher Foundation Archive
11 Seumas Milne, 'During the miners' strike, Thatcher's secret state was the real enemy within', *Guardian*, 3 October 2014
12 Lobby briefing, Margaret Thatcher Foundation Archive
13 Ingham, *Kill the Messenger*
14 Ibid.
15 *Hansard* HC Deb vol. 71 col. 211 (15 January 1985) [Electronic version]
16 Margaret Thatcher Speech at Parliamentary Lobby's Centenary Lunch, 18 January 1984, Margaret Thatcher Foundation Archive
17 Ingham, *Kill the Messenger*
18 Bernard Ingham, *The Slow Downfall of Margaret Thatcher: The Diaries of Bernard Ingham* (London: Biteback, 2019)
19 Christopher Hitchens, 'What is this Bernard?', *London Review of Books*, vol. 13 no. 10, 10 January 1991
20 Ingham, *Kill the Messenger*

Chapter 5

1 Julia Langdon, 'I shouldn't have read the papers so much when I was PM', *Observer*, 4 March 2007
2 Excerpts from Judith Chaplin diaries, published in *Sunday Telegraph*, 19 September 1999
3 Langdon, 'I shouldn't have read the papers. . .'
4 Inquiry into the Culture, Practices and Ethics of the Press (The Leveson Inquiry): Transcripts and Evidence, 2011–13, The National Archives, Kew
5 Ian Beesley, *The Official History of the Cabinet Secretaries* (London: Routledge, 2016)
6 Paul Routledge and Simon Hoggart, 'Major hits out at Cabinet', *Guardian*, 25 July 1993
7 Patrick Wintour and Stephen Bates, 'Major goes back to the old values', *Guardian*, 9 October 1993

Chapter 6

1 Kevin Toolis, 'The Enforcer', *Guardian*, 4 April 1998
2 Nick Jones, *Sultans of Spin: The Media and the New Labour Government* (London: Weidenfeld & Nicolson, 1999)
3 Jones, *Sultans of Spin*
4 Alastair Campbell, *The Blair Years: Extract from the Alastair Campbell Diaries* (London: Arrow, 2008)
5 George Jones, 'Alastair Campbell stops me from doing my job', *Daily Telegraph*, 5 July 2000
6 Campbell, *The Blair Years*
7 Jones, *Sultans of Spin*
8 Philip Webster, 'Blair rules out single currency for this Parliament', *The Times*, 18 October 1997
9 Campbell, *The Blair Years*
10 Report of the Working Group on the Government Information Service (The Mountfield report), Cabinet Office, 1997
11 Jones, *Sultans of Spin*
12 Campbell, *The Blair Years*
13 Lance Price, *Where Power Lies: Prime Ministers v the Media* (London: Simon & Schuster, 2010)
14 Campbell, *The Blair Years*
15 Tony Blair, *A Journey* (London: Hutchinson, 2010)
16 Blair, *A Journey*
17 Memorandum submitted by Alastair Campbell to Foreign Affairs Committee, 25 June 2003, www.parliament.uk

18 Blair, *A Journey*
19 Max Hastings, *Daily Mail*, 29 January 2004
20 Campbell, *The Blair Years*
21 Ibid.

Chapter 7
1 'The Guardian Profile: David Hill', *Guardian*, 29 August 2003
2 An Independent Review of Government Communication, January 2004, The National Archives, Kew
3 Government Communications Review Group Interim Report, August 2003, The National Archives, Kew
4 David Rose, 'Downing Street drops plan for TV briefings', *Press Gazette*, 30 June 2005
5 Blair, *A Journey*
6 'Blair on the media', BBC News, 12 June 2007
7 Julia Werdigier, 'Upbraided by Blair, the British press bites back', *New York Times*, 18 June 2007
8 Ann Treneman, 'I used to be a sketch writer, but I'm okay nooowwwww', *The Times*, 13 June 2007
9 Andrew Marr, 'How Blair put the media in a spin', BBC News, 10 May 2007
10 Peter Graff, 'Brown rules out early vote', Reuters, 6 October 2007
11 Patrick Wintour and Nicholas Watt, 'The election that never was', *Guardian*, 6 October 2008
12 Andrew Sparrow, 'What happens when Gordon Brown gets angry? The laser printer gets it', *Guardian*, 24 April 2009
13 Nicholas Watt, 'Economy at 60-year low, says Darling. And it will get worse', *Guardian*, 29 August 2008
14 Nicholas Watt, Steven Morris, Allegra Stratton, 'No 10 unleashed "forces of hell on me", Alistair Darling claims', *Guardian*, 24 February 2010
15 Andrew Rawnsley, *The End of the Party: The Rise and Fall of New Labour* (London: Penguin, 2010)
16 *The Brown Years*, BBC Radio 4, 2010
17 Ibid.
18 Frank Field, 'Darkness at the heart of the Labour Party', Frank Field blog, 14 April 2005
19 Helen Lewis, 'Damian McBride: Repentant sinner', *New Statesman*, 2 October 2013
20 Polly Toynbee, 'Gordon Brown must go – by June 5', *Guardian*, 11 May 2009

Chapter 8

1 David Cameron, *For the Record* (London: William Collins, 2019)
2 Cameron, *For the Record*
3 Ibid.
4 Ibid.
5 Ibid.
6 Matthew Holehouse, 'David Cameron says British press plays "vital role" in democracy', *Daily Telegraph*, 17 January 2014
7 Ibid.
8 Ibid.
9 Steerpike, 'Theresa May's former spin chief takes aim at "destructive" Fiona Hill and Nick Timothy', *Spectator*, 9 June 2017
10 Anushka Asthana, 'May removed Nick Timothy and Fiona Hill "under threat of leadership bid"', *Guardian*, 10 June 2017

Chapter 9

1 Trevor Kavanagh, 'Margaret Thatcher, the VC10, boozy journos, sing-songs and an emerald brooch from Ronald Reagan', *Sun*, 11 April 2013
2 Damian McBride, *Power Trip: A Decade of Policy, Plots and Spin* (London: Biteback, 2013)
3 McBride, *Power Trip*
4 James Lyons and Louie Smith, 'Red Arrows face axe threat', *Daily Mirror*, 2 February 2013
5 Rowena Mason, 'Theresa May "does not agree with" Donald Trump's immigration ban', *Guardian*, 28 January 2017
6 Ibid.
7 'Boris Johnson denies cabinet Brexit split', BBC News, 19 September 2017

Chapter 10

1 Kate Proctor, 'The "golden age" of female journalism was won by the nameless', *Guardian*, 1 December 2019
2 '100 years of women reporting in Westminster', Politics Weekly podcast, *Guardian*, 29 November 201)
3 Ben Davies, 'Theresa May: Shadow Education & Employment', BBC News, 22 May 2001
4 Paul Routledge, 'The insider – Paul Routledge wonders about the weather lady', *New Statesman*, 16 June 2003
5 'Michael Fallon "apologised for touching journalist's knee"', BBC News, 31 October 2017

6 *Hansard* HC Deb vol. 645 col. 632 (19 July 2018) [Electronic version]
7 Gaby Hinsliff, 'Under new management: is Carrie Symonds the real power at No 10?', *Observer*, 29 November 2020
8 Georgia Aspinall, 'The sexist headlines around Carrie Symonds' influence over Boris Johnson have "witchcraft" vibes and it needs to stop', *Grazia*, 16 November 2020
9 Charlotte Tobitt, 'Top female lobby journalists say "we need to show it's not an all-boys' club" on International Women's Day', *Press Gazette*, 8 March 2018

Chapter 11
1 Dominic Cummings, '"Two hands are a lot" – we're hiring data scientists, project managers, policy experts, assorted weirdos. . .', Dominic Cummings's blog, 2 January 2020
2 Amy Jones and Christopher Hope, 'No 10 boycotts *Today* programme citing "failure of senior management" over election bias', *Daily Telegraph*, 15 December 2019
3 Anita Singh, 'Government "punished" *Today* and wants to "diminish" power of BBC, outgoing editor says', *Daily Telegraph*, 29 July 2020
4 Tim Shipman, 'No 10 tells BBC licence fee will be scrapped', *The Times*, 16 February 2020
5 Huw Merriman, 'The people's government should not be attacking the BBC, a broadcaster the people love', *Daily Telegraph*, 16 February 2020
6 Mikey Smith, 'Amber Rudd brands Boris Johnson's Today programme boycott "a disgrace"', *Daily Mirror*, 28 January 2020
7 Freddy Mayhew, 'Every national editor signs letter to Boris Johnson urging Lobby changes rethink', *Press Gazette*, 13 January 2020
8 Matthew Moore, 'Journalists walk out of No 10 briefing after rivals barred', *The Times*, 4 February 2020
9 Andrew Grice, 'I've spent 40 years reporting from Westminster. I've never seen anything like this before', *Independent*, 4 February 2020
10 Rowena Mason, 'No 10 reporter ban: MPs across house raise concerns', *Guardian*, 4 February 2020
11 *Hansard* HC Deb vol. 671 col. 190 (4 February 2020) [Electronic version]
12 *Hansard* HC Deb vol. 671 col. 193 (4 February 2020) [Electronic version]

13 *Hansard* HC Deb vol. 671 col. 308 (5 February 2020) [Electronic version]

14 *Desert Island Discs*, BBC Radio 4, 30 November 2005

15 *Hansard* HC Deb vol. 670 col. 432 (23 January 2020) [Electronic version]

16 'Social media firms reminded of "responsibility" over coronavirus misinformation', *Express & Star*, 3 March 2020

17 Jonathan Owen, 'Downing Street comms chief calls truce with the media', PR Week, 18 March 2020

18 'Coronavirus: Dominic Cummings "made second lockdown trip"', BBC News, 24 May 2020

19 Patrick Daly, 'Dominic Cummings "not remotely bothered" by lockdown breach row, friend claims', *Daily Mirror*, 23 May 2020

20 Boris Johnson backs key aide Dominic Cummings in lockdown row', BBC News, 24 May 2020

21 Billy Kenber, 'Dominic Cummings: From Downing Street to Durham', *The Times*, 25 May 2020

22 Steven Swinford, 'Boris Johnson plans White House-style daily television press briefings', *The Times*, 3 July 2020

23 Ashley Cowburn, 'Boris Johnson to introduce White House-style televised press briefings in overhaul of No 10 communications', *Independent*, 3 July 2020

24 *World at One*, BBC Radio 4, 9 October 2020

25 James Tapsfield and Glen Owen, 'Fury at "vicious and cowardly" attacks on Carrie Symonds amid claims Cummings allies branded her "Princess Nut Nut" and accused her of "wanting to be the new Princess Diana"', *Daily Mail*, 15 November 2020

26 'Villiers: Cummings and Cain "dismissive" of MPs', BBC News, 13 November 2020

27 'Cummings' exit offers Boris Johnson a "fresh start", say Tory MPs', BBC News, 13 November 2020

28 James Slack to Lobby briefing, 17 November 2020

29 Andrew Woodcock, 'Downing Street olive branch to journalists marks apparent end to Dominic Cummings' war on media', *Independent*, 18 November 2020

30 Eleanor Langford, 'Boris Johnson Said He Was "Deeply Sorry For Every Life Lost" As UK Coronavirus Death Toll Hits 100,000', PoliticsHome, 26 January 2021

31 Heather Stewart, 'Lockdown hits No 10's plans for White House-style press briefings', *Guardian*, 6 January 2021

NOTES

32 Faith Ridler, 'Downing Street spends more than £2.6 million on refurbishments so Number 10 can hold White House-style press briefings', *Daily Mail*, 6 March 2021

33 *Today*, BBC Radio 4, 21 April 2021

34 Labour Party press release, 21 April 2021

35 *The Week in Westminster*, BBC Radio 4, 24 April 2021

36 Rules of the Parliamentary Media Lobby, 2018. See Appendix 2.

BIBLIOGRAPHY

Addison, Paul and Crang, Jeremy A. (eds), *Listening to Britain: Home Intelligence Reports on Britain's Finest Hour, May to September 1940* (London: Bodley Head, 2010)

Beesley, Ian, *The Official History of the Cabinet Secretaries* (London: Routledge, 2016)

Blair, Tony, *A Journey* (London: Hutchinson, 2010)

Cameron, David, *For the Record* (London: William Collins, 2019)

Campbell, Alastair, *The Blair Years: Extract from the Alastair Campbell Diaries* (London: Arrow, 2008)

Castle, Barbara, *The Castle Diaries 1964–76*, (London: Weidenfeld & Nicolson, 1980)

Clark, William, *From Three Worlds: Memoirs* (London: Sidgwick & Jackson, 1986)

Cockett, Richard, *Twilight of Truth: Chamberlain, Appeasement and the Manipulation of the Press* (London: Palgrave Macmillan, 1989)

Cole, John, *As it Seemed to Me: Political Memoirs* (London: Weidenfeld & Nicolson, 1995)

Dale, Iain, *Memories of Maggie: A Portrait of Margaret Thatcher* (London: Politico's, 2000)

Denison, John Evelyn, *Notes from my Journal When Speaker of the House of Commons* (London: Murray, 1900)

Franck, Thomas M. and Weisband, Edward (eds), *Secrecy and Foreign Policy* (New York: Oxford University Press, 1954)

Haines, Joe, *Kick 'Em Back: Wilson, Maxwell and Me* (London: Grosvenor House Publishing Ltd, 2019)

Haines, Joe, *The Politics of Power: The Inside Story of Life at No. 10*
(London: Jonathan Cape, 1977)

Harris, Robert, *Good and Faithful Servant: The Unauthorized
Biography of Bernard Ingham* (London: Faber & Faber, 1990)

Higginbottom, Frederick J., *The Vivid Life: A Journalist's Career*
(London: Simpkin Marshall, 1934)

Ingham, Bernard, *Kill the Messenger* (London: HarperCollins, 1991)

Ingham, Bernard, *The Slow Downfall of Margaret Thatcher: The
Diaries of Bernard Ingham* (London: Biteback, 2019)

Jones, Nicholas, *Soundbites and Spin Doctors: How Politicians
Manipulate the Media – and Vice Versa* (London: Cassell
Illustrated, 1995)

Jones, Nicholas, *Sultans of Spin: The Media and the New Labour
Government* (London: Weidenfeld & Nicolson, 1999)

King, Anthony and Sloman, Anne, *Westminster and Beyond: Based
on the BBC Radio series 'Talking Politics'* (London: Palgrave
Macmillan, 1973)

Lysaght, Charles Edward, *Brendan Bracken: A Biography* (London:
Allen Lane, 1979)

Margach, James, *The Abuse of Power: The War Between Downing
Street and the media from Lloyd George to James Callaghan*
(London: W.H. Allen, 1978)

Margach, James, *The Anatomy of Power* (London: W.H. Allen,
1979)

McBride, Damian, *Power Trip: A Decade of Policy, Plots and Spin*
(London: Biteback, 2013)

Price, Lance, *Where Power Lies: Prime Ministers v the Media*
(London: Simon & Schuster, 2010)

Rawnsley, Andrew, *The End of the Party: The Rise and Fall of New
Labour* (London: Penguin, 2010)

Sparrow, Andrew, *Obscure Scribblers: A History of Parliamentary
Reporting* (London: Politico's, 2003)

Thomson, Andrew, *Margaret Thatcher: The Woman Within*
(London: Virgin Books, 1989)

Wrigley, Chris, *Winston Churchill: A Biographical Companion*
(Santa Barbara: ABC-CLIO, 2002)

INDEX

INDEX

general elections
  1950s 38, 41
  1960s 49
  1970s 64, 72
  2000s 142, 175–7, 179–81, 188, 197,
   271
General Strike (1926) 5
Gibb, Robbie 203–4, 205, 280
Gilligan, Andrew 145–8, 154
Good Friday Agreement (1998) 136
Goodman, Elinor 76, 111–12, 128, 244,
  246–7, 249–50
Gorbachev, Mikhail 211–12
Gorman, Teresa 244
Gove, Michael 193, 199
Graham, Philip L. 1
Gray, Jean-Christophe 232–3, 234
Great Depression 8
Green, Damian 277
Greene, Sir Hugh 49
Grice, Andrew 276
Groves, Jason 234–5, 275–6, 281–2,
  291, 295, 297
Guardian 18–9, 44, 99, 106 121, 165,
  174, 176, 211,229, 233, 252, 267,
  268, 283–4
Guido Fawkes blog 169, 170, 273–4
Gulf area 213
Gunn, Herbert 35

H
'Hacked Off' campaign 185
Haines, Joe 49–51, 57–9, 64–9, 211–12
Hammond, Philip 198
Hancock, Matt 278–9
Hanrahan, Brian 81
Hardman, Isabel 262
Harman, Harriet 243
Harris, Robert 76–7, 102
Harrison, Paul 199–201, 237
Hartley-Brewer, Julia 260
Haslam, Jonathan 118–19, 218–19
Hastings, Max 148
Hattersley, Roy 158
Healey, Denis 243
Heath, Edward 47, 52, 59–60, 62–4, 85
Henderson, W. W. 6
Hennessy, Lord 2, 55–6
Heseltine, Michael 112
Higginbottom, Frederick J. 11

Hill, David 158–9, 224
Hill, Fiona 195, 196–8
Hill, Lord 56
Hitchens, Christopher 102
Hitler, Adolf 15, 17–19
Home Intelligence Department 27–9
Home Office x
horse meat scandal 231
Howard, Anthony xiii, 56
Howard, Michael 113
Howarth, Gerald 175–6
Howe, Sir Geoffrey 91, 101
HuffPost UK 275
Hussein, Saddam 144–5
Hutton inquiry 148–9, 219
Hutton, Lord 148
Hutton, Rob 156, 202, 204, 282
Huxley, Aldous 151

I
income tax policy 225–6
Independent 96–100, 148, 106, 211,
  275
India 208, 227
Information, Ministry of (MOI) 24,
  25–9, 30–1
Ingham, Sir Bernard 75–103
  on the lobby system 99–100
  style 107, 250
  on televised briefings 289
  travelling with Thatcher 209–15
International Federation of Journalists
  264
Iraq wars 143–9, 154–5, 160, 162, 165,
  220, 225
Islamabad 208, 227–8
Israel 210
ITV 63, 270, 291, 294,

J
James, Howell 116
James, Margot 256
Japan 216–17, 238
Jay, Peter 70
Jenkin, Sir Bernard 290
Jenkins, Peter 48
Johnson, Boris 269–72, 285–9
  advisers/aides 4, 57, 62
  becomes prime minister 205–6
  Covid-19 crisis 279, 283, 292–4